Nudge Marketing

Éric Singler

Nudge Marketing

Winning at Behavioral Change

PEARSON

Layout: APS-Chromostyle, Tours

© 2015, Pearson France

ISBN: 978-2-7440-6602-3

To my parents,
my wife Valérie,
my children Thomas, Baptiste and Valentine,
my brother Franck,
my friends and partners Alain, Gérard and Pascal,
and my colleagues from the BVA Nudge Unit,
Richard Bordenave and Étienne Bressoud.

Summary

Part one
A brief history of the revolution

Part two
How Homer Simpson
dethroned Superman

Part four
From Nudge to Nudge marketing

A c k n o w l e d g m e n t s

A book is the result of individual work that is both demanding and exciting. It is also the fruit of a whole range of influences drawn from lectures, discussions, encounters and experiments.

I would like to offer my sincere thanks to those people who, in one way and another, made this book's existence possible.

First of all, I'd like to mention my friends and colleagues from BVA, Richard Bordenave and Étienne Bressoud. As my fellow leaders at the BVA Nudge Unit, these are the co-designers of our Nudge creation process, and incredible discussion partners with whom to bounce around ideas. Working with them (as well as celebrating the good times and letting off steam) is a daily source of pleasure. So thank you, Richard and Étienne. And I'll see you soon for the next chapter of our adventure.

I also want to thank BVA's 'serial Nudgers', Beltrande Bakoula, Constance Dreux, Pauline Le Golvan, Odile Peixoto, Fabien Lespagnol, Aurèle Dalongeville, Christophe Bouruet, and Catherine Tanitte for their inspirational ideas that make our process as creative and effective as possible. Thanks also to those other passionate converts to the Nudge revolution for practicing it with such flair and sticking to their task with such enthusiasm: Jules Mourier, Olivier Blanchet, Carlos Gallardo, Violaine Paquet, Adélaïde Zulfikarpasic, Jean-François Levionnois, Bertrand Chokrane, Anne-Laure Gallay, Caroline Michel, Aldo Scarlata, Elisa Toscano, Sophie Mahé, Karine

Loucas, Tom Dilley, Anne-Laure de Broissia, Albert Pappen-heimer, Andy Rushforth and Valentine de Navrotzky.

And I haven't forgotten about my fellow BVA board members Gérard Lopez, Pascal Gaudin and Alain Sivan, who trusted me to embark on this beautiful adventure. But these are my friends; should one thank one's friends or not?

Dan Ariely, the remarkable Duke University professor, who I describe in these pages, has also played a crucial role. Our meeting, and the experiments that we carried our together, convinced me beyond all shadow of a doubt about the revolutionary, thrilling nature of behavioral economics. So thank you, Dan, and all that you are: an inspirational genius, if ever there was one.

But the transition from inspiration to action requires backers… If the French powers that be are converts to the Nudge approach, it's because people are convinced about Nudge's potential power to improve the effectiveness of public policy in our country. At the head of this list are Françoise Waintrop and her team at the Secretary General for the Modernization of Public Actions (SGMAP), Céline Pelletier and Laure Bonneval. To them, my warmest thanks. Françoise is a brilliant, compelling spokeswoman who has been with us since the beginning. With the active support of Céline and Laure, she has been there throughout both our experiments and our quest to convince the public authorities of their merits. It's the Public Finances Directorate General (DGFIP) who made the desire to 'give Nudge a try' a reality. The delightful problem that they gave us was how to get more people to use the impots.gouv.fr website for their tax returns. I therefore want to thank Yannick Girault, Jean-Luc Jaquet and Stéphane Albisetti from the DGFIP for having made this first Nudge experiment on French soil possible. The work itself was a success, receiving international recognition. It allowed us to win the *Marketing Magazine* gold medal in France, as well as the 'Best Case History' award at ESOMAR 2014 – the most important marketing conference on the international calendar – with entrants from 71 countries and over 250 research papers submitted. So a big thank you to SGMAP and the DGFIP!

Thanks also go to Olivier Oullier, who wrote the preface to this book, for two reasons. The first, of course, is for having taken responsibility for these vital words of introduction. And also for the major role that he has played in spreading the findings of behavioral economics throughout France. Olivier is a brilliant young professor, named a 'young global leader' at the World Economic Forum (Davos) in 2011. As well as his prolific academic research, he has used his considerable powers of persuasion to convince the public authorities to make more use of behavioral science. His 2010 report, *New Approaches to Prevention in Public Health*[1] for the Prime Minister's Strategic Analysis Centre was a fascinating, pioneering piece of French research.

For a book to exist, it needs a publisher. And in Julie Berquez and François Lantz I have two real partners. Julie was demanding, in trying to get the best out of me, as well as understanding during my moments of doubt. A source of stimulation, and of comfort. François played an important role in making my early drafts sturdier and more direct, without losing the essence of what I wanted to get across. So thank you, Julie and François!

Finally, a last word for two of the loves of my life: my eldest son, Thomas, and my wife, Valérie. In different ways, they have assisted in the writing of this book. Thomas is a young consultant fresh out of Sciences Po and Imperial College, London and now Associate at BCG. An expert in behavior himself, he helped by preparing all the documentation and rigorously proofreading my manuscript. Valérie's contribution

---

1.   Olivier Oullier and Sarah Sauneron, *Nouvelles Approches de la prévention en santé publique* [New Approaches to Prevention in Public Health], Strategic Administration Centre. French documentation, 'Reports and documents', n° 25, 2010.

was to ensure, via her own close reading of the text, that my words were clear, understandable, and as interesting as possible – for everyone not just experts in the field.

And thank you to my other loves, Valentine and Baptiste, for existing and for making my life happy!

P r e f a c e

Our society has always shown a certain aversion to uncertainty. Not knowing what will happen tomorrow is difficult for us to deal with.

As individuals, one of the ways of fighting uncertainty is to try and guess what others are thinking and feeling. Successfully deciphering the mental, emotional and behavioral state of somebody we come across gives us an indication about our future interaction with them. Similarly, mastering the way we are perceived by others reduces some of the uncertainty surrounding this interaction. At least, that's what we tell ourselves...

Another strategy involves changing habits and behavior. Our own, as well as other people's. This may involve your resolution to watch less television or lose weight, or public authorities seeking to reduce tobacco consumption as a way to save lives and reduce healthcare costs. There are many examples where a change in lifestyle can improve our health and save us money. Changing people's behavior is certainly one of the most effective ways to reduce uncertainty. Temporarily, at least.

And this is the purpose of Éric Singler's book, which aims to teach us how to change people's behavior effectively.

Traditionally, there are three levers that are used by governments to control, or modify, our good and bad habits. These are: the law; taxes and subsidies; and information. However, despite using these methods to manage public policy for many years, these levers are not quite as effective as you might believe.

Over time, people find ways to get around the law. Taxes and subsidies only affect a portion of the population. And as for information, if knowing that something was bad for you was all it took to change people's habits, there would be no doctors left who smoke…

It's a well-known fact that these three levers do not work, despite the huge amounts of money spent on their activation. The authorities' stubborn insistence on their continued use is equally well established. So should we just throw up our hands, or, for the want of anything better, keep heading down this disappointing road? Not under any circumstances! Because there is another option out there. And this new way is 'Nudge' – an approach based on reputable psychological studies, the experimental method, behavioral economics, cognitive science, and neuroscience.

When it comes to strategies for changing people's behavior, Nudge has four important benefits. It's simple, non-prescriptive, and (often) very cheap. Best of all, it works!

Since the publication of *Nudge* in 2008, the pioneering work by Richard Thaler and Cass Sunstein, many people have theorized and written on the subject. However, not many of them have successfully applied the method to both the public and private sectors.

Éric Singler is one of an elite group. This is the first book to retrace the history of the main players and core writings that brought Nudge into existence. As well as this – and this is *Nudge Marketing's* real strength – it contains a theoretical and methodological analysis that finally gives readers a set of tried-and-tested tools to formulate and implement effective Nudge strategies.

Nudge Marketing's quality lies in its substantial research, its thorough analysis, and its re-framing of the Nudge approach based on the author's own experiences in marketing and communication. No matter what the experts in psychology, economics (behavioral or otherwise), cognitive science, and neuroscience say, the people with the best knowledge and understanding of both human decisions and how to change people's 'real-life' behavior are the specialists in management sciences, management, communication, and marketing. Why is this? Because their study and practice involves humanity in its natural environment, not laboratory experiments. When it comes to the study and understanding of people's behavior *in situ* and *in vivo*, Éric Singler is a leader and a pioneer, both internationally and in France.

Starting in 1989, he set up IN VIVO and his first 'experimental store'. Based in Saint-Quentin-en-Yvelines, the store's aim was to re-create a realistic environment for the analysis of supermarket shopping behavior. As he told me during our first meeting, the idea came out of a failure. At that time, he was working as a product manager in the food industry. Studies carried out by leading institutions of the day predicted that a certain new product would have huge success. However, results did not live up to the forecast, and the failure awakened him to the fact that people's intentions are a poor way of predicting their behavior. This gave rise to the idea of observing consumers in a realistic shopping environment as a means to develop a rigorous experimental method based on people's real behavior.

Nudges are inseparable from this precise experimental process. Testing strategies on a small scale before deployment is an indispensable feature of the method, as it allows for the detection and correction of possible errors before large-scale deployment.

It's safe to say that none of the public policy reforms impacting the lives of millions of people have been tested with such scientific rigor. However, if conditions allow, they certainly should be. The benefits to doing so would be three-fold: numerous errors would be avoided; the effectiveness of the reforms would increase; and (this final point is indisputable) there would be money saved as a result.

This was the aim of the programme that I ran between 2008 and 2012 as part of the French Prime Minister's Centre for Strategic Analysis. Specifically, my remit was to use neuroscience and behavioral science to devise more effective public policies. But while we were busy writing notes and reports to persuade government departments to give us the green light for our field experiments, the United Kingdom were already performing small-scale tests that would lead to a national level rollout. As a result, our friends across the channel saw the development of more effective public health, energy saving and fiscal policies that led – crucially – to millions of pounds being saved by the government and taxpayers alike.

This British efficiency did not escape the eagle eye of Éric Singler. Like many others, he discovered *Nudge* in 2008 – the year IN VIVO joined the BVA group, of which, as one of four board members, he became CEO. Unlike most of those who read Thaler and Sunstein's book, however, Éric Singler decided to put the concepts into practice. Convinced about the benefits of Nudge, and inspired by the work of the UK Nudge Unit, he set up the BVA Nudge Unit. And in the summer of 2013 he and his team succeeded in convincing high-level French officials of its merits. Thanks to his hard work and determination, no less that fifteen separate projects are underway at the time of writing. Involved parties include the Ministry of the Interior (road safety), the Government Information Service (participation in mayoral elections), the Health Ministry (generic medicine), and the Department of Social Security (workplace satisfaction for its agents), as well as several private enterprises.

High-profile books about behavioral change very often involve a more or less interesting summary of earlier work, without suggesting any operational solutions. As for Dan

Ariely, with whom he has collaborated on various research projects, Éric Singler's *Nudge Marketing* provides both the information and the tools required for the design and application of successful strategies for changing people's behavior.

Whether you're just starting to explore this field or seeking to perfect your art, a practitioner or a theoretician, you will find this book a joy to read. The French Nudge revolution is underway, and Éric Singler is its undisputed standard bearer.

Nudge Marketing proves it in the strongest terms. Of this, there is no doubt.

Olivier Oullier

Olivier Oullier is a professor at the University of Aix-Marseille. His research uses psychology, neuroscience, complex systems and behavioral economics to understand the mechanisms behind decision making, influence and persuasion. He was named a 'young global leader' by the World Economic Forum (Davos). He advises both private and public organizations on strategies related to commitment, behavioral change, communication, and crisis management.

I n t r o d u c t i o n

Changing people's behavior – it really is possible...

How can you convince 100,000 more people in the United Kingdom to become organ donors in the space of just a year? Easy! All it takes is changing a single phrase on the gov.uk website suggesting that people join the programme.

How can you double sales of a brand of soup on special offer without altering either the price, the in-store placement, the product itself, or the packaging? Again, it's easy. Simply limit the number of products that consumers can buy rather than making it a limitless offer.

These two real-life examples, as well as the many others that we will look at together in the course of this book, illustrate two simple but important facts:

1. It *is* possible to produce significant changes in people's behavior;
2. These deep changes can be achieved as a result of seemingly minor modifications, which are both inexpensive and easy to implement.

The first fact is exciting for all those working in specific target areas. Whether you are an entrepreneur, a marketer, an advertising executive, a political decision-maker, a high-ranking official, the director of a public body or a humanitarian organization, a sales rep or the manager of a sustainable development programme, if you aspire to change the behavior of your target you must accept you have a major role to play. Your influence can be huge – without doubt bigger than you think!

The second point is no less thrilling. Not only is it possible to bring about significant changes in behavior but also, even more surprisingly, these changes can be achieved by slight *a priori* modifications that all share one important feature: they come at no additional cost. Changing the phrasing on a webpage or adding a line to the offer on a billboard generates no extra expense. And be it public policy or private enterprise – in this world where we are forced to operate to such tight margins, this is quite a promise to make!

However, the promise comes with a flipside. Altering our behavior, as highlighted by one of the heroes of this book, Professor Dan Ariely, is a major challenge for human beings, who in general don't like change[1]: 'People generally avoid changes, even if there are minor and even when another path is clearly better.' The flipside of this, is the requirement to combine a perfect mastery of both the decision-making process itself and the necessary tools for effectively changing behavior. And as we shall see, it's rare for such a perfect storm to come about.

...but the name of the game is failure!

Facts are stubborn and when it comes to behavioral change, the facts are indisputable. Failure is the norm, and success is the exception. Or, to put it a little more subtly, the correlation between efforts made, resources deployed and effectiveness is weak.

---

1. Dan Ariely, 'A Beginner's Guide to Behavioral Economics', online course, 2013.

You're unconvinced? Don't worry – that's normal! As we shall see, you – just like me – are victim to a 'confirmation bias' that makes us extremely attentive and sensitive to evidence which consolidates our belief in ourselves – in our judgment and our actions – and far less receptive to other evidence that calls these into question.

Let's look at the facts.

In the world of public policy, partial success or failure is sadly par for the course. This is true across the board, be it the financial sector, with its frequently recurring economic crises; the environment, with its problems of how to fight for and protect our planet; public health, with the increase in obesity across the western world, as well as high levels of dangerous behavior such as alcohol consumption and smoking; or, even more fundamentally, the failures of the global fight against poverty.

The evidence is equally apparent when it comes to private enterprise. For major global industries with mass consumption and clear evidence of high success rates in launching new products, failure is both widespread and on the increase. All the experts agree about this point. Philip Kotler, the godfather of global marketing and author of the marketing bible, *Marketing Management*, refers to an 80% failure rate for new products. The *French Marketing Review* puts this number at 95% – a figure which has doubled in the past ten years. And while new products are the visible tip of the failure-related iceberg – think, for instance, about the disappearance of Danone's Essensis, Coca-Cola BlāK, or Nestlé's Nesfluid – the phenomenon affects the whole spectrum of marketing activities. Other examples include the failed changes to Tropicana's packaging, or Coca-Cola Bear's promotional pack that died a death in the USA.

These failures, or at least, the difficulties involved in bringing about significant changes in behavior despite the effort made and resources used, suggest an insufficient grasp of the factors really influencing the decisions people take in the course of their daily lives.

When making decisions, humans do not think like homo economicus

Why is there this broad miscomprehension about how we perceive citizens and consumers and their and decision-making processes? Because the premise on which we base them is largely false. Unbeknown to their creators, the vast majority of actions designed to change people's behavior rely on an obsolete view of the factors influencing our decisions. We have all been instilled with the long-dominant theory of decision making, stretching from Descartes to the classical and neo-classical economists: that of the rational man.

According to this theory, our decisions are the result of a type of balancing act. Blessed with a clear view of our objectives – so it goes – we are able to carry out a rational evaluation of the pros and cons within a spectrum of available choices. We then proceed to choose the option that maximizes our satisfaction based on a set of coherent preferences that are stable over time. To change the behavior of this cold and calculating being who acts solely according to his objective, selfish interests, should hence be enough to add some facts and tip the scales. For example, stop smoking because 'smoking kills'. And yet what do we see? In France, over 25% of doctors smoke.

The behavioral economics and neuroscience revolution

This image of the rational *homo economicus* has been fundamentally called into question by behavioral economics – a revolutionary discipline combining psychology, sociology, economics, cognitive science, and decision-related neuroscience. As a result of its findings, our understanding of human decision making and behavior is currently in a phase of rapid increase and radical change. Belief in the rational man has imploded, making way for a contradictory, multi-faceted individual who is both emotional and intuitive, reflective yet constrained – a product of our species' evolutionary journey whose instinctive reflexes, habits and ways of thinking are moulded by their immediate environment. This individual is very different from the long-accepted model. And so, assuming that they want to do their job effectively, a radical rethink is required by those responsible for changing the behavior of citizens or consumers.

The lessons learned from the revolution mean we have to more or less start from scratch. You will have to forget everything you know (or rather, everything you *think* you know) about the human decision-making process. You will need to open your mind completely. Cast aside your preconceptions and convictions. And allow yourself to discover the often surprising and always fascinating insights flowing from the revolution. Using scientific evidence, we will see how unexpected yet extremely powerful action levers can be used to alter people's behavior – although we need to acquire some knowledge first, before we put them into action.

To illustrate the power of these levers, let's return to the two examples mentioned earlier. The question of donating organs in the event of an accident does not seem like a trivial decision. It brings into play some important considerations such as religion, the relationship with our body, our attitudes to death and to other people, in particular our close family. For each and every one of us, this decision should follow a period of deep reflection in which we weigh up the pros and cons of making such a choice. Economists talk about cost-benefit analysis. And it is on these grounds that we base our choice to donate or not donate our organs when presented with the option. And yet, a simple change in the phrasing of a webpage is enough to significantly increase the number of people joining an organ donation programme. Here is the phrase, as displayed on the gov.uk webpage: 'Everyday thousands of people who see this page decide to register.'

It was conceived and tested by the Behavioural Insights Team (BIT), or so-call Nudge Unit, a group affiliated to the British Prime Minister, David Cameron. In partnership with several other UK agencies involved in tackling public health, the BIT carried out a five-week study to measure the impact of this additional phrase on the behavior of more than a million visitors to the site. To evaluate the performance of each message being tested, visitors were randomly assigned to one or two of the pages. Seven messages ended up being tested (as well as the control page) by over 135,000 people. The results for the winning phrase were statistically significant and unequivocal: more than 1,300 additional donors signed up during the test period – a potential 96,000 per year. The BIT's report concluded that[2]: 'The findings show how small changes in specific public service contexts can have big impacts.'

Why does a modification so insignificant when you consider the serious personal issues linked to the donation of one's organs have such a major impact? For one simple reason: the Nudge Unit applied an effective lever that pushed visitors to the site from intention to action. When it comes to organ donation programmes, we know that the problem lies in the transition from word to deed, not in the ability to convince people of the soundness of their decision. The gov.uk project showed that over 90% of the British public, are already convinced! Even when we know that we should do something – either for ourselves, for the community, or for the planet – there are many times we still don't act. We just don't change our behavior or put our intentions into practice. The question

---

2. The Behavioural Insights Team (ed.), *Applying Behavioural Insights to Organ Donation: Preliminary Results from a Randomised Controlled Trial*, Cabinet Office, December 2013, p. 8.

is hence not to convince people – either by publicity stunts or via expensive yet ineffective information campaigns – but to come up with actions based on real levers that ease the passage from thinking to doing. We need to understand both why this transition doesn't happen, and what we should change to ensure that it does. This is what the Nudge Unit achieved by applying social norms – a major lever identified by behavioral economics. Those times we hesitate when faced with a decision, we are highly influenced by other people's behavior. Put simply, the Nudge Unit brought into play the one element it knew would motivate people to act. And it did so thanks to the findings of this new science of decision making and behavior that we are about to discover together.

The second example – a promotional offer from the consumer goods sector – is deliberately taken from a very different field. A team of American academics[3] conducted an experiment comparing sales of Campbell's soup during a promotional campaign in which prices were cut from 89 to 79 cents per can using the following three methods:

♦ alongside the offer price, it was stated that there was no per-person limit to the number of cans that could be purchased;
♦ a maximum limit was set at 4 cans per person;
♦ a maximum limit was set at 12 cans per person.

The resulting sales figures were telling: 3.3 cans per person were purchased in the first instance; 3.5 in the second; and 7 in the third – more than a twofold increase. And the reason? The 12-can limit acted as a reference point for potential buyers seeking to gain maximum benefit from the offer. The introduction of a limit hence brought about a significant

---

3. Brian Wansink, Robert J. Kent and Stephen J. Hoch, 'An Anchoring and Adjustment Model of Purchase Quantity Decisions', *Journal of Marketing Research*, vol. 35, February 1998, p. 71-81.

increase in the number of cans purchased. In behavioral economics, this psychological phenomenon is known as 'anchoring'. In the course of our daily decisions, we often act according to a series of reference points – anchors – which, consciously or otherwise, we use to make comparisons and take decisions. And the presence of these anchors can have a strong influence on our behavior.

The Nudge revolution: how to change people's behavior effectively

In 2008, Richard Thaler and Cass Sunstein published a book[4] entitled *Nudge*. This seminal work gave its name to an approach, which, drawing on the lessons of behavioral economics, seeks to design effective actions aimed at encouraging behavioral change. These changes may be to the benefit of the individuals themselves, to the wider community, or to the planet.

My intention here is to carry on the work of the authors of the trail-blazing *Nudge*. At the same time, I will provide a deeper understanding of both the approach itself and the behavioral economics theory on which it is based. By re-examining landmark cases from the past five years, I will arrive at a methodology. That is, an action plan for creating effective ways to produce desired behavioral change – the 'Nudge marketing' of the title – in the fields of public policy and private enterprise.

In a nutshell, this is what Nudge marketing means for me: a type of knowledge, a state of mind, and a method for mastering strategies to change people's behavior.

---

4. Richard Thaler and Cass Sunstein, *Nudge: Improving Decisions about Health, Wealth and Happiness*, Yale University Press, 2008.

The aim of this book is hence to allow you to go about your professional life with greater effectiveness. This may entail real-life behavioral changes, or simply an improved understanding of the mysterious, enchanting world of decision making and human behavior.

The first two sections of the book will furnish you with a detailed understanding of the behavioral economics revolution and its key lessons:

◆ In Part one, I will give a brief history of the revolution. This will involve a quick-fire portrait of its key figures, as well as a description of its major milestones and the tools it has employed.

◆ In Part two, I will describe, via a range of experiments both astonishing and informative, how ordinary people such as you and I go about taking real-life decisions. We will examine the ways in which our 'illogical selves', our emotions, our relations to others, and the context of our decisions all affect our eventual behavior.

Armed with this new information, you will be ready for action. The third and fourth parts have an identical objective applied to two distinct worlds – public policy and private enterprise. These parts are both centred on the same basic question: How can we come up with effective strategies for changing people's behavior?

◆ Part three will address the following problem: What is the best way to apply these important findings to public policy? How can we use our knowledge of levers governing people's behavior to more effectively produce the desired changes? The aim is to understand how the Nudge revolution might assist policymakers, public administrations, humanitarian groups, or those promoting sustainable development to succeed in modifying people's behavior. The beneficiary may be the individuals themselves or the wider community.

◆ Part four will address the same question as applied to the world of business and marketing: What new mental framework does the Nudge marketer have to adopt in order to be more effective? How can the lessons drawn from behavioral economics be practically applied to marketing? It's a question of understanding how behavioral economics and the Nudge approach can assist marketers in overcoming their greatest challenges. These include such things as launching a successful new product; coming up with convincing publicity material; designing a website or social networking page that really connects with its target audience; creating successful brand architecture; or producing appropriate pricing strategies.

Parts three and four will also include:

◆ studies involving real-life examples;
◆ general findings aimed at identifying the key factors for success;
◆ suggested action plans.

The ultimate aim of the book is both simple and highly ambitious: to be more successful in changing people's behavior, and to improve the return on investments for actions undertaken.

PART ONE

A BRIEF HISTORY OF THE REVOLUTION

The behavioral economics revolution

The revolution didn't happen overnight. And the revolutionaries had to work together to overthrow their victim. Ousting a centuries-old dominant theory is no mean feat. All the more so when the attack is aimed at something as fundamental as our understanding of the way that humans take decisions.

A challenge of this scale generally takes years, even decades. A combined effort is needed to first shake the throne and finally topple the king.

For a long time, the theory of the rational man was firmly embedded in the general consciousness. Over the course of the twentieth century, it gradually imposed itself on neoclassical economic theory, which postulates an individual who is wholly rational in his choices. Let's call this individual 'Superman', on account of the superpowers he is meant to possess. Indeed, the Superman of neoclassical theory is endowed with no less than four otherworldly gifts: he is perfectly informed about every feature of the options facing him; he is able to process this information in a logical, statistically sound, and unemotional manner; his sole motivation is his personal interest (not that of others) and he seeks to maximize his own satisfaction according to the calculations he has made; his preferences are stable over time and independent of the way in which his choices are presented to him. From these four superpowers, all of which are axioms of economic theory, economists created mathematical models of the decision-making process. Their aim was to reliably predict both our behavior as economic agents and the overall effect of individuals' behavior on the market. Over the decades, these models have become the basis of economic policies designed to anticipate the outcome of a given range of options.

The Superman of neoclassical theory has a thick skin. He continues to attract powerful supporters – and their influence endures. Significantly, he still has an impact on the day-to-day decision making in areas such as public policy and private companies. However, these actions are generally ineffective in producing the desired changes in behavior. We are hence still under the daily influence of a theory that is largely false, and which we unwittingly apply when designing actions aimed at changing the way that people take decisions.

Overthrowing Superman has been a difficult and drawn-out process – a progressive poisoning which took close to 60 years between 1950 and 2010, and which involved the joint efforts of many revolutionaries. The groundwork for the overthrow was laid by the godfathers – the pre-revolutionaries – who craftily implanted the ideas, those most dangerous of seeds, into the heads of the protagonists.

I will now give you the brief history, in two acts, of this great 'thought revolution'.

The first act involves a presentation of the revolutionaries. Also, their brothers in arms, their fellow radicals from other disciplines such as psychology and neuroscience, and the Nudge practitioners who are their spiritual sons. These are the rebels, many of them touched by genius, who did away with the presiding theory of the rational man.

The second act concerns the various stages of the revolution, particularly the weapons that the revolutionaries forged and later put to use. You will learn how and why Homer Simpson came to dethrone Superman and take up power. To wit, Dan Lovallo and Olivier Sibony[1] assertion that: 'Once heretical, behavioral economics is now mainstream.'

And so to our discovery of this thought-shattering revolution!

---

1.   www.mckinsey.com/insights/strategy/the_case_for_behavioral_strategy

1

The main players

There are barely twenty of them. Men, for the most part. All academics. Almost all are American, although some are of Israeli origin. All are geniuses in their field. But above all, these are rebels. Revolutionaries, who confronted the established order, identified its weak points, set them in a modern context, and then gradually came up with an alternative theory of decision making and human behavior that would become known as behavioral economics.

The pioneers: Herbert Simon and the proponents of bounded rationality

Herbert Simon is not a 'behavioral economist' per se. Indeed, the term did not even exist when he was engaged in his early work. Born in 1916, Simon was an American economist and sociologist. He studied at the University of Chicago, where in 1943 he defended his political science thesis on decision making in organizations. In 1949, he joined the Carnegie Institute of Technology, and he began publishing in the 1950s. He received the 1978 Nobel Prize in Economics, and was highly active through the end of the 1990s. He died in 2001.

Simon is considered the pioneer of the behavioral economics revolution, as it was he who first called into question the theory of the rational man. He sowed the seeds, which subsequently flowered under the real revolutionaries, much as the Enlightenment philosophers inspired the French revolutionaries in 1789 or the Americans in 1776. It was Simon who, beginning with the principles of the rational economic agent, identified significant limitations that would call into question the fundamental axioms on which the entire theory was based.

Herbert Simon conceived and circulated the first critiques of human rationality – critiques which the next generation would use to fan the flames of the revolt. The Carnegie Mellon professor laid the foundations by inventing what would go on to become the theory of bounded rationality. Beginning with the axioms of neoclassical theory, he set out to highlight the limitations of real people acting in the real world. He states[1]: 'Because of the psychological limits of the organism (particularly with respect to computational and predictive ability), actual human rationality-striving can at best be an extremely crude and simplified approximation to the kind of global rationality that is implied, for example, by game theoretical models.' In other words, we are not rational beings. We are not always able to make the choice that maximizes our personal satisfaction – that is, the best available decision – since this is does not always match our desire. We cannot be rational, as we are psychologically incapable of processing the full range of information at our disposal and, even more importantly, evaluating it according

---

1. Herbert A. Simon, 'A Behavioral Model of Rational Choice', *The Quarterly Journal of Economics*, vol. 69, n° 1, February 1955, p. 99-118.

to the canons of statistical analysis and probability. As well as this limitation in our ability to process information, we are also hampered by external constraints. For example, we either do not have the necessary time to process the information in question, or we opt to not invest this time – by definition limited – in deliberating over small decisions. In the end, we choose an option that is satisfying in light of the time and effort required to identify the perfect solution for our overall objectives; and this is not necessarily the best solution. Herbert Simon hence opens the door for subsequent researchers by showing that our rationality is, at the very least, restricted.

During the same period, Maurice Allais, a French economist who received the 1988 Nobel Prize in Economics, also contributed to the progressive splintering of the theory of rationality. In 1953, Allais presented what would come to be known as the 'Allais paradox' to the American Economic Society. The paradox demonstrates that the independence axiom – one of the fundamental axioms of neoclassical expected utility theory – is often flouted in the course of people's everyday decisions. In short, the theory stipulates that in an uncertain environment, for example a lottery, when you prefer option A to option B, then the addition of a third option – option C – should not alter your original preference (A or B). The change represented by option C does not generate a change in the original preference for option A or option B. However, Allais demonstrated experimentally that in certain cases people do not act like this, thus contradicting the independence axiom. And if a fundamental axiom of expected utility theory is false, what does this mean for the theory as a whole and for the soundness of its predictive capabilities?

Taking the lead from Simon and Allais, younger economists and psychologists continued the quest for a deeper understanding of the limits of human rationality. For the first time, economists had drawn serious attention to the structural limitations of the axioms on which the dominant economic theory was based.

Under the direct influence of Simon's earlier research[2], Reinhard Selten, who would also receive the 1994 Nobel Prize in economics, continued and expanded upon this re-examination of the theory of rationality.

Selten worked towards developing a theory of limited rationality. In 2002, he coordinated the publication of *Bounded Rationality*[3] – a work that came out of the Dahlem Konferenz, a German interdisciplinary forum whose aim is to infuse economics with a greater amount of psychology. Here, the significance of reasoning shortcuts – decision-making logic that is extremely simplified and rapidly employed in the course of our everyday choices – is shown to be in direct conflict with a rational process that weighs the pros and cons of each option before identifying that which maximizes satisfaction. For example, if the price of a carton of orange juice is the main variable for a decision maker, he can, according to reasoning shortcuts, go straight to the product on offer at the end of the aisle. By this logic, there is no reason to view all the other items on the shelves.

For bounded rationality theoreticians, the axioms of classical economic theory do not hold water. Our desire is still to make rational choices – what Simon terms 'intentional rationality'. We seek to maximize our personal interest. But we are continually hampered by these inherent limitations that prevent us from reaching our goal.

---

2. Mie Augier and James G. March (dir.), *Models of a Man: Essays in Memory of Herbert A. Simon*, MIT Press, 2004, p. 162.
3. Gerd Gigerenzer and Reinhard Selten (dir.), *Bounded Rationality: The Adaptive Toolbox*, MIT Press, 2002.

Paul Slovic and the psychology of decisions

Psychologists played a central role in the development of what would gradually become behavioral economics.

Indeed, behavioral economics represents psychology's big comeback in decision theory. Its role has been to inject some life, some reality, and some flesh and blood into the essentially mathematical decision models drawn up by economists in the first half of the twentieth century.

As one closely involved with the revolution, Paul Slovic is without doubt psychology's most iconic figure. Concerned in particular with ideas of risk perception and its consequences for decisions and choices, Slovic's work spans the mid-1960s up to the present day, with his publication in 2010 of *The Feeling of Risk*.[4] In 1982, along with Kahneman and Tversky, he was one of the three co-directors of *Judgment under Uncertainty: Heuristics and Biases* – a major work in the nascent field of behavioral economics. As the title suggests, the experiments brought to light what is considered 'bias' by classical decision theory in regard to expected behavior. In situations of uncertainty – that is, the majority of decisions that we take in the course of our everyday lives – we make choices that often do not correspond to those predicted by the theory of the rational man.

Five psychologists have had a particularly strong influence in the field of behavioral economics: Robert Zajonc, Richard Nisbett, Robert Cialdini, Timothy Wilson, and Barry Schwartz. They are all professors – and of psychology, of course. Robert Zajonc worked on the concept of familiarity, in particular, the link between repeated exposure to a stimulus and the corresponding unconscious emotion.

Robert Cialdini, with his important 1984 publication, *Influence: The Psychology of Persuasion,* is the most well known

---

4. Paul Slovic, *The Feeling of Risk*, EarthScan, 2010.

outside of academic circles. In particular, he stresses the role of social norms (as seen earlier in the example of organ donors) and reciprocity in our behavior. Cialdini continues to publish successful popular science books such as *Yes! 50 Scientifically Proven Ways to Be Persuasive,*[5] and, more recently, *The Small Big.*[6] His contribution is to open people's minds to the psychological, non-rational aspects of decision making.

Richard Nisbett and Timothy D. Wilson have worked both together and individually on an issue that is central to our understanding of decisions: our limited capacity to explain our choices and behaviors while being persuaded of the contrary. Their important research paper, 'Telling More than We Can Know: Verbal Reports on Mental Processes', to which we shall return to later, was published in 1977 in the *Psychological Review* and demonstrates the strong limits in the explanation of one's own choices.

Barry Schwartz is the psychology professor with the highest media profile. He regularly contributes editorials to the *New York Times* and has given several remarkable, much-discussed TED[7] lectures, most notably the one in which he presents the theories contained in his celebrated 2004 publication, *The Paradox of Choice: Why More is Less.*[8] His main area of interest is the way that wide choices affect our decisions and behavior. Once again, Schwartz's experiments show that our choices differ according to the nature and complexity of the various options at our disposal.

---

5.   Robert Cialdini, *Yes! 50 Scientifically Proven Ways to Be Persuasive*, Simon and Schuster, 2008.
6.   Steve Martin, Noah Goldstein and Robert Cialdini, *The Small Big: Small Change That's Spark Big Influence*, Grand Central Publishing, 2014.
7.   Technology, entertainment and design.
8.   Barry Schwartz, *The Paradox of Choice: Why More Is Less*, Harper Perennial, 2004.

Experiment after experiment, these psychologists continue to chip away at the foundations of utility theory. Time and again, they demonstrate that beneath the desire for rationality there lurks a human reality involving deep psychological influences that have a major impact on the decisions taken by real people in the course of their everyday lives.

The founding fathers: Amos Tversky and Daniel Kahneman

The most prominent of these psychologists, Daniel Kahneman, and his friend and intellectual travel partner Amos Tversky, are the founding fathers of behavioral economics.

Their collaboration began in 1969, at the Hebrew University of Jerusalem, where Amos completed a BA in human sciences in 1961. He later returned after receiving his doctorate from the University of Michigan, and the two researchers worked together from then until Tversky's death some twenty-five years later.

Their research period spanned the end of the 1970s until the end of the 1990s. It laid the groundwork for what would go on to become behavioral economics, as well as inspiring a whole generation of researchers who themselves would become important players in the revolution. Together, the pair wrote three of the four most-cited papers in the field[9].

Kahneman and Tversky – later Kahneman alone with his masterpiece[10] *Thinking, Fast and Slow* – gradually revolutionized our understanding of human decisions, notably by providing an overall vision of what it is that these entail.

---

9. Mark Egan, in *Stirling Behavioural Science Blog*: economicspsychology-policy.blogspot.fr
10. Daniel Kahneman, *Thinking, Fast and Slow*, Farrar, Straus and Giroux, 2011.

Drawing on their own research while integrating knowledge gleaned from that of other psychologists, they arrived at an overview of the decision-making process. That is, a general operating method based on an increasingly precise set of rules. Kahneman and Tversky created the framework on which behavioral economics was built. This framework – published in 1979 and called 'prospect theory' – puts forward two revolutionary ideas with respect to traditional decision theory.

- First of all, choice is not measured in absolute terms but with regard to a reference point. The decision maker uses this reference point to evaluate potential gains and losses associated with the available options. However, we, as humans, do not evaluate gains and losses in the same way. Generally speaking, we feel losses much more keenly than gains of a similar magnitude. We are thus averse to loss. All things being equal, for instance, we prefer not to take the risk of losing 100 dollars, even when we have the equivalent chance of winning the same amount. In making our decision, the same value hence has two different weights – which completely contradicts utility theory.
- Secondly, Kahneman and Tversky's experiments show that decision makers have a poor grasp of probabilities. We overestimate low probabilities and underestimate high probabilities. This leads us to make decisions in the course of our daily lives that are erroneous in terms of the pure mathematical logic on which classical decision theory is based.

Prospect theory hence fundamentally alters previous ideas about decision-making logic. And this pioneering work is the breach into which subsequent researchers have directed their best efforts. Their collective goal: to enrich and enhance our understanding of the way that humans take decisions.

Richard Thaler and Cass Sunstein: the Nudge-men and the public policy revolution

Richard Thaler and Cass Sunstein are both American professors. Thaler, Professor of Economics at the esteemed University of Chicago; Sunstein, Professor of Law at Harvard.

Nudge was a huge publishing success, allowing behavioral economics to finally scale the hallowed walls of academia. The book presents a practical application for 40 years of university-based decision-making research. It seeks to answer questions including: How to turn knowledge into action? How to create more effective public policy for the big issues currently at hand – public health, for instance, or the environment – based on the real factors governing people's behavior?

Following *Nudge*'s phenomenal impact, the authors dedicated themselves to raising awareness of their ideas among public policy decision makers and this also went far better that they could have hoped.

In 2010, Richard Thaler was closely involved in the creation of what journalists quickly coined the 'Nudge Unit' – the Behavioral Insights Team put together by David Cameron's UK government.

A short time earlier, in 2009, Barack Obama, the recently elected president of the most powerful country in the world, named Cass Sunstein as head of the White House Office of Information and Regulation Affairs (OIRA). Created in 1980 under the Reagan administration, OIRA's initial function was to oversee authorization for federal agencies seeking to collect information about American citizens. In 1981, this role was extended to ensuring that all regulatory action sought by the administration was only undertaken if collective benefits outweighed potential costs.

The experience was positive, and in summer 2013 the Obama administration decided to set up a team charged with applying the findings of behavioral economics to improving public policy effectiveness. This new team, directed by Maya Shankar, commenced operations in January 2015.

Sunstein continues to publish numerous works aimed at making the power of Nudge more widely known, while Thaler travels the globe spreading the word.

George Loewenstein and the leading academics

Some important teacher-researchers are at the heart of the behavioral economics revolution. Younger than the founding fathers, and for the moment lacking the same media presence as that gained by Richard Thaler and Cass Sunstein with *Nudge* and its follow-up publications, these are nevertheless important members of the uprising. For 30 years, they have been carrying out experiments that have considerably enriched behavioral economics' current knowledge base.

George Loewenstein is without doubt the most iconic of these academic heavyweights whose research and discoveries have seen behavioral economics thrust into the mainstream. Like almost all behavioral economists, he is a professor of economics and psychology. The gradual integration of these two long-separate disciplines – a distinction that is still the case in many institutions – is in itself an example of behavioral economics at work. The Herbert Simon chair in the Social and Decision Sciences department of Carnegie Mellon University, held by Loewenstein, is itself highly symbolic. Loewenstein also directs the Center for Behavioral Research; and his ambition is that which lies at the heart of all behavioral economics: to introduce psychology to the study of economics and human behavior.

Loewenstein has made major contributions to our understanding of the decision-making process in three specific areas: choice over time; the role of emotions in decisions; and the problem of negotiation. Behind Kahneman-Tversky, whose work has been cited more than 150,000 times according to Google scholar, and Thaler-Sunstein, who can boast over 60,000 citations, it is Loewenstein with 40,000 who is the most-cited behavioral economist.

Matthew Rabin and Ernst Fehr should also be counted among those outstanding researchers who continually push forward our understanding of human decisions. They too have played an important role in the development of behavioral economics.

Matthew Rabin, among the most brilliant of the new generation of behavioral economists, is Professor of Economics at UC Berkeley. In 2001, he received the John Bates Clark medal for the best economist under the age of 40. His contribution to the development of behavioral economics is significant both in terms of the research that he carries out, and also in his ability to publicize his findings. As a researcher, Rabin's main area of interest concerns perceptions of fairness in decision making, and procrastination. His work in these areas once again demonstrates the limitations of utility theory in explaining decision-related behavior. Humans, as he shows, are not solely concerned with their selfish interests. Rather, they take into account the interest of their fellow man when making decisions. Regarding the promotion of behavioral economics, Rabin, along with George Loewenstein and Colin Camerer, was behind the 2004 publication of *Advances in Behavioral Economics* – a key work bringing together the most important research in this ever-expanding field.

Ernst Fehr is another iconic example of a teacher-researcher to have played an important role in improving our understanding of the factors that influence decisions and behavior. Fehr, an Austrian, is a professor of microeconomics and experimental economic research at the University of Zurich. He specializes in analyzing the role of social interaction in decisions. In particular, he is concerned with reciprocity and fairness. His research demonstrates that the selfish quest for personal gain does not sufficiently explain a large number of the decisions that we make in the course of our daily lives. Fehr also plays an important role in bringing together behavioral economics and decision neuroscience – a topic we'll come back to.

Dan Ariely: behavioral economics marketer-in-chief

There had to be one, and it's undoubtedly Ariely. Rabble-rouser, agitator – marketer, in a word, for the whole behavioral economics movement. With the 2008 publication of *Predictably Irrational,*[11] which has since been translated into 30 languages, Ariely produced the one thing that behavioral economics needed to burst out of the tight-knit world of academic research: public recognition. He achieved this – especially in business circles – via a clear, easy-to-read book founded on strong academic principles.

Aside from being a fabulous marketer for behavioral economics, as well as a tremendous, inspirational storyteller, Dan Ariely is a brilliant psychologist and renowned academic seeking to further our understanding of the way humans take decisions in real life. His experiments highlight the role of emotions, particularly those relating to possession and social interaction. As such, Ariely, in whose hands the most complex mechanisms become clear, takes his place in the pantheon of behavioral economists.

Ariely also uses all the modern tools to generate publicity for both the field and for his own ideas. He has a website, danariely.com, as well as a blog, both bursting with short, amusing videos explaining the concepts, as well as TED talks

---

11. Dan Ariely, *Predictably Irrational: The Hidden Forces that Shape our Decisions,* HarperCollins, 2008.

with almost four million views on YouTube. There is also the first free online course on Coursera with over 140,000 subscribers, myself among them. While he may not be a pioneer per se, he is one of those men – and by my reckoning the best of them – who have made huge strides in taking behavioral economics out of its ivory tower and into the mainstream.

In 2008, Ariely set the cat among the pigeons by writing: 'We are really far less rational than standard economy theory assumes. Moreover, these irrational behaviors of ours are neither random nor senseless. They are systematic, and since we repeat them again and again, predictable.' If behavior is predictable, it is possible to estimate the outcome and then find effective strategies to bring about change.

With Ariely at the helm, behavioral economics has truly broken free of the closed circle in which it was conceived.

Antonio Damasio and neuroscience

Behavioral economics is by nature multidisciplinary, and decision neuroscience, as one of these disciplines, has an important role to play. Traditionally, behavioral economists are drawn from backgrounds in psychology, economics, sociology and experimental economics. However, Antonio Damasio, Michael Gazzaniga, Joseph LeDoux and Read Montague have taken a radically different starting point – biology – to invent what has become known as 'neuroscience'. Conceived under the same name at the end of the 1960s – around the same time as behavioral economics – neuroscience has developed at a spectacular rate over the last 50 years. The phenomenon is such that we can now, and with good reason, speak about the 'neuroscience revolution'. Decision neuroscientists are concerned with the same subject as behavioral economists, although their starting point – analysis of brain function and the nervous system – is somewhat different. The goal, however, is similar: to understand the workings of the human mind.

For all their common ground, the neuroscientists' approach is very different to that of other behavioral economists. The former is concerned with observing the brain function of an individual engaged in a specific task. It may also involve an attempt to understand behavioral dysfunctions in a person suffering from brain damage. The development of increasingly accurate, sophisticated observational tools has resulted in great strides being made since the 1970s. This is particularly true in the case of functional magnetic resonance imaging (fMRI), which allows us to see the working brain 'in action'.

Experiments carried out by neuroscientists enrich, improve, amend, confirm, and overturn the observations and conclusions of behavioral economists. In search of their common goal, to understand what underlies behavior and decision making, the fusion of these two approaches serves to heighten their collective insight. This integration is hence a mutually fruitful source of knowledge.

Antonio Damasio is without doubt the most famous neuroscientist. For many years, he directed the Department of Neuroscience at the University of Iowa, while also teaching at the Salk Institute for Biological Studies in La Jolla, California. Later, he went on to join the University of Southern California as Professor of Neuroscience and Director of the Brain and Creativity Institute. His book, *Descartes' Error: Emotion, Reason and the Human Brain*, (published in the USA in 1994) has been translated into over 30 languages. Its landmark contribution, contained in the title, is its assertion that reason and emotion are intimately linked. They work in harmony with one another: there is no reason without emotion. For better or worse, emotion is at the core of all human decisions.

Joseph LeDoux, professor at the Centre for Neural Science at New York University, has one objective in regard to emotions[12]: 'To give a scientific account of what emotions are, how they operate in the brain, and why they have such important influences in our lives.' As for Damasio with *Descartes' Error*, LeDoux would also publish a seminal work in 2005, *The Emotional Brain*. Thanks to the work of Damasio and LeDoux, there is no longer any doubt that our decision making is heavily influenced by our emotional state.

Michael Gazzaniga is another big name in the world of decision neuroscience. Director of the SAGE Center for the Study of the Mind at the University of California, and President of the Cognitive Neuroscience Institute, Gazzaniga has demonstrated that we have a basic need to explain our behavior, even when such explanations are physiologically impossible. His experiments and their conclusions confirm psychologists' findings regarding the limits of our ability to understand, and to articulate for others, our choices and behavior.

Read Montague represents the young generation of neuroscientists working on our understanding of decisions. Born in 1960, he is a professor in the Department of Neuroscience at the Baylor College of Medicine. He is also a director of the Human Neuroimaging Lab and the Centre for Theoretical Neuroscience in Huston. In 2006, Montague published *Why Choose this Book? How We Make Decisions*. Here, he seeks to understand the physiological framework supporting the decision-making process. He asks, how can we explain our decisions by examining the working of our brains? To what extent are the decisions we make physiologically derived?

---

12. Joseph LeDoux, *The Emotional Brain: The Mysterious Underpinnings of Emotional Life*, Phoenix, 1998, p.15-16.

Colin Camerer and the rise of neuroeconomics

The complementary nature of neuroscience and behavioral economics has found quasi-formal recognition in the birth of 'neuroeconomics' – a new line of research whose manifesto *Neuroeconomics: Decision Making and the Brain*[13] was published in 2009 under the co-direction of Paul Glimcher, Colin Camerer, Ernst Fehr and Russell Poldrack. The basic concept behind the merger was straightforward: to gain a better understanding of decisions and behaviors and it seemed sensible for neuroscientists and behavioral economists to pool their respective expertise and approaches. Both parties would be stronger as a result, allowing for a deeper understanding of the phenomena at hand. And so behavioral economists became interested in neuroscience and its tools – in particular the steady emergence of neuro-imaging – as a means to improve their understanding of the psychological and neurological foundations to their experiments. And, conversely, neuroscientists and cognitivists were happy to take the findings of behavioral economics and psychology and apply them to neurological and cerebral functions.

Colin Camerer, Professor of Behavioral Finance and Economics at the California Institute of Technology (Caltech), is the perfect example of a brilliant researcher who has used the fusion of these disciplines to advance scientific knowledge about decisions and behavior. Camerer, who started out as a behavioral economist, increasingly turned his attentions to neuroscience, and in the end oversaw the new line of research known as 'neuroeconomics'. In 1997, in collaboration with George Loewenstein, Camerer organized the first meetings at the University of Carnegie Mellon between behavioral

---

13. Paul Glimcher, Colin Camerer, Ernst Fehr and Russell Poldrack, *Neuroeconomics: Decision Making and the Brain*, Elsevier, 2009.

economists and neuroscientists specializing in the decision-making process.

Thus conceived, neuroeconomics continued its phenomenal growth, which has matched the giant leaps made in neuro-imaging techniques over the last 20 years. Following the meeting at Carnegie Mellon, other symposia were organized bringing together behavioral economists and neuroscientists and culminated in the 2003 conference at Martha's Vineyards, organized by Greg Burns. Here the birth certificate was stamped and the official status of the discipline confirmed.

All of the big 'discoveries' in behavioral economics have been re-examined using neuroscientific techniques in an attempt to understand the physiological foundations of behavioral reactions and the decision-making process. The neuroeconomics contingent has given weight to their work and the advancing revolution. Their contribution has been to provide a deeper understanding of the physiological conditions underlying the science of behavior and decisions.

David Halpern, Esther Duflo and the behavioral economics practitioners

This final group would not exist without their predecessors. Nevertheless, it is without a doubt the most important of them all. They are, of course, the behavioral economics practitioners. Without the academic research conducted over the last 40 years, it is indeed true that there would be no results to apply. Then again, what good are the results without a real-world application? What is the purpose to the research whose honourable goal is the improved understanding of everyday decisions made by real people in the course of their real lives? What is the point of going on about its value in order to build a better world?

Behavioral economics practitioners are all about action. Their mission is to come up with a programme aimed at changing behavior in a specific target area. Be it those using a particular service (hospital patients) or any other segment of the population. The practitioners' goal is simply this: to change observed behavior 'A' into desired behavior 'B'.

The current group is small, albeit quickly growing as behavioral economics becomes more widely known. I think of myself – on a modest level – as one of them. And my hope is that this book might persuade you to join up.

By way of a family photo, if you will, I've chosen two very different personalities: David Halpern and Esther Duflo.

David Halpern directs the Behavioural Insights Team attached to David Cameron's British government. He is also in charge of the What Works Network in the role of 'national advisor'. Established in 2013, the network is responsible for gathering and identifying – with accompanying scientific proof – good practice in the fields of education, crime reduction, upstream policy interventions, and local-level economic growth stimuli. According to a recent announcement, the What Works Network will be funded to the tune of 200 billion pounds. This is a hence a project of genuine substance – an example of real behavioral economics in action.

In an interview with Christian Jarrett for *The Psychologist*, David Halpern makes a clear link between his work for the Behavioural Insights Team and the book, *Nudge*. In a more general sense, he also highlights the relationship between behavioral economics research and the leading thinkers under his direction.

The aim is to work on people's behavior. Moreover, politics is precisely this: eliciting changes in citizens' behavior, and steering these changes in the desired direction. The Nudge Unit's goal is simple: to apply the teachings of behavioral economics to re-orient citizens' behaviors, with a view to improving both individual and collective well-being. David

Halpern, as one entrusted with its practical application, is hence a true son of the revolution.

The same is true of Esther Duflo, whose role and function and are nevertheless very different. First, she is a woman, which is something of a rarity in current behavioral economics circles. She is also French, something similarly rare, for which my country should hang its head. Her area of key interest is understanding and combatting world poverty – which is also different to the topics studied by her predecessors.

My point in introducing Esther Duflo is to shine a light on the broad area of study that is behavioral economics. In the beginning, it was about understanding commonplace behaviors and decisions that people take in the course of their everyday lives. An intellectual quest for improved comprehension. However, the emerging practitioners have dramatically shifted the goalposts. Now, it is all about applying these findings to expedite the desired changes for increased effectiveness in an improving world. Esther Duflo is the embodiment of a new generation of men and women turning this knowedge into action.

A specialist in development economics, she applies a specific method drawn directly from experimental economics. To understand poverty, she begins with individual behaviors and decisions taken from a narrow range of real-life situations. Her aim is to identify the reality of the factors preventing economic development in people's everyday lives, and then to come up with a substantive, effective plan of action. The aim of doing field experiment after field experiment is to understand poverty through an analysis of observed decisions and behaviors. By isolating the foundations of these behaviors it is possible to identify potential actions, and, most importantly, to test their effectiveness under real-life conditions.

In 2003, Esther Duflo founded an action laboratory for fighting poverty (the Poverty Action Lab, which will be renamed the Abdul Latif Jameel Poverty Action Lap, or

J-PAL), the aim of which is to spread and promote her method among other researchers, NGOs and governments. Duflo has hence made the transition from theory into action and she now leads a parallel existence as both research professor and someone right at the heart of the action. On 21st December 2012, she was appointed to the President's Global Development Council responsible for advising President Obama and senior officials in the American administration on issues relating to economic development.

Now the behavioral economics practitioners are in place, let's turn our attention to the various phases of the revolution. We'll begin by taking a look at the revolutionaries' weapons, before examining some of their main conclusions regarding human behavior.

Chapter *2*

The stages of the revolution

From the early questions of the 1950s to their practical application in 2010

The behavioral economics revolution can be broken down into four main phases. These span half a century, from the early signs of incipient revolt to its dramatic appearance on the public stage:

- The prerevolutionary period: 1950-1970
- The underground revolution: 1970-2002
- The acknowledged revolution: 2002-2010
- The revolution in action: from 2010 until today

The prerevolutionary period: 1950-1970

This prerevolutionary phase involves the opening of minds. A fresh perspective, beginning at the end of the 1950s and ending at the beginning of the 1970s, which allowed the next generation to question the principles on which the dominant theory was based. Essentially, this spanned the first papers of Herbert Simon and Maurice Allais through the early work of the founding fathers, Kahneman and Tversky.

It was a time when a handful of individuals were pitched against the all-powerful neoclassical economic theory. Rather than questioning the entire theory, Simon and Allais focused on specific areas. In particular, a number of axioms fundamental to utility theory. Their thinking was that in repudiating these axioms, the models themselves would be rendered unstable, and thus incapable of translating the reality of decisions made by economic agents.

For Herbert Simon, this involved questioning our unlimited capacity to process information. For Maurice Allais, it was about proving that the independence axiom crucial to utility theory does not reflect the reality of human decisions. Supporters of classical theory thought that these amounted to minor criticisms: trivial deficiencies revealed by special cases that did not undermine the model's overall solidity. At worst, they said work was required to optimize the basic templates.

These early critiques were largely ignored by the majority of influential economists. But it wasn't all for nothing; their voices had been heard! In particular, by some young economists and psychologists just starting out at the end of the 1960s. The seeds of the revolution had been sown.

The underground revolution: 1970-2002

Daniel Kahneman, Amos Tversky, Paul Slovic, and Richard Thaler made up the first battalion of this new generation.

For three decades, these men, who would go on to found a completely new discipline, carried out a wide range of experiments to understand the reality of human decisions. Their aim was to methodically identify the heuristic principles used in the course of people's daily lives. This decade saw the discovery of the main factors that had a systematic influence over behavior. It also saw the nascent organization of the highly diversified field now known as behavioral economics, as well as the appearance of decision neuroscience and the integration of psychology.

Naming key dates always feels a little arbitrary. However, important revolutionaries such as Colin Camerer and George Loewenstein all concur[1] that the 1974 publication in *Science* of an article by Kahneman and Tversky was a defining moment. Here, the two authors gave evidence that we use mental shortcuts – simplified logical processes to evaluate the probability of each choice option. In so doing, we distance ourselves from the principles of statistical calculation postulated by classical theory – a cornerstone of dominant economic thought.

The second era-defining moment can also be given a date, as it concerns the 1979 publication of an article on prospect theory[2] that earned the authors a Noble Prize. This time, the argument was not concerned with a point-by-point critique of a single axiom. Rather, the establishment of a substantively different logic according to which humans are not capable of acting as 'mathematically' rational beings. Kahneman and Tversky hence put forward an alternate view of human decisions that is largely based on psychology.

And so the path was cleared to carry out this research whose aim was to identify, by means of experiment, the real factors influencing our behavior.

Towards the end of this period, the collective findings gave a perspective on the logic of decisions that was both entirely new and in direct conflict with utility theory. In 1997, the *Quarterly Journal of Economics* ran a special edition to mark this

---

1. Colin Camerer and George Loewenstein, 'Behavioral Economics: Past, Present and Future', *Advances in Behavioral Economics*, Russell Sage Foundation, Princeton University Press, 2004.

2. Daniel Kahneman and Amos Tversky, 'Prospect Theory: An Analysis of Decision under Risk', *Econometrica*, vol. 47, n° 2, March 1979, p. 263-291.

radical shake-up. And like that, behavioral economics was born. Conceived by a few isolated scholars considered heretics by their peers, it would go on to become, over the next 20 years, a recognized and highly organized global discipline.

With the publication of their research, the main players gradually became more widely known and more closely involved with each other's work. In 1986, a Chicago conference brought together those who would become the main behavioral economists. In same year, two American foundations – the Russell Sage Foundation and the Alfred Sloan Foundation – set up behavioral economics research programmes. In 1992, the Russell Sage Foundation increased its commitment by launching the Behavioral Economics Roundtable, which brought together and provided funding for the main researchers in the field. Still active today, the Roundtable counts almost all the most important behavioral economists among its twenty-eight members, including six Noble Prize winners.

The 1990s also saw the birth and swift development of decision neurosciences, and their subsequent integration into behavioral economics. Some of the big-name behavioral economists such as George Loewenstein and Colin Camerer were instrumental in this process.

And so it was that at the beginning of the 2000s, behavioral economics, solidly grounded in 30 years of scientific research, was braced to conquer hearts and minds beyond the close-knit world of academia.

The acknowledged revolution: 2002-2010

The first step on the road to wider recognition came when Daniel Kahneman was awarded the Nobel Prize in Economics in 2002. Tversky-Kahneman's joint endeavours were acknowledged at the highest level, and the whole field benefited as a result.

Anomalies regarding the supposed rationality of human decisions, demonstrated in experiment after experiment, were no longer thought of as exceptions. No more were they dismissed as special cases within an otherwise functional theory. Rather, they were a means to the complete uprooting of this theory, and its replacement with a new core concept in the form of prospect theory.

The Nobel Prize was certainly a magnificent springboard from which to launch behavioral economics into the mainstream; but it was also just the beginning. The prize itself would be supplemented by many publications over the following years by leading behavioral economists.

At the head of these publications was *Predictably Irrational* by Dan Ariely, which came out in February of this pivotal year. With his innovative style that rejects complex academic phrasing, the Duke professor found a way to make the principal findings of thirty years of scholarly research available to the general public. Translated into over thirty languages, the book was a huge international success. It disseminated those ideas long championed by behavioral economics, among which the most fundamental of them all: that our irrationality is both systematic and, at the same time, predictable. Ariely's easy-to-read style, backed up by concrete scientific findings, touched a nerve with both business decision makers and, especially, marketers.

Less than two months after the release of *Predictably Irrational*, Richard Thaler and Cass Sunstein published their own globally acclaimed *Nudge: Improving Decisions about Health, Wealth, and Happiness*. The aims of this book were somewhat different. Rather than describing how individuals take decisions, the authors were concerned with showing how it's possible to come up with 'Nudges' based on a subtle understanding of decision-making mechanisms. That is, gentle incentive systems encouraging individuals to take decisions that are better for themselves or for the wider community. The 'Nudge in the right direction' of the title signifies the key transition from knowledge into action. And it was with this book that behavioral economics truly entered the fray, especially in the case of public decision makers.

In a fitting conclusion to a decade that begins and ends with him, the third work establishing behavioral economics' definitive presence was once more written by its founder, Daniel Kahneman. From the start, *Thinking Fast and Slow*, published in 2011, was viewed as something of a decision-making bible. For all the demands of these impatient, image-oriented times, Kahneman's 500-page tome was still a global bestseller. Behavioral economics had emerged as a major force, and its practitioners would waste no time in seizing the reins.

The revolution in action: from 2010 until today

The period 2002-2010 was a wonderful sounding board for behavioral economics. Over the next five years, that noise translated into action. Practitioners seized the revolutionary moment, with public policy and private enterprise both squarely in their sights.

When it comes to public policy, the ideas set out in *Nudge* have had a progressive influence on numerous governments – something that has happened with unprecedented speed. This really is the perfect moment for an approach that places heavy emphasis on not only the capacity to change peoples' real-life behavior but also on the simple, inexpensive means by which the actions leading to such changes can be implemented. What could be more appealing to those governments, whose hands are tied by budgets linked to the ubiquitous debt of the major western economies, than a joint discussion about increasing effectiveness and reducing costs?

The governments of David Cameron and Barack Obama, as we have seen, were the first to formally endorse the Nudge approach. Cameron's Behavioural Insights Team is responsible for applying 'insights from academic research in behavioral economics to public and social policy'. The UK Nudge Unit works alongside the full range of government departments, as well as local authorities linked to towns and regions. The unit's role is to help implement 'Nudges' aimed at generating behavior that has a positive effect on individual or collective welfare.

Barack Obama is no novice when it comes to behavioral economics. During his 2008 presidential campaign, he was supported by what *Time*[3] magazine termed a 'behavioral dream team', composed of not only Thaler and Sunstein but also Dan Ariely and even Daniel Kahneman!

Convinced, no doubt, by the role played by the 'dream team' in his electoral campaign, as well as OIRA's success under Sunstein and the experiences of the British government, Obama decided to set up a US version of the Behavioural Insights Team in 2013. His belief in behavioral economics itself, and in the results it has produced, are highlighted by the title of the government document announcing the deployment: 'Strengthening Federal Capacity for Behavioral Insights'.

Barely five years after the publication of *Nudge*, and three years after the creation of the Behavioural Insights Team by the British government, the enthusiasm for behavioral economics, has gone global. The Singapore government has jumped aboard, and the Australian, Danish, and Canadian governments seem likely to do the same. In autumn 2014, Angela Merkel's Germany announced the creation of a team of behavioral psychologists drawn straight from the British

---

3. Michael Grunwald, 'How Obama Is Using the Science of Change', *Time*, 2nd April 2009.

and American examples. As well as nation states, certain global organizations have also shown an interest. For instance, in autumn 2013, the EEC organized its first behavioral economics conference. In 2014, the OCDE published a paper written by Peter Lunn and entitled *Regulatory Policy and Behavioural Economics*. And, in December 2014, the World Bank put out its own document on the subject[4].

In 2013, the French government, who were initially hesitant despite the pioneering work presented by Olivier Oullier to the Centre for Strategic Analysis in 2010,[5] conducted its first experiments in the field. This work, carried out by the BVA Nudge Unit on behalf of the Public Finances Directorate General and sponsored by the Prime Minister's Secretary General for the Modernization of Public Actions (SGMAP), is a significant step for the approach's development in France. Several new experiments are currently underway on important subjects such as the reduction of cell phone use while driving by the Traffic and Road Safety Directorate, and the promotion of generic drugs by the Ministry of Health. Consideration is also being given to the formal introduction of a programme leading to a French Nudge Unit, for which I hope to be the spokesperson with my colleagues from the 'change tank' NudgeFrance[6], as well as the creation of a training programme at the École Nationale d'Administration (ENA)[7] for future high-level officials.

It's not only at government level that behavioral economics strikes a chord. New establishments of different shapes and sizes and with different objectives have been set up to accommodate the latest research. Among these are Sendhil

---

4.   World Bank, *World Development Report 2015: Mind, Society, and Behavior*, International Bank for Reconstruction and Development/The World Bank, 2015.

5.   Olivier Oullier (2010), *op. cit.*

6.   Éric Singler, 'Towards a French Nudge Unit', *Libération*, 12th May, 2014.

7.   National Administration College.

Mullainathan's Ideas42, Dan Ariely's IrrationalLabs, and Pelle Hansen's iNudgeyou in Denmark. As well as these, there are the private institutes such as the BVA Nudge Unit in France, or Rory Sutherland's Brain Juicer and OgilvyChange in the UK.

The revolution, it seems, is in full swing.

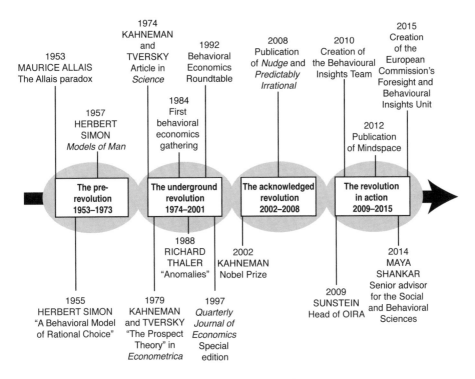

Figure 2.1 The behavioral economics revolution

Chapter 3

The weapons

Throughout the behavioral economics revolution, the same weapon has been used time and again to demonstrate the irrelevance of the dominant theory. And what is this simple, albeit highly scientific weapon, of considerable persuasive force? It is an experimental method applied to daily decisions to measure the impact of hypotheses on behavior.

The atomic bomb: the experimental method

This method was not invented by behavioral economists. In fact, it dates back to the nineteenth century, when it was popularized by the Frenchman Claude Bernard through his study of medicine and biology. The principle is very simple: you put forward a hypothesis, then you come up with an experiment to either prove or disprove it. The method is generally composed of the following elements:

- a 'control' group – a sample of people who are not submitted to the action being tested;
- a 'test' group – a sample of statistically comparable people, who are submitted to a specific intervention.

Let's return to the case of organ donation for a straightforward example. If you want to know whether adding a phrase to a webpage will have an effect on the behavior of visitors to the site, you create an 'experiment design' comprising the following elements:

◆ the intervention: the addition of the phrase 'every day thousands of people who see this page decide to register' to the webpage;

◆ the hypothesis: the addition of this phrase will increase the percentage of donors from their current number via social norms;

◆ the original state: the current webpage, without the phrase being tested;

◆ the test state: the new test page;

◆ the variable tested: the number of donors for each state.

As stated previously, this technique is nothing new. It has been an important part of scientific methodology for almost three centuries. Nevertheless, the experimental method represents a major innovation in the world of classical and neo-classical economics.

Here, researchers develop and rely on mathematically constructed macroeconomic models. Behavioral economists are hence proposing a complete methodological U-turn. They are not looking for global models – the 'big theory' that explains everything via a series of established axioms. Rather, their research is based upon experiments whose results have individual explanations. It's worth noting that when Daniel Kahneman won the Nobel Prize in Economics, the award was shared with Vernon Smith – one of the founders of experimental economics as a systematized way of testing hypotheses under real-life conditions. And, although purists such as George Loewenstein stress[1] that behavioral economists are

---

1. George Loewenstein, 'Experimental Economics from the Vantage-Point of Behavioural Economics', in George Loewenstein (dir.), *Exotic Preferences: Behavioral Economics and Human Motivation*, Oxford University Press, 2008.

more 'eclectic' in their approach, the experimental method is undeniably at the heart of the great strides made in understanding human behavior.

Taking aim: everyday individual decisions

Behavioral economists see the world in microcosm. They want to understand how we ordinary people take decisions in the course of our everyday lives. Their goal is hence not to arrive at some all-encompassing conception of human decisions via a single universal model. Rather, they want to identify and understand the factors underlying these decisions through the study of individual behaviors in specific situations. Why is it that I drink a cup of hot chocolate every morning? Why is it that I agree (or not) to donate my organs in the event of my accidental death? That I cheat (or not) in a particular situation? That I help someone whose car has broken down at the side of the road? That I take part in an energy saving plan? That I throw my rubbish into special dustbins? That I pay my fines late or on time?

The focus on everyday decisions means that behavioral economists operate at a very basic level. By varying the conditions in which the observed decision takes place, they hope to understand its underlying logic. In particular, they want to identify those factors influencing people in making these decisions. Behavioral economics is hence firmly engaged with the real world. Its core objective is to understand how *real* people take decisions in *real* life.

However, this broad range of experiments, which in and of themselves might be considered trivial, masks a larger ambition: to discover the common, constant logical (and illogical!) processes that underpin all human decisions. The aim of each experiment is hence twofold: both to understand the decision in question and, more fundamentally, to prove a hypothesis about decision logic in the given context. As a result of this ongoing process, the body of experiments is enriched, and our understanding of decisions deepened. The method used by behavioral economists thus proceeds from the particular to the general. As such, it differs from classical theories of *homo economicus* or the rational man, which set out in search of a general model by which to explain specific phenomena. So while, the quest for comprehensive understanding is therefore similar, the means by which this is achieved amounts to a true revolutionary U-turn.

The key indicator: behavior

The third element in the revolutionary arsenal concerns a key indicator being addressed by these experiments. Here, once again, there is a significant break from previous research.

This indicator is people's real behavior. Their real-life decisions rather than their attitudes, their tendencies to act, or their intentions in regard to their decisions. The *intention* to act or to decide in one direction or another is of no concern. What counts, rather, is the action *actually* taken as a consequence of a decision. The difference is huge, as we have long known that what people claim to do or to decide in a given situation has very little to do with their real-life action or decision. The vast majority of new products launched for the mass market – in the region of 80%, depending on the source – are failures that disappear inside two years. The same majority of products were subject to validation studies prior to launch, with positive results, especially with regard to purchasing intentions. Real life, however, paints a rather different picture. Purchasing intentions may be positive, but the purchasing reality is something else entirely. Wherever you look, the truth remains: our intentions are an inaccurate way of predicting behavior. The analysis of people's real behavior is hence at the heart of the experiments performed by behavioral economists in their quest to understand the fundamentals of the way we take decisions.

Putting this ambition into practice, however, can be complex. It consists of a huge methodological challenge, both from a theoretical standpoint and in terms of practical implementation. Simply asking someone a question about what their decision might be in a given situation is a simple, quick and inexpensive process. All the more so in the internet era, when you can post a questionnaire online and receive an almost instantaneous response, at hardly any cost. On the other hand, placing the same subject in context and observing their behavior is a long, complicated, and costly procedure. 'Behavioral ambition' thus presents a much more complex challenge when it relates to academic research (the bedrock of behavioral economics) and funding can be difficult to come by.

These studies are designed to benefit marketing budgets in the case of private enterprise, and state budgets in the case of public policy. The challenge facing researchers is huge. They need to fund experimental studies allowing them to study people's *real* decisions and behavior, when the same studies could – apparently – be carried out more simply and at lower cost by simply questioning these same people about their *intended* behavior. The only problem with the second method is it lacks the reliability of the first when it comes to understanding the reality of how people decide.

Behavioral economists hence find themselves faced with a dilemma. The solution involves two types of study:

- those carried out in research laboratories;
- those carried out in a real-world setting.

There are two major advantages to the studies carried out in university laboratories. The first of these is pragmatic, and concerns their relatively easy implementation. The second is methodological, and concerns the ability to control the full range of conditions of the test.

As part of his highly engaging online course 'Behavioural Economics in Action',[2] Professor Dilip Soman of the Rotman School of Management at the University of Toronto opened a debate about the relative advantages and disadvantages of the two methods. Professor Itamar Simonson (Graduate School of Business) and Owain Service, the Managing Director of the UK Behavioural Insights Team, give a good summary of the issues at the heart of the debate. For Simonson: 'Well-designed lab studies have clear advantages over field studies. Unlike field studies, well-designed lab studies can tell you why an effect that you observed happens, how it happens, and under what conditions it's either weaker or stronger. With field studies, on the other hand, you often wonder about whether they generalize, whether there are other causes for what you see.' Service, however, stresses the benefits of studying things in real life: 'I firmly believe that field studies add more insight than lab studies. And there's a very good reason for this, which is that I care about what works in the real world. So if lab studies have their place, it's really to inform the design of the field study, which, by my reckoning, makes lab studies good but not quite as good as field experiments.' Nina Mazar, Professor of Marketing at the Rotman School and a rising behavioral economics star, joins him in saying: 'The question is if the best insight is gained by field experiments. And I want to argue, absolutely. What good is it if I find an effect in a controlled lab environment when I don't know if it will hold outside of the lab in the so-called real world?'

I should state here that my own opinion – based on almost 25 years of studies carried out both in IN VIVO BVA ShopperLabs laboratories as well as 'shopper' studies performed in real stores – falls somewhere in between the two. I would also add another variable to the debate: the realism of the labora-

---

2.   Dilip Soman, 'Behavioural Economics in Action', Rotman University of Toronto, online course, BE101x, 2014.

tory setting. The greater this realism, the more the limitations rightly highlighted by the advocates of field experiments seem to fade away. If the laboratory setting closely mirrors that of real life, it follows that the results obtained should be able to predict real life results. I dare say this is the experience of the advertising companies with whom we have tested new products, made changes to packaging, or reorganized their shelving and point of sale communications in our ShopperLabs; before witnessing the same effects in the real world. On the other hand, if the laboratory conditions are poorly matched to the natural environment in which the decision takes place (it's not only a question of the physical environment but also the setting's ability to recreate the right mindset in the participants) then the results may not be reproduced. Beyond this criterion, my own feeling is that the two methods co-exist because they have good reason to. That is, they both possess significant, albeit different advantages. Depending on both the aims of the researcher and the restrictions that they have to deal with, either one or other of the two approaches may be best. But the ultimate goal – understanding how decisions are made in real life – never changes. Thus, if laboratory conditions are overly artificial, that indicates to me that this is no longer a behavioral economics-type experiment.

To sum up, the behavioral economists' arsenal consists of the following: a single research goal – to understand the ordinary decisions made by normal people in real life; a single method – experimentation, either in laboratory conditions or in the field; and a single indicator – real-life behavior and the actual decision taken. Commitment to their research and methodological goals aside, however, the revolutionaries are driven by the highest of ambitions. Their common goal is to create a better world in which people take decisions that improve conditions for themselves, their community, or the planet. In terms of public policy, this means political leaders will be able to take more effective decisions to benefit of their fellow citizens.

A revolution in search of a better world

A better world! Many people, I'm sure, would consider this a naïve or at best utopian ambition. Utopian or naïve, that is, for all those pessimists who can't believe a set of ideas and a scientific approach can help with such a lofty goal. Inappropriate, too, for those who think that it is not for the state, however democratic, to guide the individual's behavior – even when this brings about an increase in their happiness. This is an important ethical question, and I will return to it at the end of the book.

Nonetheless, the writings and pronouncements of our revolutionaries all resonate with the same desire: to make the world a better place. As Richard Thaler and Cass Sunstein state,[3] 'We argue for self-conscious efforts, by institutions in the private sectors and also by government, to steer people's choices in directions that will improve their lives.' For Dan Ariely, it's also about improving our lives:[4] 'Behavioral economists believe that people are susceptible to irrelevant influences from their immediate environment (which we call context effects), irrelevant emotions, shortsightedness, and other forms of irrationality. What good news can accompany this realization? The good news is that these mistakes also provide opportunities for improvement. If we all make systematic mistakes in our decisions, then why not develop new strategies, tools, and methods to help us make better decisions and improve our overall well-being?'

And so, let's throw ourselves into the inner workings of the revolution by sharing its findings and examining how these factors affect our real-life decisions and behavior.

---

3.   Richard Thaler and Cass Sunstein (2010), *op. cit.*, p. 5.
4.   Dan Ariely, *Predictably Irrational: The Hidden Forces that Shape our Decisions*, HarpersCollins, 2008, p. 318.

PART TWO

HOW HOMER SIMPSON DETHRONED SUPERMAN

What are the factors that influence our decisions?

Chapter 4

The Superman illusion (and the Homer Simpson reality)

The basic challenge of understanding human decisions contains two viewpoints. These viewpoints are vigorously, sometimes violently, opposed. It's a conflict that could be compared to a battle between two symbolic characters. In the blue corner, the current titleholder; Superman. A one-of-a-kind, long-standing champion, his star may be fading but he is still very much a force. And in the red corner, the young pretender; Homer Simpson. A newcomer whose steady progress over the last 30 years makes him a viable contender for the crown.

The question they are fighting over is a big one: Which theory leads us to better understand and hence be able to predict human behavior?

Superman, the perfect specimen, is the darling of traditional decision theoreticians: the famous *homo economicus*. He represents the theory of rationality, and is the agent on which classical and neoclassical economics are based – from Adam Smith to Oskar Morgenstern to John von Neumann. He is close to perfection. Technical perfection, at least. Above all, this is a being that acts and decides in an eminently rational manner. He achieves this via certain undeniable qualities, which constitute the premises upheld by supporters of human rationality theory.

Let's quickly remind ourselves of his quasi-supernatural powers. He has a clear objective, which is to maximize personal satisfaction for the decisions he takes and the behavior he adopts. To accomplish this, he has a mental capacity that allows him both a perfect knowledge of the range of options facing him, as well as the ability to accurately assess (using his finely tuned mathematical brain) the value of each option. Using these skills, he can identify which option is best. Every one of his decisions stems from a rational cost-benefit assessment of each option, which he uses to identify the choice that maximizes his utility (so say the economists). As well as this, Superman is highly coherent and stable in the preferences that guide his choices. He is a constant force who doesn't change from one day to the next. He is also someone in possession of free will, unaffected by his environment, whose only influence is his often selfish, money-driven interests.

All in all, *homo economicus* is not a man at all – which is why I've called him Superman. He is more of an optical illusion, a cold-hearted monster, or a robot than flesh and blood.

However, there is a problem with all this. Superman is not of this world, just as real people are not like *homo economicus*. Cass Sunstein and Richard Thaler sum it up as follows: 'If you look at economics textbooks, you will learn that *homo economics* can think like Albert Einstein, store as much memory as IBM's Big Blue, and exercise the willpower of Mahatma Gandhi. Really. But the people who we know are not like that.'[1]

---

1. Richard Thaler and Cass Sunstein (2010), *op. cit.*, p. 26.

The six fundamentals of human decisions

Forty years of behavioral economics experiments have resulted in a radically different picture of the human reality. And the conclusion is extremely clear: we are much closer to Homer Simpson than we are to the notorious, imaginary Superman.

The decisions taken by the Homer character include the following six characteristics (see Figure 4.1). Note that they are all some distance from the tenets of classical theory.

◆ Our logical process is highly chaotic
◆ We are emotional beings
◆ We are social beings
◆ We are creatures of context
◆ We are creatures of habit
◆ We have intuitive natures that we do not understand

Figure 4.1 The six fundamental traits of human decision making

These six fundamental traits shared by all of us – albeit with significant individual variations – form the basis for the process by which we arrive at our decisions.

Understanding these traits is central to being able to design actions aimed at steering people's behavior in the desired direction. Only via a deep knowledge of each will it be possible for practitioners to identify the relevant, effective levers that they need to reach their goal. But before delving deeper into a description of the human reality, let's kill off, once and for all, this rationality by which we are supposedly defined.

Rational? You said rational?!

Of course we all think we are rational. And since you're convinced of it, let's start by looking at some amusing – but scientifically rigorous – examples that might shed some new light on this famous rationality.

This experiment was carried out by a trio of important behavioral economists: Dan Ariely, Drazen Prelec and George Loewenstein.[2] The aim was to evaluate the influence of an arbitrary number on perceptions about the price of consumer goods. The researchers began by presenting a number of products to a sample of students. Among these were chocolates, wine, a wireless computer keyboard, etc. Next, they asked the students to perform the following tasks:

- ◆ write the final two digits of their social security number at the top of the page containing the various products;
- ◆ re-write this number opposite each product in the form of a price. For example, if the social security number ends in 35, write 35 dollars;

---

2.   Dan Ariely, George Loewenstein and Drazen Prelec, 'Coherent Arbitrariness: Stable Demand Curves without Stable Preferences', *Quarterly Journal of Economics*, vol. 118, n° 1, 2003, p. 73-106.

- for each product, state whether they would agree to buy it at the marked price;
- finally, write the maximum price that they would be prepared to pay for each product.

Of course, we cannot believe that a random number – the two final digits of a social security number – can influence the price that someone is prepared to pay for something. And yet… Here are the results comparing the prices given by the students with the lowest and highest social security numbers:

- wireless keyboard: 16.09 dollars versus 55.64 dollars.
- book: 12.82 dollars versus 30 dollars.
- chocolates: 9.55 dollars versus 20.64 dollars…

There is hence a statistical correlation between the price given for each product and the last two digits of the social security number. Furthermore, this is true for every one of the objects! Once again, we find ourselves some distance from the theory of the rational man. It appears we are influenced by factors that we would not even consider, and if we did consider them, we would never imagine they could have such a strong effect on our perceptions and decisions. In a moment, we will look at the phenomenon known as 'anchoring' which we talked about previously in the example of the Campbell's soup promotion.

Another example is an experiment carried out by Daniel Kahneman himself. Here, the goal is to measure if the value we assign our time is stable and independent of the way in which we use it. Participants in the study were asked to choose one the following:

- buy a pen for 25 dollars in the same shop that they found it;
- or, buy the same pen in a shop located 15 minutes' walk away for 18 dollars.

In this instance, the majority chose to walk for fifteen minutes and pay the lower price, saving seven dollars. The respondents thought that 15 minutes of their time was worth the extra seven dollars. Nothing irrational, so far.

But things got interesting when Kahneman offered the participants a second choice regarding the purchase of a suit, with the following options:

+ buy a suit for 455 dollars in the same shop that they found it;

+ or, buy the same suit in a shop located 15 minutes' walk away for 448 dollars.

In this instance, the majority chose the first option – to pay the higher price. They thought, at least implicitly, that it was not worth walking 15 minutes for the sake of seven dollars.

For both these decisions, the question concerns the estimated value of our time. In the first case, this is seven dollars. In the second, more than seven dollars, as we're not willing to walk 15 minutes to save this amount. Once again, both our assumed rationality and the stability of our preferences claimed by utility theory are undermined. I could cite many more such examples, using concrete scientific studies, to illustrate this basic human 'irrationality'. Forty years of experiments carried out by behavioral economists have made it abundantly clear that we are not the rational economic agents – the Supermen – that classical and neoclassical economists have long held us to be. Amos Tversky pithily sums up this fundamental difference: 'My colleagues study artificial intelligence; I study natural stupidity.'

Given that we do not act rationally, it is even more important to understand that behind each example of 'irrational' decision making or behavior there lurks an identifiable logic – or non-logic – which is possible to explain. This is the central issue for practitioners responsible for coming up with actions aimed at changing people's behavior. If the logic underlying our 'irrational' decisions is stable and predictable, it is hence possible (since we understand the decision-making mechanisms) to pre-empt this logic and integrate it into an action plan aimed at encouraging people – be they citizens, end users, clients or consumers – to alter their decisions.

So if human decision making isn't rational, how did it develop? And how can it be influenced in the future?

5

Chapter

Our logical process is highly chaotic

The eleven logical illusions

Our decisions can be both surprising in regard to our own interests and deviant in terms of purely rational criteria. The reason for this is that despite their many incredible abilities, our brains are not foolproof super-computers. And this causes us to make systematic logical 'errors'.

These systematic errors are grounded in an underlying, perhaps even biological structure that the majority of us share. This is not a question of IQ, training, or self-discipline. Rather, it is something innately human. We are subject to logical illusions, similar to optical illusions, of which we are largely unaware and which are extremely difficult to correct, even when they are explained to us.

Behavioral economists refer to these logical illusions as 'biases' or 'mental shortcuts'. From the seminal work of Herbert Simon and Maurice Allais, through that of Kahneman-Tversky to the present day, the vast majority of their experiments aim at uncovering the principles of these biases. That is, the causes of our deviation from this mythic, perfectly rational decision that maximizes our interests. And practitioners require an understanding of these principles. They are the levers on which effective strategies for changing behavior are constructed.

So let's turn our attention to the eleven bias principles (see Figure 5.1), whose scientific validity is without question and whose influence on our behavior and decisions is immense.

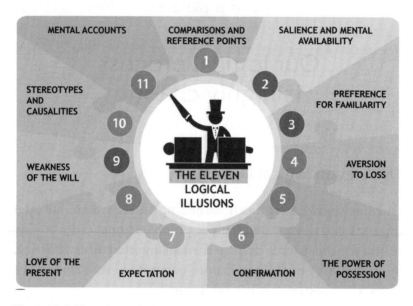

Figure 5.1 The eleven logical illusions

Illusion 1: we are creatures of comparison, not reason

Let's return to Kahneman's experiment, described above, which shows that we value our time comparatively. In the case of a pen worth 25 dollars, we are prepared to invest 15 minutes to save seven dollars. On the other hand, we are not prepared to make the same effort to save the same seven bucks in the case of a suit worth 455 dollars. From a theoretical point of view, this is irrational. However, it is explainable providing that we understand a basic concept regarding the way we think. We do not reason in absolute terms: *what is the value of 15 minutes of my time*. Instead, we are heavily influenced by a reference point that may or may not be intentional, and of which we may not even be conscious. Take, for instance, the initial price of the product we would like to buy (25 or 455 dollars). The reference point will be the starting block from which we evaluate the advantages and disadvantages of the decision. We use this reference point as a means of arriving at an estimated worth, as it's too complicated to calculate value in absolute terms. As creatures of comparison, our decisions are affected not by our absolute interest – to save seven dollars in exchange for 15 minutes of our time – but by our interest *relative* to this reference point. And of course, as practitioners – that is, as choice architects – we often have the chance to create or suggest a reference point to be used by clients or consumers in a manner that we can predict. As we shall see, a well-chosen reference point can have a powerful impact on people's behavior.

Kahneman and Tversky were the first to highlight this new way of thinking, where the influence on decision making is often an unconscious one, known as 'anchoring'. The first study demonstrating the effect was published in a seminal paper,[1] the premise of which is extremely simple. The researchers gave two groups of students two different multiplication sums, and asked them each to give an answer within five seconds:

- the first sum was written as follows: 8 7 6 5 4 3 2 1;
- the second sum (whose result is identical to the first) was written: 1 2 3 4 5 6 7 8.

1. Daniel Kahneman and Amos Tversky, 'Judgment under Uncertainty: Heuristics and Biaises', *Science*, New Series, vol. 185, n° 4157, 27th September 1974, p. 1124-1131.

With insufficient time to perform the calculation, the students tried to come up with an estimate based on the first few numbers of the sum. In the first group, the median result was 2,250; and in the second group it was 520! Both numbers are a long way from the real answer of 40,320. But the interesting thing is the extent to which the first few numbers influenced the calculation. For the first sum, the high initial numbers led to a substantially higher result than for the second sum, which began with low numbers. The first few numbers of the two multiplication hence 'anchored' the students' reasoning. Initial information regarding new decisions often functions as an anchor, or a reference point – that is, a point of basic comparison around which we form the analysis that leads to our final decision.

In the above experiments, it may seem that the reference point – the price of the product we intend to buy or the sum that we have to work out – is conscious, and the choice rational. But this reference point can be far less obvious; its influence, not always visible.

This is the case for Ariely's experiment, described earlier, regarding the effect of the final two digits of a social security number on the price the students were prepared to pay for various products. The higher the random number, the happier the students were to pay a higher price. Here, again, we see a reference point at work. But this time it was unconscious – none of the students could make the link between their pricing decision and their recall of their social security number. And it was also completely arbitrary. The anchoring effect is also evident in the startling results that I described in the introduction for the Campbell's soup promotion. We can hence be influenced by anchors that work as implicit reference points, particularly in cases where we have no prior experience of the new decision facing us.

Whether these reference points are explicit or implicit, whether we use them consciously or otherwise, the key point is that as human decision makers we have a greater gift for comparison than we do for evaluating the inherent interest of the options facing us.

Illusion 2: the impact of salience

An airplane falls out of the sky causing the deaths of several dozen people. The facts are reported in television news programmes and again on the internet. This information is hence salient: many people are made aware of it for a fixed amount of time, until another news item comes along to take its place. The objective risk of dying in a plane crash is not changed by this event. It remains infinitesimal. On the other hand, the perception of this risk is greatly magnified for those being fed this information. And the salience of this – that is, our heightened mental awareness of the information at a given moment – has a disproportionate effect on our decisions. It's as if the probability of an event occurring is somehow linked to its position at the forefront of our mind. If there has just been an air disaster, this means that air disasters often happen, and the probability of a plane crash happening is high. The 'rational' decision is hence to avoid this means of transport – the safest in the world – going by the only information that should really be considered according to rational logic, which is that a plane is statistically less likely to experience an accident than any other means of transport. Gerd Gigerenzer[2] highlighted the reality of this type of behavior in the wake of 9/11. Not many other events in the course of human history have generated such a media reaction as this. The salience of the information – in this case, the risk of being killed by an

---

2. Gerd Gigerenzer, 'Dread Risk, September 11, and Fatal Traffic Accidents', *Psychological Science*, vol. 15, n° 4, 2004, p. 286-287.

airplane that had been diverted by terrorists, particularly in the USA – was very great. And this brought about a change in air transport-related behavior. Compared to the same months of the previous year, sales per airline passenger decreased by 20%, 17% and 12% for the months of October, November and December respectively. At the same time, since Americans still had to get around, the volume of road traffic increased by 2.9% over the same period. And the result of this choice of favouring cars over planes? Three hundred and fifty additional car-related deaths compared to the stable trend observed over the preceding years. The salience of the information about the risks attached to air travel translated into a change in behavior whereby cars were preferred to planes. This turned out to be a poor collective decision, as it resulted in a much higher death count than would have been caused by the status quo. Of course, this is an unusual case, linked as it was to a global event with an exceptional level of salience. Nevertheless, it serves to emphasize the basis bias affecting our behavior. In considering the consequences of or alternatives to a decision, we are disproportionally influenced by events of which we are especially aware.

Salience is not only connected with external communications. It can also be 'internal' – what is known as the 'mental availability' of a piece of information. If information is readily mentally available – that is, if we can summon it without any particular effort – then it has a disproportionally high effect on our judgment. If, for example, there are lots of divorced people in my immediate social circle, I will tend to overestimate the divorce rate of the population as a whole. The ease with which we are able to recall information causes it to have a disproportionate influence, which can lead us into forming judgments that may turn out to be false. Once again, Kahneman and Tversky were the first to highlight this 'availability' bias with an extremely simple experiment that was nevertheless informative. The following two lists of 39 names were presented to the groups participating in the study:

◆ the first list contained the names of 20 high-profile male celebrities (Richard Nixon and the like) and 19 less well-known women;

◆ the second list contained the inverse: 20 high-profile female celebrities (Elizabeth Taylor and the like) and 19 less well-known men.

Participants had to listen to an audio recording in which a name was stated every two seconds. Clearly, when it came to memorization, they found it easier to remember and repeat the names of the well-known celebrities on each list. Hence, more men for the first list, and more women for the second. More interesting, however, was the participants' judgments regarding the proportion – in reality almost identical, 20 versus 19 – of men and women in the lists. Here, the results show a clear difference: 80% thought that there were more men in the list containing famous men, and the same percentage for women in the list containing famous women. The availability of the information hence caused the participants in the study to make erroneous judgments.

To sum up, we tend to think that our immediate reality – the environment in which we live, whose details we witness on a daily basis – is statistically representative of the true state of things. If 80% of couples in my circle of friends are divorced, it follows that divorce must be very common in the rest of the population. If I've just heard that a plane has gone down, this can't be such a rare occurrence, and so on. This is a mental shortcut that we use very often and which leads us to making 'irrational' decisions based on a false understanding of reality.

Salience and the mental availability bias hence play a 'quantitative' role, in that they modify respective probabilities as they appear. However, they can also have a modifying effect on our 'qualitative' perception, as demonstrated by Robert Zajonc through what he terms the 'familiarity effect'.

Illusion 3: our preferences are driven by familiarity

Robert Zajonc, an American psychologist, performed many experiments[3] on both humans and animals to demonstrate that familiarity with a stimulus, whatever it may be, causes a gradual, positive appreciation of this stimulus. In an early experiment, Zajonc picked out 12 Turkish words (*iktitaf, afworbu, sarcik…*) that would not have any meaning for non-Turkish speakers. He presented them to participants, whose task was to listen to the researcher pronounce the words whilst watching them being written on a card. Participants then had to repeat the words out loud, before ranking each one on an appreciation scale according to whether they perceived it positively or not. Zajonc's experiment was designed such that the words came up at different frequencies (0, 1, 2, 5, 10 and 25 times). The exercise was supposed to be about the pronunciation of foreign words, but its real objective was to measure the effect of repetition on the words' perception – positive or otherwise. And the results were clear. The appreciation of each word increased in line with the number of times it was repeated. Unknown words with no significance for the participants thus acquired a positive value as they became more familiar.

Next, Zajonc modified these stimuli to see to what extent familiarity linked to repeated exposure was universal. In another experiment, he switched the Turkish words for Chinese characters. In this case, the participants didn't have to pronounce the words in question (which they would not have been able to do) but simply observe them closely. As before, they then had to rank them on an appreciation scale. And once again, the same effect was observed: the higher the exposure to a character, the greater the level of appreciation for it.

3. Robert Zajonc, *The Selected Works of R. B. Zajonc*, Wiley, 2004.

Finally, in a third experiment, Zajonc swapped the Chinese characters for photographs of unknown peoples' faces (in fact, these were photos taken from the Michigan State University yearbook). Applying the same procedure, he presented the faces at different frequencies before asking participants to note to what extent they could love each of them. Of course, the results were the same as for the previous studies. Affection varied for each face according to the frequency with which it was viewed. The more frequently a photo was seen, the more favourably it was perceived.

Since Zajonc's ground-breaking research, this familiarity effect via repeated exposure to a stimulus – be it a word, an object, a person, or a brand – has been confirmed on numerous occasions.

Zajonc revealed another effect of familiarity via repetition. Not only does this familiarity have a positive effect in regard to the person, object or situation in question, but it also positively alters our own mood. Once again, this can happen without our being conscious of it, as demonstrated by Zajonc and colleagues in the following study.[4] Students from the University of Georgia were asked to view Chinese characters projected at five millisecond intervals – faster than the eye can see. To test the effect of repetition, the first group was shown each character once, while the second group saw each character five times. When it was over, the researchers evaluated the mood of the participants in each group, using both direct questions and a choice of faces to illustrate the way that they were feeling. And the results were startling. The mood of the participants in the group to whom the characters were shown five times was significantly better than that of those who saw the characters just once. Simple contact with stimuli that has become familiar due to repeated exposure is hence enough to bring about a positive change in mood. And without us even being aware of it! Again,

---

4.   Jennifer L. Monahan, Sheila T. Murphy and R. B. Zajonc, 'Subliminal Mere Exposure: Specific, General, and Diffuse Effects', *Psychological Science*, vol. 11, n° 6, November 2000.

'evolutionary' psychology can explain this apparently surprising phenomenon. The familiar – as opposed to the unknown – is not dangerous! If a stimulus becomes familiar, it is because we didn't avoid it in the first instance, as would have been the case had we known it to have negative consequences. Therefore, in terms of the survival of the species, it may be logical to feel affection towards familiar objects, people and situations; and this affection may translate into a more general feeling of well-being. And so whilst irrational when it comes to individual logic, as our preferences are supposed to result from a cost-benefit analysis, the impact of familiarity via repeated exposure may be rational in terms of evolutionary survival.

Illusion 4: loss aversion - we prefer not losing to winning

Loss aversion is one of the first and most important biases revealed by Daniel Kahneman and Amos Tversky. It is one of the central pillars of prospect theory, which earned its authors the 2002 Nobel Prize in Economics, as well as forming the basis for a large number of our everyday decisions. So what does this aversion to loss involve? It is really quite simple. Contrary to what is suggested by rational behavior, we don't value equivalent gains and losses in the same way. Losing a sum of money is perceived in a proportionally more negative manner than the positive perception attached to winning the same amount. Loss aversion has been demonstrated on many occasions by experiments in which the participants are asked to play lottery games in which they can win or lose a given amount according to specific probabilities. They have to choose two options of the following type:

◆ win a given amount – say, 100 dollars – with a 50% chance of success;
◆ lose the same amount (100 dollars) with the same probability (50%).

Taken together, the results of these experiments show that the majority of participants are risk averse. They prefer not to take the chance when the potential gain is equivalent to the risk incurred, and only start playing when the potential gain significantly outweighs this risk. On average, Kahneman states that the ratio is 1.5 to 2.5,[5] which indicates that we are happy to play a lottery only when the potential gain is almost double the possible risk. In situations where we are uncertain of the result of a decision – something which is true for the majority of choices that we make in the course of our daily lives – we tend to favour the less risky option, unless the potential gain is significantly greater. Risk aversion hence reveals that the psychological cost of losing is greater than the psychological benefits derived from an equivalent win. Once again, this leads us to take decisions that are irrational in purely logical terms. However, there is a logical explanation – a human explanation, at any rate – for this illogicality.

Illusion 5: we have excessive affection for things we own or which we make with our own hands

We afford more value to objects we own than to those we don't. Possessing an object, it seems, gives it a special value in our eyes – the result of an emotional transfer whose sole cause is the fact of ownership. Dan Ariely and his colleague Ziv Carmon[6] provide a deeper understanding of the phenomenon via an amusing (and informative) study carried out not in a laboratory but at the 1994 American college basketball

---

5. Daniel Kahneman, *Thinking Fast and Slow*, Farrar Straus and Giroux, 2011, p. 284.
6. Ziv Carmon and Dan Ariely, 'Focusing on the Forgone: How Value Can Appear so Different to Buyers and Sellers', *Journal of Consumer Research*, vol. 27, December 2000.

finals in which Duke was taking part (the NCAA Final Four Basketball Tournament). The participants in the experiment were Duke students who had drawn lots for tickets to the match. Ariely and Carmon contacted a group of students who'd missed out, and asked how much they would be prepared to pay for a ticket. They then contacted the winners to find out what price they would be willing to accept for their tickets. Confirming the results of previous studies, the prices offered for a semi-final ticket and the prices suggested by the owners of these tickets were very different:

- 1,500 dollars for those selling;
- 150 dollars for those buying.

Membership of the two groups – winners and losers – was obtained by drawing lots, and thus completely random. They were all students, basketball fans, and keen to buy tickets to watch their team. The perceived value of a ticket to the match should hence have been the same for members of both groups. However, possession of a ticket changed everything: the winners gave it a value that was ten times greater than that of the losers. Carmon and Ariely tried to understand the factors underlying this effect. By interviewing the students according to whether they won a ticket or not, researchers showed that possession shifts the focus of our attention. The winners were focused on the rarity and exceptional nature of the event they were about to watch. They had already engaged with the pleasure that the basketball match would bring them. The prospect of selling their ticket was hence felt as a serious emotional loss and was reflected in the extremely high asking price. As we saw with loss aversion, we are highly sensitive to all losses – a sensitivity which amplified the effect and resulted in the extraordinarily high asking price of 1,500 dollars. For their part, the losers, as they didn't have a ticket, did not immerse themselves in the anticipation of a future pleasure. They were simply focused on the fact that they would have to spend a sum of money. Their attention was more concentrated on the money than the match, as well as on those other things they'd miss out on once they had spent it. The different prices offered by potential sellers and buyers were hence caused by a joint shift in focus to a single aspect of the trade: the thing each party had to lose.

This excessive affection for objects we possess can also apply to our thoughts and actions, as demonstrated by Ariely, Michael Norton and Daniel Mochton in an experiment that they named 'the Ikea effect'.[7] They called it this because the researchers – just as for purchases made at the world's leading interior decoration store – asked the participants to assemble or make the objects with their own hands. The aim was to evaluate the impact that the fact of having assembled or made the objects had on the participants' appreciation of them, as well as the perception of their value. The initial task examined the extent to which assembling an object affects the value that we give it. Participants were split into two groups as follows:

◆ members of the first group had to assemble a 'Kassett' Ikea storage box;

◆ members of the second group had to inspect an identical pre-assembled box.

Following this task, both groups were asked to come up with a price for the box. The result was clear, and confirmed the researchers' intuition: the price given by the 'assemblers' was significantly higher than that given by the 'inspectors'. The fact of having assembled an object is enough to raise its value in the eyes of those who have sweated over it. And when the participants were asked to rank their appreciation of the object in question, the score given by the 'assemblers' was once again superior. They had a greater appreciation of the object and hence gave it a higher monetary value.

---

7. Michael Norton, Daniel Mochton and Dan Ariely, 'The "IKEA Effect": When Work Leads to Love', *Harvard Business Review*, Working Paper 11-091, 2011.

In another experiment, Ariely and colleagues wanted to assess the additional value linked to the simple possession of an object, compared to that created by the fact of having worked on it. Results showed that while possession adds value, the fact of having worked on something increases the effect still further. When the researchers asked participants to create origami figures (a crane or a frog) or to make things out of Lego, the price that they placed on their 'creations' was greater than for that of mere possession. It seems we believe that the time and effort we expend on an object should be reflected in its price. This extra value also causes a change in our perception of the objects themselves, which we find more appealing than those made by other people.

The 'Ikea effect' is thus a part of our illogical decision-making process. It leads us to allocate an economically irrational value to an object in which we have some personal investment, and which, as a result, we think of as superior to other identical objects. And this overvaluing is not limited to things we own or make. It also applies to things we think, as a look at the following bias will show.

Illusion 6: we love it when our existing beliefs are confirmed

We have a strong tendency to believe that our own opinions and judgments are correct, and those of others less relevant or simply wrong. In short, we think we're right about most things. We are also convinced that the accuracy of our thoughts extends beyond the fact that this is our opinion. Rather, there are solid arguments that we can make. Hard evidence to back up our position! The problem is that we are highly inclined to only see the evidence that confirms our opinion, while ignoring or discrediting that which might call it into question. As such, we are both convinced of what we think and confident that our judgment derives from an objective analysis of the situation and the foreseeable options.

A study on the subject of the death penalty[8] by three Stanford professors illustrates this mechanism by which we confirm our own opinions, even in the face of counter arguments. For this experiment, carried out in the USA, the researchers formed a group of participants in which half were for the death penalty and half against it. Participants were all asked to read a text that was supposed to give the results of a study into the consequences of introducing the death penalty. There were two versions of the text, with conflicting conclusions:

◆ conclusion 1 confirmed the deterrent effect of the death penalty;
◆ conclusion 2 stated that the death penalty had no effect.

Participants were split into two groups. One was given the text supporting the death penalty; the other was given the text that was against it. The procedure was then reversed, meaning all participants were exposed to both texts.

After reading the texts, participants had to respond to two questions. The first of these concerned any potential change of opinion on the death penalty. The second was about their stance in regard to its deterrent effect. Next, participants were given a supplementary document containing more detailed information about the results of the study. This included the study data, criticisms levelled after publication, the authors' responses, etc. They were then subjected to a final series of questions regarding the quality of the study and the extent to which they found it persuasive.

Those in favour of the death penalty thought that the study demonstrating its lack of effect was far less convincing, and

8.   Charles G. Lord, Lee Ross and Mark R. Lepper, 'Biased Assimilation and Attitude Polarization: The Effects of Prior Theories on Subsequently Considered Evidence', *Journal of Personality and Social Psychology*, vol. 37, n° 11, November 1979, p. 2098-2109.

less well carried out, than the study with the opposite conclusion. Correspondingly, those against the death penalty thought the inverse. The same studies were hence evaluated in fundamentally different ways depending on the original attitude of each participant.

Many studies on a wide range of subjects have demonstrated the significance of this effect. We cling to our opinions – a stubbornness that comes about because we either pay no attention to potentially destabilizing information, or because we perceive such information negatively. Hence, we process identical information not on its own terms but through the filter of our own subjective agenda.

Illusion 7: our perception is guided by expectation

It's not just our opinions that alter the way we analyze situations and information. Our prior expectations play an equally important role in the way that we perceive experiences, as demonstrated by another study carried out by Dan Ariely, Shane Frederick, and Leonard Lee on the refreshing subject of beer drinking.[9]

Their aim was to assess the impact of a piece of information – the presence of drops of balsamic vinegar in a glass of beer – on our organoleptic perception. Does knowing this information change our perception of the way the beer tastes? Does knowing it before or after the tasting alter what we have to say about the product? The researchers performed the experiment in the real-life context of two Boston bars. They offered clients a free tasting of two different beers: 'MIT Brew', the regional specialty, and another

9. Leonard Lee, Shane Frederick and Dan Ariely, 'Try it you'll like it', *Psychological Science*, vol. 17, n° 12, 2006.

regular beer (Budweiser or Samuel Adams). Participants were split into three groups and then subjected to the following test protocol:

- those in the first group ('blind') were invited to taste the two beers without any extra information;
- those in the second group ('before') were told about the drops of balsamic vinegar in the MIT Brew prior to the tasting;
- those in the third group ('after') were told which one contained the balsamic vinegar, but only after tasting both beers.

Following this, the drinkers had to say which beer they preferred. In theory, the preference for one or other of the beers should have been the same for each group. Since the same two beers were tasted by all three groups and the question referred only to taste, there shouldn't have been any difference. But of course, this wasn't the case. The extra information significantly altered perceptions and resulting preferences. In the 'blind' group, 59% of participants preferred the local beer, MIT Brew. However, when warned beforehand that the MIT Brew contained drops of balsamic vinegar, only 30% said they preferred it. Finally, when the information was received after the tasting, the preference rate rebounded to 52%. The participants were hence clearly influenced by the information, but only when it was received beforehand. In the second group, the information about the presence of the vinegar – a substance that is *a priori* unpleasant – caused them to perceive the MIT Brew less positively. The expectation created by the information altered their experience. On the other hand, as soon as the tasting had finished, and the participants had formed their opinions, the presence of the vinegar was no longer significant.

Our prior expectations are hence a key factor that can significantly alter our perception of an experience. We do not evaluate our experiences in absolute terms, but in relation to our expectation.

Illusion 8: we prefer the present to the future

This bias is without doubt the one that causes us most harm. Why can't we resist a delicious candy when we are well aware that it contains more calories than we should reasonably consume? Why don't we save enough to give ourselves a comfortable pension? Why do we continue to smoke when we know – it is written on the back of every pack of cigarettes – that 'smoking kills'? Why don't we do a bit more physical exercise when we know it's so good for our long-term health? And why don't we go – or go more often – for the screening tests that can save our lives by spotting illnesses that are curable if you catch them early?

The above questions all have the same simple answer. We are affected by a major bias: our excessive focus on the present. Faced with a choice between a small short-term effort and a significant long-term benefit, or even between a small short-term benefit and a large medium-term benefit, we have a very high propensity to take the short-term option.

George Loewenstein, who did a lot of work on the role that time plays in our decisions, designed an amusing experiment[10] to demonstrate the way we favour short-term pleasure over efforts whose reward comes further down the road. He asked participants to choose from a list of videos. The movies they chose were to be watched the same day, the following day, and the day after that. The list contained two types of movies. Some were easy to watch but of limited interest (these represented vice, or easiness); others were more demanding but intended to be more interesting (these represented virtue, for example *Schindler's List*). Researchers asked half of the participants to

---

10. Daniel Read, George Loewenstein and Shobana Kalyanaraman, 'Mixing Virtue and Vice: Combining the Immediacy Effect and the Diversification Heuristic', *Journal of Behavioral Decision Making*, vol. 12, n° 4, December 1999, p. 257-273.

choose movies for the three days all at the same time. The other half were asked to choose to the movies sequentially – one movie for the first day, one for the next, and so on. When selecting the movies simultaneously, participants chose a sequence that went vice/virtue/virtue. Hence, easiness for today, and effort for tomorrow and the day after that. In the case of the sequential choice, where a movie was watched on the same day that it was chosen, the majority made a different selection: vice/vice/vice. So when making a choice whose consequences are felt on the same day, we favour immediate pleasure over exigency. In a supplementary study, Loewenstein showed that we are more inclined to choose exigency (virtue) when there is a delay between the choice being carried out and its consequences being felt. When participants were asked to choose movies that they would watch in a few days' time, the result was: virtue/virtue/virtue. For each of our daily decisions, we thus place a disproportionate value on the short term. We are both eager to grab short-term benefits – the instant pleasure of a cigarette, an alcoholic drink, or unprotected sex – and very willing to delay the necessary costs and efforts until tomorrow (or longer, if possible). Which is why we often reject the best option: it is either too costly in the short term or its benefits are too distant and drawn out. Imagine, if you will, the consequences of this bias when it comes to protecting the planet!

Illusion 9: our willpower is generally not all that strong... and it gets weaker over time

We generally know the thing we have to do to achieve our aims. Work hard to pass the exam that allows us to get the good degree and then the dream job. Do more daily exercise to get in better physical shape. Eat less fat and sugar to avoid cardiovascular problems. Save money so as not be in the red at the end of the month and so on. It's clear, then, that we have goals. And according to the theory of *homo economicus*, we act in order to achieve them. But when it comes to the Everyman, who puts off until tomorrow what he should really do today, this is often not the case. This is known as procrastination, and it is one of the big problems confronting our willpower. The fact of the matter is we don't behave in accordance with our own interests, even when they have been clearly identified to us as such.

Procrastination comes about when the salience of costs linked to an intended action is high in relation to the salience of benefits linked to the same action. We can clearly see the benefit of not doing what we intended to do; or, conversely, the drawbacks to doing it. From a rational perspective, it makes no sense to act against our interests. Nevertheless, this type of behavior is commonplace. This is hence another illogical aspect of the decision-making process: we know what we *should* do, but we can't bring ourselves to do it! Our willpower is far from being infallible. And what's more, it quickly evaporates. In the same way that a tool wears out with time, the power of our will diminishes with use. The more we apply it, the weaker its response to new requests, as shown by an amusing study carried out by Roy Baumeister and colleagues.[11] In this experiment, the researchers gave their hungry participants (they had missed a meal) a tricky challenge: to eat radishes rather than the chocolates that were placed in front of them. After this slightly inhumane first act, they were asked to solve some rather boring puzzles. Another group then had to solve the same puzzles, without being previously tempted by the chocolate. The aim was to see whether the willpower used by participants from the first group in not eating the chocolate had a subsequent effect on their ability to complete the

11. Roy E. Baumeister, Ellen Bratslavsky, Mark Muraven and Dianne M. Tice, 'Ego Depletion: Is the Active Self a Limited Resource?', *Journal of Personality and Social Psychology*, vol. 74, nº 5, 1998, p. 1252-1265.

OUR LOGICAL PROCESS IS HIGHLY CHAOTIC 83

slightly frustrating puzzles compared to that of the control group. Did their earlier use of willpower cause it to diminish? This was, in fact, the case. Participants who had already demonstrated willpower in resisting the chocolate gave up on the puzzles significantly faster (after eight minutes) than those who had not previously used up their reserves (these stuck at it for over 20 minutes).

Procrastination, and the gradual evaporation of our willpower, are thus two more significant impediments to our quest for rational behavior. Generally speaking, however, the effort needed to correct them is not one that we like to make.

Illusion 10: we are influenced by stereotypes and assumed causalities

We don't like complex choices. More precisely, we don't like to make the necessary effort involved in making a rational decision when faced with a complex choice. A rational choice supposes that we weigh, in rigorous and balanced fashion, the advantages and disadvantages of each choice option. More often than not, however, we avoid doing this as it places significant demands on our attention and our time.

So how do we go about it? By simplifying the information provided and using stereotypes drawn from experience that allow us to quickly interpret situations. Daniel Kahneman performed an experiment[12] on this topic in which he gave participants the following scenario:

A taxi was involved in a night-time accident. Two taxi companies – green and blue – operate in the city. You are given the following information:

◆ 85% of taxis are green and 15% are blue;

---

12. Daniel Kahneman (2011), *op. cit.*, p. 166.

♦ a witness identified the taxi as being blue. The court tested the witness's reliability under the circumstances of the night of the accident. They concluded that the witness would have identified the colour correctly in 80% of cases and incorrectly in 20% of cases.

What is the probability that the taxi involved in the accident is blue rather than green?

The problem isn't easy – at least, it isn't easy for me – as it requires a probability calculation to arrive at the correct answer, which is a 41% chance that the offending taxi is blue. And what figure did the participants come up with? 80%! Why did they get it wrong? Because in simplifying the problem they only took account of the information they considered easiest to process and most concrete – that of the witness. A logical error stemmed from the desire to simplify.

Next, Kahneman subjected participants to a variation on this first experiment. In this version, the information provided was as follows:

♦ two companies operate the same number of taxis, but the green taxis are involved in 85% of accidents;
♦ the information relating to the witness is the same as that given in the previous version.

This time, participants completely ignored the witness' information implicating the blue taxi. Why? Because the evidence took over. If 85% of accidents are caused by green taxis, our logical minds want the guilty taxi to be of this colour. We like simple causality and logical shortcuts. And when a cause seems obvious, we immediately favour it over information that is more solid but also more difficult to integrate into our thought process. As Kahneman puts it, 'causes trump statistics'!

Stereotypes – our relatively firm belief in the specific characteristics of a group of individuals – are often the cause of these reasoning errors. We frequently interpret situations in light of these stereotypes, which are present in our minds and which allow us to make a very quick – and often false – analysis of what is going on. They act as communication shortcuts that are processed rapidly and with ease. And as we shall see, they can be used in marketing as an extremely effective way of communicating information.

Illusion 11: 'mental accounting' – how we compartmentalize our money

When it comes to our own money, we act like company accountants. We work out spending budgets, more or less strictly, for different categories according to our income: food, hobbies, housing, etc. This mechanism, highlighted by Thaler,[13] is one such 'mental account' whose benefit is fairly clear. That is, to have a tighter attitude to spending money and help us manage our resources. But this outlook has an impact both on our spending habits and on our behavior. Our decisions can be altered depending on the mental account to which we have assigned our money. Thaler demonstrates this via a simple example. Imagine you've bought theatre tickets. On the way to watch the play, you realize that you've lost the ticket that cost you 100 dollars. However, you have a 100-dollar bill in your wallet. The question is now whether you use it to buy another ticket. In this instance, the majority of people decide not to, as they perceive the total cost of seeing the play to be 200 dollars. But now consider the following scenario: you go to the theatre to buy a ticket, and you realize that you've lost 100 dollars from your wallet. In this case, the majority decide to buy the ticket anyway. However, the loss in both instances is identical – 100 dollars. The only differ-

---

13. Richard Thaler, 'Mental Accounting and Consumer Choice', *Marketing Science*, vol. 4, n° 3, 1985, p. 199-214.

ence is that in the first example it concerns a ticket, and in the second, a bank note. Our behavior differs because, having assigned an amount of money to a spending category, we no longer perceive it as fungible. The simple fact of an amount being 'framed' for spending in a certain way induces a particular type of behavior. As we shall see, the use of mental accounting, and the ability to frame our money in this fashion, can generate significant changes in behavior – and with no change in a person's overall income.

In taking decisions, we are thus confronted by logical biases that detract from a pure rationality – one that would otherwise allow us to act as super-computers, maximizing our interest every time we make a choice. But we aren't capable of being this rational. Our inner-calculator suffers from a fundamental bias. And it doesn't stop here. We are also deeply emotional – another factor with a serious impact on the decisions that we take.

Chapter 6

We are emotional beings

Human irrationality does not begin and end with reasoning errors. There is another force at play — a force so powerful it affects our lives daily and influences all of our decision-making processes. This force, is our emotion.

The impact of emotions on our decisions and behavior depends on both their type and their intensity. We can understand their roles by grouping them according to the five main influencing mechanisms (see Figure 6.1).

Earlier in the book, I introduced you to a neuroscientist called Antonio Damasio who drew everybody's attention to the important role emotions have on our decision making. The case that brought him worldwide fame was that of Phineas Gage, as described in *Descartes' Error: Emotion, Reason and the Human Brain*.[1] Gage, who lived in nineteenth century New England, was involved in a terrible accident. An iron bar went straight through his skull. Somehow, despite the hole in his head, he survived. Even more surprisingly, his cognitive and rational faculties remained intact. But not his personality. What neuroscientists refer to as the ventromedial

---

1.   Antonio Damasio, *Descartes' Error: Emotion, Reason and the Human Brain*, Odile Jacob, 1995.

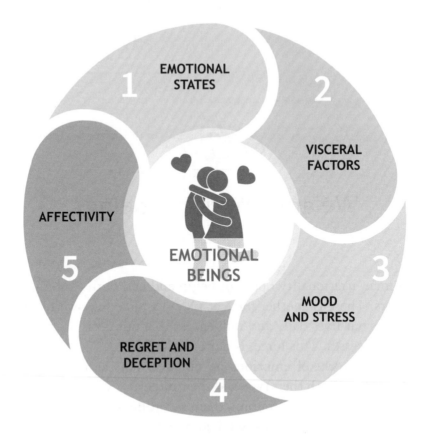

Figure 6.1 The five main influencing mechanisms of emotions

region of the frontal lobe was destroyed, and Gage was no longer able to plan his actions, follow social conventions or, ultimately, take decisions that would aid his own survival.

In order to make good decisions – that is, decisions by which we can adapt to our environment and to other people – requires more than mere cognitive function. As well as an ability to think logically, we need a working emotional faculty. There is no reason without emotions. Or, more precisely, there are no rational decisions. Reason and emotion work in interaction with each other. Their intimate connection allows us to formulate decisions adapted to our environment. As such, our emotional capacity lies at the heart of the decision-making process. By setting aside the role of emotions, cognitive science and the theory of the rational man omitted a vital element. Without emotions, a large number of our daily, human decisions cannot be understood. This was Damasio's main revelation – and it is one about which all decision neuroscientists agree.

Our emotions can overwhelm us, or influence us in subtle ways, according to their type and their intensity.

Emotional states change our behavior

When great minds come together, the results can be astonishing. This was indeed the case for George Loewenstein and Dan Ariely, who worked together at Berkeley in 2001 studying the influence of emotional states on behavior. The two friends decided to work on one of the most powerful emotions experienced by all human beings – sexual arousal – and the resulting study was both provocative and enlightening.[2] To evaluate its effect on behavior, the pair recruited 25 exclusively male Berkeley students and told them about the subject of the study: 'decision making and sexual arousal'. Each student was handed an iBook with a twelve-key keyboard. Once they were back home and in bed, they were instructed to answer three series of questions while imagining themselves in a state of sexual arousal. For each question, they had to state whether they liked the activity described or not. The first series of questions concerned sexual preferences; the second, sexually unethical behavior, for example encouraging a woman to drink during dinner to increase their chances of sleeping with her; and the third was about unprotected sex.

---

2. Dan Ariely and George Loewenstein, 'The Heat of the Moment: The Effect of Sexual Arousal on Sexual Decision Making', *Journal of Behavioral Decision Making*, vol. 19, n° 2, April 2006, p. 87-98.

The experiment took place in two stages:

◆ first, the students were only required to answer the questions asked;

◆ second, several days later, the students were given a much more specific set of instructions. They had to respond to the same questions in a state of real, rather than imaged sexual excitement. They were asked to look at erotic pictures while masturbating before giving their answers.

Table 6.1 The effect of sexual arousal on sexual decision making

	Non-aroused	Aroused
Are women's shoes erotic?	42 %	65 %
Can you imagine being attracted to a 12-year-old girl?	23 %	46 %
Can you imagine having sex with a 40-year-old woman?	58 %	77 %
Can you imagine having sex with a 50-year-old woman?	28 %	55 %
Can you imagine having sex with a 60-year-old woman?	7 %	23 %
Can you imagine having sex with a man?	8 %	14 %
Could it be fun to have sex with someone who was extremely fat?	13 %	24 %
Could you enjoy having sex with someone you hated?	53 %	77 %
If you were attracted to a woman and she proposed a threesome with a man, would you do it?	19 %	34 %
Is a woman sexy when she's sweating?	56 %	72 %
Would it be fun to get tied up by your sexual partner?	63 %	81 %
Would you take a date to a fancy restaurant to increase your chance of having sex with her?	55 %	70 %
Would you tell a woman that you loved her to increase the chance that she would have sex with you?	30 %	51 %
Would you encourage your date to drink to increase the chance that she would have sex with you?	46 %	63 %
Would you keep trying to have sex after your date says "no."?	20 %	45 %
Would you slip a woman a drug to increase the chance that she would have sex with you?	5 %	26 %

Source: Dan Ariely and George Loewenstein, 'The Heat of the Moment', *Journal of Behavioral Decision Making*, April 2006.

The aim was to compare the answers according to whether the state of sexual arousal was imagined or real. And, what the researchers found was, the results were poles apart. These were the same people, faced with the same questions; however, their emotional states were different, and this caused a dramatic change in their responses (see Table 6.1).

The effect of sexual arousal on assumed behavior was very clear. A decision is therefore not simply an individual person faced with various choices. Rather, it's an individual in a *particular emotional state* faced with these choices. And the same individual, faced with the same choices, can react very differently depending on their emotional state. What's more – and this is another major finding revealed by the study, which I'll come back to – the people in question are not able to predict their own behavior when sexually aroused, even when you try to make them focus on this state. The instructions in the first stage of the experiment tell the students to image they are sexually aroused before answering the questions. But imagining yourself aroused and really being aroused are not the same at all. Our behavior is therefore very difficult to second guess.

Visceral factors: how our basic emotions can overwhelm us

Sexual arousal is one of what George Loewenstein terms 'visceral factors'[3] – states that have a strong influence on behavior once they reach a certain level of intensity. As well as emotions, these visceral factors include hunger, thirst, fear, anger, and physical pain. As in the above experiment describing the effect of sexual

---

3. George Loewenstein, 'Out of Control: Visceral Influences on Behavior', *Organizational Behavior and Human Decision Processes*, vol. 65, n° 3, March 1996, p. 272-292.

arousal on behavior, these visceral factors bring about a loss of self-control that spans from moderate to all-consuming. At a heightened level of intensity, visceral factors have such a per-suasive effect on our desires that they become extremely diffi-cult to resist. Even when we are aware that our decision will turn out to be a bad one. It's like the drug user with the shakes whose can't resist the need to give himself a hit, in full knowl-edge of the negative effect the drug will have on him. Visceral factors can be activated by a lack or deprivation of something – for instance, not having had a drink in a long time. Equally, the stimulus can be external – an image we perceive as erotic that triggers our sexual desire, or a comment we find personally insulting that ignites our anger. Our visceral factors awakened, emanates our desire for the object or the action that has stirred them into life. Our focus tightens on the need to satisfy this desire, and our feelings towards it become urgent. We must fulfil the need right here, right now! And at any cost! With the level of intensity so heightened, we're prepared to accept poor terms in order to achieve this. We pay over the odds. We take unnecessary risks. We make huge efforts with very little thought for how the potential consequences may affect other people.

Another study[4] complements Ariely and Loewenstein's research into behavioral change caused by the level of sexual arousal. The aim this time was to assess the way in which the intensity of the arousal affects our ability to take risks, and to gain a better understanding of the factors influencing our deci-sion. Here, once again, the conclusions were clear cut. At their most aroused, participants showed a significantly higher pro-pensity to take risks (in this case, having unprotected sex with a woman they didn't know) than when in a less turbulent emo-tional state. The intensity of our emotions hence alters our

---

4.   Peter H. Ditto, David A. Pizarro, Eden B. Epstein, Jill A. Jacobson and Tara K. MacDonald, 'Visceral Influences on Risk-Taking Behavior', *Journal of Behavioral Decision Making*, vol. 19, n° 2, April 2006, p. 99-113.

behavior. We act differently to how, in the cold light of day, we imagine that we would – including actions that place our own health at risk. The study also shows that we perceive situations differently according to our level of sexual arousal, and that this influences our decisions. For participants in the group with high arousal levels, the reasons for succumbing to temptation – for example, a partner's physical attractiveness or the sexual attraction that they feel for her – were greater than those in the other group. Conversely, the risks associated with the situation were seen as significantly inferior. The 'aroused' group thought the level of risk to be far lower than the 'unaroused' group. The resulting decision hence has a certain logic to it. Due to their perceiving situations as more attractive and less risky, 'aroused' people, make decisions differently to others. Their emotional state produces a change in behavior caused by different perceptions of the same underlying situation.

The influence of our prevailing emotions: from humour to stress

We could assume that this is all about extreme emotions or those related to our innermost desires. It might follow that less intense emotions don't have the same effect on our behavior. But this is not the case at all, as demonstrated by three other experiments concerned with emotional states of mind less powerful that those linked to sexual desire.

We all know that at any given moment, short-lived or otherwise, we can experience a subtle positive or negative emotion. We have good and bad moods. We feel a certain sadness, or, conversely, joy. The aim of a 2004 study[5] carried

---

5. Jennifer Lerner, Deborah Small and George Loewenstein, 'Heart Strings and Purse Strings: Carroyer Effects of Emotions on Economic Decisions', *Psychological Science*, vol. 15, n° 5, May 2004, p. 337-341.

out by Lerner, Loewenstein and Small was to understand the effect that sadness or disgust have on our choices. Participants were shown the following three types of video:

- the first group watched a 'neutral' movie that was not intended to produce a specific feeling in the viewer;
- the second group watched a movie showing the death of a child that was intended to cause sadness;
- the third group watched a movie showing a man using a dirty bathroom that was intended to cause disgust.

After watching the movie, they asked the participants to reply to questions about the price of a highlighter pen they had been given at the start of the experiment. The aim was to see if the feelings of sadness or disgust resulting from the movie reflected the price at which they were prepared to buy or sell the highlighter pen. According to rational choice theory, there should be no change in price. At any given moment, the price of an object is determined by variables that have nothing to do with the emotions of those buying or selling. But in real life? Here are the results. The prices given by sellers and buyers were influenced by their prevailing emotions as follows:

- for 'sad' participants, the price was significantly lower than the 'neutral' group when selling (around 3 dollars versus 4.5 dollars) and higher when buying (4.5 dollars versus 3.5 dollars);
- for 'disgusted' participants, the prices given for both buying and selling were lower than in the control group.

Once again, our emotional state plays an important role in our decisions, even when the emotion itself is not especially strong. And this includes our economic choices.

This is equally the case for stress — a feeling that is more drawn out, but nevertheless very common in our personal and professional lives. A series of studies presented by Karolina

Lempert and Elizabeth Phelps[6] have shown how stress alters our decisions. In particular, we are more cautious in situations with potential gain, but more adventurous when faced with risk (Porcelli and Delgado, 2009). We also make less use of available relevant information when formulating our decisions, and we are quicker to fall back on habits and automatic responses.

Regret, deception, and the impact of emotions on our future choices

The emotions that we feel while taking decisions have a major impact on the decision-making process and ensuing results. This is true for more than just our immediate emotions. Certain emotional states such as regret and feeling deceived can have a deferred influence whose effect is felt in future choices that we make. Anticipating this potential for regret or for being deceived, we seek to minimize the chance that it arises, and alter our decision making accordingly. Regret and deception are similar in nature and involve the same behavioral goal – to avoid unpleasant feelings. However, studies[7] have revealed their effects on the decision-making process to be different. When faced with a situation in which we can foresee a bad decision leading to regret, we research the relevant information more deeply. Our decision-making process is more thoughtful and attentive. We make a special effort to identify

---

6. Karolina Lempert and Elizabeth Phelps, 'Neuroeconomics of Emotion and Decision Making', in Paul W. Glimcher and Ernst Fehr (dir.), *Neuroeconomics: Decision Making and the Brain*, 2nd edition, Academic Press, 2013, p. 219-236.

7. Marcel Zeelenberg, Wilco W. van Dijk, Anthony S. R. Manstead and Joop van der Pligt, 'On Bad Decisions and Disconfirmed Expectancies: The Psychology of Regret and Disappointment', *Cognition and Emotion*, vol. 14, n° 4, 2000, p. 521-541.

the right decision and avoid regrets associated with bad choices. In instances where we anticipate the possibility of being deceived, we try to match our expectations to the outcome. That is, we reduce our expectations to ensure there's a greater chance of them being met. If our expectations are lower, then the risk of deception is also less severe. We use this as a way to maximize the psychological well-being emanating from our choices.

The study into regret and deception hence contains some interesting points. The impact of emotions on decisions can be immediate or deferred. And these closely held emotions have different influences on our decision-making processes, according to their type.

Rokia, and the identified victim effect

When handled correctly, emotions can be much more effective that more rational arguments, as demonstrated by an experiment known as 'the identifiable victim effect'.

This experiment concerns donations made following a humanitarian disaster. The aim was to compare participants' behavior when confronted with a donation request with the following different emphases:

◆ either, the number of potential victims of a humanitarian disaster (a rational argument);

◆ or, a specific victim, with a name and accompanying description (the 'identifiable victim').

In the first instance,[8] participants read a letter highlighting the number of people in various African countries at risk of

---

8. Deborah A. Small, George Loewenstein and Paul Slovic, 'Sympathy and Callousness: The Impact of Deliberative Thought on Donations to Identifiable and Statistical Victims', *Organizational Behavior and Human Decision Process*, vol. 102, n° 2, March 2007, p. 143-153.

starvation if they didn't receive aid. The figures given were 3 million children in Malawi, 3 million Zambians, and 11 million Ethiopians. In the second instance, the letter contained a detailed description of a single person. A girl called Rokia, aged seven, from Mali.

I imagine you can guess the result. Participants receiving the first letter made an average donation of 1.17 dollars, while those reading about Rokia gave an average of 2.83 dollars – more than double the amount. How on earth can this be rational? We give more to save one person's life than we do to save the lives of hundreds or even millions! But to think of it this way is to ignore the role of emotions in our decisions. We can see little Rokia with our own eyes, and reading her description produces an emotional response that translates into a greater level of altruism. The lesson is clear: emotion is a powerful motivating factor for our behavior. This study gives a scientific demonstration of a commonplace behavior pattern. As mentioned by the authors, when 'Baby Jessica' fell down a Texas well in 1989, more than 700,000 dollars was sent to help finance her rescue.

Emotions are thus at the heart of decisions great and small, life-changing or banal. And, whether we're aware of it or not, their influence is enormous. So here we find ourselves, plagued by bias and logical inconsistency, swayed by the emotions that permeate our daily lives, and also in the grip of yet another important factor: social norms and interactions.

Chapter 7

We are social beings: a biological phenomenon?

Mathew Liebermann, Professor of Psychology, Psychiatry and Biobehavioral Science at the University of California, writes:[1] 'Our brains are built to practice thinking about the social world and our place in it.' This claim results from studies of IMRF imaging highlighting the extent to which we are biologically oriented towards others. Of course, we think about our family, our friends and our loved ones; but we also consider people we don't know personally. And we often act according to the social environment in which we find ourselves.

Psychologists have long being able to demonstrate the role of this uniquely human quality on our behavior – a point I will come back to. However, the exciting new aspect of this research on brain function is the way it shows the social connection to be biologically derived. Liebermann gives us a series of ground-breaking studies in support of this idea. The experiments involve participants completing tasks while being scanned; showing which part of their brains are actively in use. His idea was to compare the brain's active zones when participants were asked

---

1. Matthew Liebermann, *Social: Why Our Brains Are Wired to Connect*, Crown Publisher, 2013, p. 22.

to think of other people, as opposed to times that they were asked to think of nothing in particular. This comparison gave rise to the idea of the 'social brain'! A simple explanation is that the active zones are very similar. In other words, when we aren't thinking about something in particular, our minds turn to other people. Our brains are social by default. Equally interesting is that this is not linked to our gradual socialization – a learning curve via which we come to realize the importance of social relations. Rather, it's a physiological reality that is present from birth. In a study carried out on babies aged between two weeks and two years,[2] researchers showed that these infants also possessed a default brain activity. As children of this age group have yet to develop social interests, this indicates that our brains are hardwired to develop socially oriented thought processes.

Social awareness is hence at the heart of our daily thoughts and concerns. You could even say at the heart of our brains, as the 'social brain by default' hypothesis suggests. It is also an important subject in that social suffering – as shown by other studies[3] – can be conflated with physical pain. Certainly, if we accept that we are fundamentally social beings, this will have a significant impact on our daily decisions.

Studies carried out by behavioral economists have allowed us to identify the six main mechanisms (see Figure 7.1) with a systematic influence on our everyday decision-making process resulting from social interactions:

◆ Social norms
◆ The role of the messenger
◆ The role of our peers

---

2.   Wei Gaoa, Hongtu Zhub, Kelly S. Giovanelloc, J. Keith Smithe, Dinggang Shenc, John H. Gilmoref and Weili Lin, 'Evidence on the Emergence of the Brain's Default Network from 2-Week-Old to 2-Year-Old Healthy Pediatric Subjects', *PNAS*, vol. 106, n° 16, 21 April 2009.
3.   Naomi Eisenberger, 'The Pain of Social Disconnection: Examining the Shared Neural Underpinnings of Physical and Social Pain', *Nature Reviews Neuroscience* | *AOP*, published on the internet 3rd May 2011.

- ◆ The role of the group
- ◆ Reciprocity and fairness
- ◆ Pre-commitment

Figure 7.1 The six mechanisms of social influence

Social norms: the burden of behaving as we're meant to

I just love the example Ariely[4] uses for explaining social norms. As usual with him, it's both entertaining and inform-ative. Imagine having Christmas dinner with your in-laws.

---

4.   Dan Ariely (2008), *op. cit.*, p. 75.

After eating your way through a magnificent turkey, you offer to pay your mother-in-law for it! And, I can't resist the pleasure of repeating the imaginary question posed by Dan to his mother-in-law: 'Mom, for all the love you've put into this, how much do I owe you? Do you think 300 dollars will do it? No, wait, I should give you 400!' I don't know what you think about it, but the idea of posing a similar question to my own mother-in-law, Monique, fills me with dread! I love her, and I've got on very well with her for over 30 years – a feeling that I hope is mutual (yes, there are exceptions to the son-in-law-mother-in-law relationship). However, I suspect a question such as this might do some serious damage to our bond! And what does this signify? Simply, that there are unwritten rules that govern our behavior and the decisions we make.

The very first example given in this book, if you recall, was about the organ donation programme promoted by the UK Nudge Unit via the rewording of a webpage. The new phrase they introduced was as follows: 'Everyday thousands of people who see this page decide to register.' So why did it have such an impact on the decisions of those reading it? Simply because, in referencing the adherent behavior of thousands of other people, gov.uk communicated an image of the prevailing social norm. And this gave new visitors a stronger incentive to adhere to it themselves.

Social norms encourage conformist behavior, as people belonging to the social group in question (or who would like to belong to it) want to show, consciously or otherwise, that they share the culture and values of that group. We call this 'compliance bias'.

An understanding of the organ donation example is very useful in order to appreciate the underlying mechanism in more depth. Our starting point can be the one who speaks: the messenger.

The importance of the messenger and the authority figure

For a message to have an effect on our behavior, the person delivering it – the messenger – must have some credibility. In this instance, there are in fact two messengers: gov.uk, who deliver the message, and the NHS (National Health Service), who are mentioned in the introduction and under whose name the offer is being made. We can assume that visitors to the site consider these messengers to be especially credible. The British government is behind the programme, and as such legitimizes both the action proposed to its citizens and the status of the NHS – an organization with a known expertise in organ donation. The messenger hence plays an important role in decisions that we take. This role can be for the better, as in the current example; and for the worse, as shown by the following series of experiments demonstrating the impact that authority figures have on ordinary people's behavior.

These studies, carried out by Stanley Milgram in the 1960s, are among the most well-known and talked about in the history of psychology. Their aim was to measure people's obedience to instructions coming from an authority figure. Participants were told the study was to find our whether punishment leads to improvements in learning, and the experiment involved three distinct roles:

♦ The experimenter, who represents authority, which is shown in his appearance (white shirt, etc.) and his behavior (rigor, authority, etc.). He is positioned alongside the participants and tells the 'teacher' what to do.
♦ The 'students', who are supposed to be doing the learning (these are in fact actors).
♦ The 'teachers', who are the real participants invited to take part in the study. After signing up, they are informed that

the 'students' have understood the subject and consented to take part in the experiment.

The students were told that they should learn a list of words. The teachers had to dictate these words then check the accuracy of the students' answers. In the event of a wrong answer, the teachers had to push a lever designed to give the offending student an electric shock. The force of this shock increased from 45 to 450 volts, according to the number of incorrect answers given. The 'students' (who did not, of course, receive any electric shocks) pretended to be in greater amounts of pain. For a 75-volt shock, they let out a groan; at 120 volts they complained to the experimenter about how much it hurt; at 135 volts they asked to quit the experiment; at 270 volts they screamed; and over 300 volts they refused to answer any more questions.

The results were shocking. Over 60% of 'teachers', at the instigation of the experimenter, completed the experiment and thus administered a likely fatal 450-volt electric shock.

The same experiment has been repeated across different countries, eras, and involving different themes. And sadly, these have all produced identical results. On each occasion, researchers found that around two-thirds of participants were prepared to inflict serious pain on other people when acting under the influence of an authority figure.

The messenger can thus have an impact far beyond the simple, neutral communication of a message. They can shape this message to their own image, and strengthen or reduce its weight according to the way that the receiver views them. The messenger is hence a potential lever in the change architect's armoury. However, authority figures are not are the only ones to have an influence. The same is true for other people's behavior and decision making – including those who we perceive as ordinary or anonymous.

Peer influence

There are times when the messenger may not take the form of an authority figure but still, by virtue of his presence or behavior, be the unwitting bearer of a message. Such is the inadvertent influence that others – our peers – exert on our behavior and decisions.

In an experiment carried out with Francesca Gino and Shahar Ayal,[5] Dan Ariely takes on a subject that concerns us all: dishonesty. Not the large-scale dishonesty of 'professional' thieves, but normal people's workaday dishonesty – the little tricks and white lies that are a part of our routine. To examine this behavior, Ariely came up with a series of experiments for a sample of Carnegie Mellon students, who he asked to take part in a game called 'the matrix test'.

This game involved 20 grids on a sheet of paper. For each of these, the students had to find two numbers that added up to one. For example, 0.67 and 0.33. There was a five-minute time limit for the task, which was insufficient to complete all 20 grids. For each correct answer, the students received a financial reward. The aim of the research was to understand the role of social interactions in deceitful behavior. What happens when people openly cheat? What happens when the one who cheats is on our side? Or when they're affiliated to a rival group? To what extent, therefore, do other people influence our own decisions? Ariely and colleagues formed four groups of comparable students who were each placed in a specific scenario aimed at answering these questions.

◆ In the first group ('control'), the students were brought together in a classroom and given the exercise. Afterwards,

---

5. Francesca Gino, Shahar Ayal and Dan Ariely, 'Contagion and Differentiation in Unethical Behavior: The Effect of One Bad Apple on the Barrel', *Psychological Science*, vol. 20, n° 3, 2009, p. 293-298.

they had to hand in their completed grids to an examiner who counted the number of correct answers. The examiner also checked that the students, who had received 10 dollars at the beginning of the experiment, kept the amount of money that corresponded to their correct answers, and no more. For example, if they completed all 20 grids, they could leave with the full 10 dollars. However, if they only completed 15 grids, they had to give back two dollars and 50 cents. It was hence impossible for students in this group to cheat in terms of either the number of completed grids or the amount of money returned.

◆ In the second group ('shredder'), students had to correct the completed grids themselves. They made a note of the number of correctly completed grids, then put the grids through a shredder. They then sealed the money to be returned in an envelope and slid it into a box. The experimenter, who remained in the room, had no control over the process. The students were thus able to cheat.

◆ In the third group ('shredder with in-group confederate'), the general procedure was identical to that of the second group, with one notable exception. After 60 seconds, a student wearing a Carnegie Mellon T-shirt got up and said out loud that he had completed all the grids – which was impossible. He added that he did not have to return any money. The experimenter then told him that he was free to go. He hence openly cheated and pocketed the money, without any problem.

◆ In the fourth group ('shredder with out-group confederate'), the procedure was identical to that of the third group. However, in this instance, the T-shirt worn by the 'cheat' was of a competing university.

Results revealed that on average, students in the 'control' group completed almost 7 grids. Those in the 'shredder' group, around 12. Those in the 'shredder with in-group confederate' group, around 15. And those in the 'shredder with out-group confederate' group, only 9. The conclusions are thus clear. The rate of cheating, which we can think of as the difference in completed grids between the 'control' and 'shredder' groups, was high – over 70%. However, it was even worse in the 'shredder with in-group confederate' group, where the number of grids declared complete was almost double. One bad apple on our own side hence heightens the general level of cheating. It's as if the cheating student establishes the act of cheating as a social norm. On the other hand, when the same thing happens in a group who we dislike – in this case, the rival university – it has the opposite effect. Here, the rate of cheating diminished, although it didn't stop entirely, as the number of completed grids was still greater than that of the control group.

Ariely and colleagues showed, sadly, that the students cheated when presented with the opportunity to do so. As well as this, the cheating behavior was heavily influenced by the behavior of others, and the social norm that they constructed as a consequence. In a 2012 publication on the same subject[6], Ariely shows via numerous experiments that this is true for all of us. We cheat – a little bit, but not too much – in a manner that allows us to retain a positive self-image. In such a way, we reap the 'spoils' of cheating, without having to question the essential honesty we tell ourselves that we possess.

Other people's behavior hence plays a major role in all that we do. And this is even more true when we find ourselves confronted by the behavior, not of a single individual, but of a group.

6. Dan Ariely, *The (Honest) Truth about Dishonesty*, Harper, 2013.

Group pressure

Very often, our daily lives lead us to take personal decisions or express opinions that are observed by other people. This may be in a professional context, for example, being asked to give an opinion in front of colleagues – or in a more personal situation, such as our choice of food when in a restaurant with our family. And in these instances where we express our decision in front of a group, the latter's influence can be very great – even when we have no prior relationship with the people in question.

Salomon Asch's[7] well-known experiment provides a simple demonstration of the group's effect on an individual's decision. Asch assembled a group of seven to nine students in the same room. He then gave them a straightforward exercise, as shown in Figure 7.2.

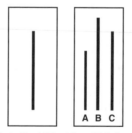

Source: Salomon Asch, in Harold Guetzkow (dir.), *Groups, Leadership and Men*, 1951.

Figure 7.2 Salomon Asch's experiment

The students had to compare the line on the left (the 'model') with three other lines on the right. Their task was to identify the line of the same length as the model (in this case, line C). They were then questioned by Asch, one by one, and asked to state the answer for the rest of the group to hear.

---

7. Salomon Asch, 'Effects of Group Pressure upon the Modification and Distortion of Judgments', in Harold Guetzkow (dir.), *Groups, Leadership and Men*, Carnegie Press, 1951.

However, all of the students were actors – the experimenter's associates – apart from one ('the subject') who was questioned second to last.

For the first two exercises, the associates all gave the correct answer. The subject did the same. In the third exercise, however, the associates all gave the same wrong answer. And what did the subject do? In 37% of cases, the subject conformed to the group's opinion and gave a wrong answer – one that ran contrary to their own opinion. Asch performed many variations of this basic experiment to gain a better understanding of the variables that make the effect so powerful. A key feature here is the unanimous nature of the associates' response. If one person gives a different answer, prior to the question being put to the subject, the subject is far less influenced by the group and in the vast majority of cases states the correct response. The size of the group is also an important variable. Asch showed that groups of four people led to more than 30% of subjects giving a wrong answer. In groups with two associates and one subject, however, the rate was only 13.6%.

Other researchers have also demonstrated that the cohesion of the group, the individual's desire to belong to it, or other members' perceived expertise are all factors that increase the influence the group exerts.

However, this influence is not restricted to isolated individuals making true or false judgments. It can also be seen in the course of our everyday decision making, such as the type of beer we order when with friends. As an experiment performed by Dan Ariely and Jonathan Levav[8] has shown, other people's orders have a significant influence over the type of drink that we select. Customers choose different beers accord-

---

8. Dan Ariely and Jonathan Levav, 'Sequential Choice in Group Settings: Taking the Road Less Traveled and Less Enjoyed', *Journal of Consumer Research*, vol. 27, December 2000, p. 279-290.

ing to whether they are making a strictly individual choice or whether this choice is made in front of others. When the order is made verbally, rather than on a private basis where members of the group can't know what the others are having, the range of beers selected is significantly more diverse. In this case, the explanatory hypothesis concerns the desire for individual expression – the opposite to group conformity.

Reciprocity and fairness

Our daily lives involve us being in constant contact with other people. These include members of our family, of course, as well as work colleagues, friends, retailers, and, in a more general sense, those unknown folk whose daily paths we cross on public transport, in stores, in recreational areas and simply on the street.

We are observed continuously by others and engaged in all kinds of social interaction. And, the way other people act towards us has a strong influence on our own behavior, whether we're aware of it or not. From the simplest, most commonplace behaviors – saying 'hello' or 'thank you', holding the elevator door open, doing somebody a favour or offering our help – to more formal engagements such as business negotiations, all social interactions induce specific reactions that have an influence upon our subsequent decisions. In short, the fairness, or kindness with which we believe we have been treated generates reciprocal behavior that falls some distance from the pure logic of our own self-interest. As Adam Smith said: 'Kindness is the parent of kindness.'[9] One good turn deserves another.

Numerous experiments have highlighted the role of fairness and reciprocity in our behavior and decisions. The con-

---

9. Adam Smith, *The Theory of Moral Sentiments*, 1759.

tributions of one of the world's foremost experts in this area, Professor Ernst Fehr of the University of Zurich,[10] are especially noteworthy.

The basic principle of these experiments is to pit two individuals against each other. The first of these ('the offeror') has an amount of money – say, 10 dollars – while the second ('the respondent') has nothing. The transaction that takes place between these two is very simple. The offeror has to suggest an amount to give to the respondent. If the respondent accepts, they both get to share the money according to the terms agreed. If the offer is rejected, however, neither party receives any money. Hundreds of studies of this type of have been performed, with the following results: the majority of offers are for between 40 and 50% of the available amount. These offers are generally accepted. But the respondent's decision, when the amount offered is less than 20% of the total, is more interesting. In this case, the majority turn down the offer. They prefer an 'irrational' solution (gaining nothing) over one that is financially preferable (receiving something, however small) but which they believe to be unjust. Our decisions are hence not purely a function of our interest. Rather, they involve some other more subjective elements. The perceived fairness of an action or an offer by an individual, an organization, or a brand thus has a strong influence on our behavioral response – to the extent that we may decide to act against our interest.

In another version of this game – the so-called 'dictator game' – the offeror is placed in a position of power. Once again, he has to suggest a way to split the money in his possession. This time, however, the money is shared according

---

10. Ernst Fehr and Klaus M. Schmidt, 'The Economics of Fairness, Reciprocity and Altruism: Experimental Evidence and New Theories', in Serge-Christophe Kolm and Jean Mercier Ythier (dir.), *Handbook of the Economics of Giving, Altruism and Reciprocity*, vol. 1, Elsevier, 2006.

to the stated offer, irrespective of the response. It is actually a false transaction, as the offeror alone decides the terms of the distribution – hence the word 'dictator' used here in the title. Maximizing his interest would therefore involve the offeror keeping the whole amount. For example, 10 dollars for himself, and none for the respondent. However, this is not what our 'dictators' do. The majority offer some money. Why, since it isn't in their interest? Because they foresee the perceived unfairness of a zero offer, and the resultant image it creates, both in their own eyes and those of the respondent. On average, the 'dictators' offer an amount between 10 and 25% of the total. They pursue their own interest while trying to conserve that of the other person. However, there is no specific benefit in doing so, as participants generally have no prior knowledge of one another and no future relationship to consider.

Professor Fehr's conclusions show that we don't take decisions purely as a function of our interest. Rather, that we incorporate a range of other, more subjective elements. Our perceived fairness of an action or proposal made by a person, an organization, or a brand has a strong influence on our behavioral response. So strong, in fact, that it can occasionally lead us to act against our own best interests.

Another conclusion is that we often pursue our own interests while trying to preserve other people's, even when there is no particular benefit to us. Fairness is hence a value that has a very strong influence on the decisions that we take.

Pre-commitment

Other people's influence on our own behavior can also take place indirectly via self-image and ego validation. We all seek an image of ourselves, in both our own eyes and in those of others, that is as positive as possible. And this influences our decisions and behavior through the commitments that we make. By making a public commitment to do something, our ability to keep to it is strengthened. This was the basis on which two Yale professors created StickK in 2008. The company's approach is very simple. You commit to undertake an action – for example, lose weight – and then you deposit an initial amount of money. If you fail, this money will be transferred to an organization of your choice. And if you succeed, you get it back. The beneficiary can be a charitable organization, a friend, or even – to give you more incentive to stick to your commitment – an organization that you hate.

We hence really are social beings. We are guided not only by our own interest but also by the fact we care about other people's interests too – including those we do not know. And the influence of these external factors doesn't stop here. Our surroundings or a particular situation in which we find ourselves at the time of taking a decision plays an equally important role.

Chapter 8

We are creatures of context

Our preferences are meant to drive our choices. From a range of available options, we are supposed to choose the one that brings us the most satisfaction. At least, this is how we'd go about things if we really were the rational decision makers that utility theory wants us to believe we are. However, as stated previously, there is a whole raft of reasons to indicate that the reality is far more complicated. We are subject to a range of subtle or less subtle influences. The illogicality of our decisions, the emotions that we feel, and the presence of others all have a strong effect on the choices that we make in the course of our everyday lives.

But there's still more to it than this. Our preferences are neither as strong nor as stable as we would have ourselves believe. Rather, these beloved preferences, which we think of as the expression of our individuality, are burdened by the way in which our choices are presented. They are *not* independent of what Thaler and Sunstein call 'choice architecture'. Quite the opposite, in fact: they are very much a product of the environment in which the decision is taken. This is a concept that behavioral economists call 'framing'.

Below are the eight main features influencing our decisions in the moment they are taken (see Figure 8.1).

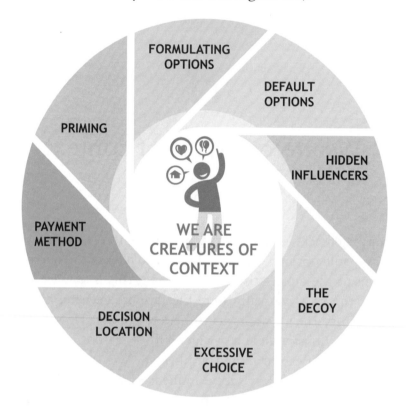

Figure 8.1 Eight influencing factors in our choice environment

Our preferences change according to the formulation of the options

The most well-known experiment[1] to demonstrate the effects of framing comes once again from Daniel Kahneman and Amos Tversky. The two researchers presented students from

---

1. Amos Tversky and Daniel Kahneman, 'The Framing of Decisions and the Psychology of Choice', *Science*, New Series, vol. 211, n° 4481, 30 January 1981, p. 453-458.

the universities of Stanford and British Columbia with the following fictional scenario: the USA has been hit by an outbreak of a disease liable to kill 600 people. Two treatment options are being considered:

- the first of these is worded: 'If programme A is adopted, 200 lives will be saved (72%)';
- the second: 'If programme B is adopted, there is a one-third probability that 600 people will be saved and a two-thirds probability that no people will be saved.'

In this instance, the majority of students said that they would go with programme A. The uncertainty attached to programme B worked against it, due to the risk aversion previously demonstrated by the same researchers. For the students, 200 lives saved for certain seemed preferable to 600 lives with a just a one-third probability of being saved.

But this wasn't the main focus of the experiment. The aim was to know how the students would choose when confronted by another wording of these same two programmes. It was merely a question of changing the form, as the mathematical basis was identical to the previous two options:

- this time, the first option (identical to programme A) was worded as follows: 'If programme C is adopted, 400 people will die (22%)';
- the second option (identical to programme B) stipulated this time that: 'If programme D is adopted, there is a one-third probability that nobody dies and a two-thirds probability that 600 people die (78%).'

In this instance, the majority of students went for programme D. The new wording of the two programmes hence caused the students' preference to be reversed. In the first example, programme A (200 people saved for certain) was preferred to programme B. In the second configuration, however, programme D (identical to programme B) was chosen over programme C (400 people die), despite the fact that the only difference between programmes C and A was the way that they were written!

And this type of influence doesn't only affect students making theoretical selections unrelated to their everyday decisions. The way the options are worded can also influence experienced professionals in their day-to-day choices.[2]

Our choices and preferences are thus heavily impacted by the way in which they are presented. This is not a set of stable, internal preferences that determines our eventual selection, but actually, a combination of *both* our preferences and the choice architecture that we are faced with.

However, the concept of choice architecture goes far beyond the simple formulation of choice options. More broadly, it concerns the way in which a choice is presented to us that has a major impact on our decisions. This is also reiterated in the results of another famous study[3] carried out by two researchers at the Center for Decision Sciences at the University of Columbia, Eric Johnson and Daniel Goldstein.

Default options: a powerful way of steering decisions

When we find ourselves presented with a choice, it is not uncommon for one of the options to be favoured by the person doing the presenting. Our everyday lives are surrounded by choice architectures containing default options as seen in the technology we use, such as our phones and our computers;

2. Barbara McNeil, Stephen Pauker, Harold Sox and Amos Tversky, 'On the Elicitation of Preferences for Alternative Therapies', *New England Journal of Medicine*, vol. 306, n° 21, May 1982, p. 1259-1262.
3. Eric Johnson and Daniel Goldstein, 'Do Defaults Save Lives', *Science*, vol. 302, 21st November 2003, p. 1338-1339.

the social networks we frequent (not to mention confidentiality and the sharing of personal information); the forms that we fill out, etc.

Johnson and Goldstein examined the power of default options in guiding our decisions. Starting with organ donation, they asked, 'Do default options alter our decisions?'. Is the acceptance rate for organ donation affected by the presence of a default option? To find out, they carried out the following three experiments and compared the results according to the type of default option used:

◆ an experiment involving students;
◆ a study of the rate of consent in European countries;
◆ a fact-based study of European organ donations between 1991 and 2001.

For the first of these, students were asked to decide about their participation in an organ donation programme. It was put to them that they were living in a new state. This new state stipulated – by default – either, a) adherence to the programme, or b) a non-adherence option. The students had to either accept or decline the given default option. When the default was adherence, 82% consented to take part in the programme. But when the default option was reversed, this number dropped to 42%! To confirm these results over a larger sample representing real-life attitudes and not those generated in a lab, researchers performed a second analysis of consent rates in European countries. And once again, the results were very clear. In countries such as France, Austria, Belgium, or Portugal, where citizens participate by default and have to check a specific box to opt out of the programme, consent rates are over 85%. However, in countries such as Germany, Holland, and England, where people have to check a box to opt *into* the programme, the rate falls to less than 30%. That's more than a 50% difference! And the cause of it is simply the way that people are presented with the choice!

However, these numbers merely reflect people's attitudes – and we are well aware of just how big the gulf can be between intention and behavior. For their third study, Johnson and Goldstein hence decided to examine organ donation statistics in European countries from 1991 to 2001, according to the default option given by each country. Yet again, results confirmed the significant influence of the default option, which was the sole cause of 16.1% more real-life organ donations. In real terms, this amounted to more than two million additional donors. And so in reply to the researchers' original question, we can say, with some certainty: Yes! The default policy saves lives!

'Hidden drivers': an important factor in decision making process

Brian Wansink and Pierre Chandon are two of the world's leading experts in food consumption. Their experiments have revolutionized the way we understand our relationship with food and the choices we make on a daily basis. Why do we consume more of one product than another? Most importantly, what determines the quantities that we consume?

Brian Wansink is Professor of Marketing at Cornell University and Director of the Cornell Food and Brand Lab (www. FoodPsychology.Cornell.edu). Pierre Chandon is Professor of Marketing at INSEAD, where he holds the L'Oréal chair and directs the Social Science Research Centre. Their research, which is based on studies that are at the same time fascinating and amusing, focus on the factors that determine our consumption habits. Contrary to what we may think, our tastes and appetite are not the main lever in determining the quantity of food that we consume. Yet again, it's the choice architecture, that we are presented with (or which we present to ourselves), and our environment, that urge us to continue eating, or, just as importantly, let us know when to stop! Most of the time, we are not consciously aware of these 'hidden drivers', to use Wansink's term from the bestselling *Mindless Eating*[4].

In the following study led by Wansink, experimenters offered a bucket of popcorn and a soft drink to people who had just bought movie tickets to see *Payback*. Some received a medium-sized bucket, while others were handed a giant-sized bucket. Even the medium-sized bucket, however, contained more popcorn that it was possible to eat. The aim was to see the effect that the size of the bucket had on the way the popcorn was consumed. The popcorn had been deliberately prepared five days before the test was carried out, and was hence not as tasty as it could have been. So consumption was not fuelled by the quality of the product. Furthermore, the movie was being screened at 13:30, meaning that the majority of viewers would have just eaten lunch and shouldn't have been hungry.

When the movie was over, researchers collected the buckets to measure how much popcorn had been eaten. The moviegoers were also asked to reply to some quick questions about their consumption. Once again, the results were both clear and enlightening:

◆ viewers who received the giant bucket ate much more than those who received the medium-sized bucket: 173 additional calories, or 21 more handfuls – around 53%;
◆ and of course, responses showed that participants did not believe that the size of the bucket had any effect on the amount of popcorn they consumed!

Wansink repeated his popcorn study with a number of different variables, and the results were always the same. We

---

4. Brian Wansink, *Mindless Eating: Why We Eat More than We Think*, Bantam Books, 2006.

are influenced by factors that either stimulate or slow down our consumption – and most of the time this process is unconscious. Environmental factors either activate the urge to eat (or find something to eat), or, conversely, tell us that enough is enough.

In a more general sense, Wansink and Chandon highlight the importance of what they call 'normative benchmarks' for the quantities of food that we consume, such as the size of the bucket in the popcorn study. Our consumption is strongly linked to these indirect influencers. Other examples include the size of a plate or glass, a product's packaging, or even the name given to each serving.

In a study of the consumption of French fries, Chandon[5] demonstrated the important role of the name given to each portion size. When bags of fries weighing 71, 117 and 154 grams were named 'small', 'normal' and 'large' respectively, participants consumed an average of 93 calories. When the same portions were named 'mini', 'small' and 'normal' this number rose to 114 – an increase of 22%! We hence tend towards the 'normal' portion, whatever quantity this actually represents.

Why are we so sensitive to these external influences when, on one hand, we are supposedly able to judge the amount of food that we need or want, and, on the other, we have an internal regulation system – the feeling of satiety – that is designed to tell us when we're full? The fact is that these regulation systems are easily misled, as demonstrated by another of Wansink's experiments.[6] Here, the subject was the quantity of soup eaten during a 20-minute meal by four guests seated at the same table. The goal was to measure the

5. Pierre Chandon *et al.*, 2013.
6. Brian Wansink, James Painter and Jill North, 'Bottomless Bowls: Why Visual Cues of Portion Size May Influence Intake', *Obesity Research*, vol. 13, n° 1, January 2005, p. 93-100.

quantity of soup consumed in this timeframe, with two different setups. The four customers at each table were given a bowl filled with the same amount of soup. However, two of them had a 'rigged' bowl that was attached to a pipe running underneath the table and providing a continuous refill. The other two had normal bowls. The researchers used this as a means to calculate the difference in consumption according to the type of bowl being used. The result was that the majority of people with a 'rigged' bowl continued eating after the 20 minutes were up. More significantly, the quantity of soup that they ate was over 400 grams, as opposed to 250 grams for those with a 'normal' bowl – around 73% more. And – even better – did the 'duped' customers feel any fuller than the others? No! Did they think they had taken on any more calories? No again! They thought they had ingested an equal number, when they had, in fact, consumed 113 more.

This shows how badly equipped we are to evaluate the quantity of food we take on board. Wansink and Chandon conclude that we are victims of two different phenomena that lead us to a poor assessment of reality. First, we tend to evaluate quantity visually – and we do this particularly badly. We also trust our eyesight when deciding whether or not to stop. Hence, the customers with the rigged bowls kept on eating as long as the soup bowl wasn't empty. At the same time, we are easily distracted. When we eat while doing something else, as if often the case, we pay less attention to our food. Several studies[7] have shown the effects of this. Watching television while eating, or eating with a friend, leads us to consume 18% and 14% more, respectively, compared to the occasions when we eat without these same distractions.

---

7.   Marion M. Hetherington, Annie S. Anderson, Geraldine N. M. Norton and Lisa Newson, 'Situational Effects on Meal Intake: A Comparison of Eating Alone and Eating with Others', *Psychology and Behavior*, vol. 88, n° 4-5, July 2006, p. 498-505.

The 'decoy effect': how to change people's choices by offering them something they don't want

Our preferences and choices are strongly influenced by the way that they are presented to us; by the formulation of the given options, by the presence of a default option (that we are inclined to follow), and by hidden drivers such as food packaging. In addition to this, these preferences can also be destabilized by a choice option in which we have no interest. This is what behavioral economists call the 'decoy effect', and is demonstrated by Dan Ariely's well-known example.

The Economist magazine offers three different types of subscription:

- online only for 59 dollars;
- paper only for 125 dollars;
- online *and* paper for 125 dollars.

The middle package – the paper only subscription – is of course not very appealing. Why pay 125 dollars for just the paper version of the magazine when you can have the online version as well for the same price? This was precisely the reasoning adopted by Ariely's students when presented with the choice, as none of them chose the former. The majority (84%) went for the online and paper option for 125 dollars, while a minority (16%) chose the online only version for 59 dollars. But, what happens to these numbers when you take away the option nobody is interested in? In this instance, the students' preferences were reversed! Now, 68% chose the 59 dollar option (as opposed to 84% previously), while the 125 dollar option was chosen by just 32%. The presence of the option in which nobody was interested – and that nobody chose – hence had a significant influence on the students' decisions. The reason for this was that it altered their relative perception of the other two options. Faced with three possible choices, the presence of two competing 125-dollar offers highlights the value of one relative to the other. However, when the choice was limited to two options, students focused more on the price difference, which led them to the cheaper package. So there you have it – the decoy effect in action!

Our behavior is not only altered by the type of options presented but also by the number of available choices. Choice and preference can be cleverly controlled by the careful design of choice architecture.

Too much choice can kill desire

In the 1950s, Herbert Simon, one of the founders of behavioral economics, drew attention to the limits of human rationality by highlighting the problems we have in dealing with large volumes of information. And this difficulty translates to paradoxical behavior when we are confronted with decisions that involve a wide range of choice options. We might expect being spoilt for choice to lead to greater feelings of satisfaction. That is, our range of preferences is better catered for where there is broader choice to satisfy the spectrum of our needs. However, this is not always the case.

Initially, the richness of the offer may appear attractive. But, when it comes to making a choice, this can make things more complicated. It requires a greater effort to be certain of picking whichever option is best for us. And, this ends up leading to anxiety and indecision. Contrary to imagined logic, an abundance of choice does not necessarily result in an increased motivation to purchase. This is the major theme explored by the psychologist Barry Schwartz in his wonderful book, whose title says it all, *The Paradox of Choice: Why More is Less*.[8] The unexpected effect of excessive choice on behavior can be explained by our fear of choosing badly. Faced with so many options, are

---

8.   Barry Schwartz (2004), *op. cit.*

we really able to identify the exact reference that matches our preference? All the more so when we have no specialist knowledge of the product, and when we imagine our choice to be important. What's more, this excessive choice can lead to greater feelings of post-purchase dissatisfaction. When it turns out that our choice is not as gratifying as we expected – for example, if the product is merely good rather than exceptional – Schwartz shows that the regret experienced increases in line with the importance of the choice. There were so many possibilities, and yet we still weren't able to pick the perfect one – which by the law of averages has to be there surely – and that would have led to greater satisfaction. Once again, the choice architecture – in this case, the relative abundance of options – reveals itself to be a fundamental influence on our behavior.

Choice architecture is not limited to the type of offer, its features, and the number of options it contains. The overall environment – that is, the place in which the decision takes place – plays an equally pivotal role in the choices that we make.

The impact of the decision location

In the introduction to *Nudge*, Richard Thaler and Cass Sunstein – who together came up with the concept of choice architecture – highlight the importance of the physical space in which a decision takes place. That is, the potential impact that it has on both our preferences and our behavior. The authors tell the story of their friend Carolyn, the director of school lunchrooms for a large US city, who changed children's eating habits simply by altering the way in which food was presented. These changes did not involve removing dishes and replacing them with new ones. In fact, it was simply a case of changing their physical positioning and making them more or less salient to the children's choice process. Managing the lunchroom space so that healthy foods were more salient produced a significant change in the children's decisions – Thaler puts it somewhere in the range of 25%. It wasn't the children's food preferences that changed, but their choices. This was caused by there being a stronger visual incentive for some products than for others. The underlying behavioral logic is easy enough to understand. If the first thing that I see is a beautiful bag of fries, or a bowl of spaghetti bolognaise, there's a strong chance that I will give in to temptation. I experience an emotional release, which produces an often irresistible desire to take one of these dishes – even though I know that they are not good for my health – not to mention my waistline. But when the situation is reversed, and the first thing that I see are healthy dishes – a beautiful tomato salad, for example, which is not in direct visual competition with the bag of fries – then there's a good chance I'll be steered towards the 'good choice'. Of course, the healthy dish in question has to match my tastes, although it doesn't have to be my all-time favourite food. The salience of the healthy dish hence creates a decision point that no longer exists if the unhealthy dish is given visual priority.

Many behavioral studies, particularly those aimed at finding better ways to fight obesity, have confirmed that salience of a product is most influenced by the way a space is organized.[9]

Choice architecture, however, entails more than the salience of a product or specific piece of information. When it comes to payment, for instance, there are different ways of organizing things – and their respective functions are not neutral.

How we pay affects what we decide to buy

Drazen Prelec and Duncan Simester have demonstrated the surprising impact of the method that we use to pay for things.

---

9. B. Wansink, J. E. Painter and Y. K. Lee, 'The Office Candy Dish: Proximity's Influence on Estimated and Actual Consumption', *International Journal of Obesity*, vol. 30, n° 5, May 2006, p. 871-875.

The pair set up an experiment[10] involving two big sporting events – a basketball game between the Boston Celtics and the Miami Heat, and a baseball game between the Boston Red Socks and the Toronto Blue Jets. Their cohort was a group of MBA students, and the objective was to measure the effect of the payment method (credit card, cheque or cash) on the price that students were prepared to pay for a ticket at auction. When payment had to be in cash, the average reserve price suggested by the students for the Celtics match was 28.51 dollars. However, when payment was by credit card, the reserve increased to more than 60 dollars. Likewise, an identical effect was observed for the baseball game. Here, the average price suggested for a Red Socks ticket was 9 dollars in cash, and almost 16 dollars by credit card.

Dilip Soman[11], a specialist in payment methods from the University of Toronto's Rotman School of Management, has a very good explanation for the psychological phenomenon behind this seemingly 'irrational' – or at least surprising in terms of payment transparency – behavior. Payment in cash, Soman says, is highly salient. We can see the dollar bills we use to make the purchase. We have to count them to arrive at the correct amount. When paying by cheque, however, we don't see the money physically pass through our hands, although we take great care in writing out the price of whatever we are paying for. Salience is hence still present in the act of writing a cheque, albeit less so than with cash. However, this salience is greatly reduced when we pay by credit card. We don't see the money slipping through our fingers, and we are less focused on the amount itself. Transparency is

10. Drazen Prelec and Duncan Simester, 'Always Leave Home without It: A Further Investigation of the Credit-Card Effect on Willingness to Pay', *Marketing Letters*, vol. 12, n° 1, 2001, p. 5-12.

11. Dilip Soman, 'The Effect of Payment Transparency on Consumption: Quasi-Experiments from the Field', *Marketing Letters*, vol. 14, n° 3, 2003, p. 173-183.

linked to our more or less strong mental awareness of the sum being spent. Cash is extremely transparent, while cheques and credit cards are far less so. There is therefore a hierarchy of payment systems based on relative transparencies – and this transparency has a significant effect on our decisions as consumers.

In another experiment, Dilip Soman confirms that credit cards are our preferred means of buying objects we consider less essential. Comparative spending on 'basic' commodities doesn't change according to the payment method used (credit card, cheque, or cash). However, there is a significant difference when it comes to secondary products: 27.5% of the shopping basket when customers pay in cash; 33% when they pay by cheque; and 43% when they pay by card.

Both laboratory and real-life experiments have confirmed the effects of payment methods on decisions. In this case, the means of payment and the product or service being purchased can be thought of as related. However, we can also be influenced by other factors that are entirely disconnected, with no obvious link between them whatsoever.

'Priming': how environmental triggers can influence behavior

'Priming' refers to the often unconscious change in our behavior, our decisions, or our perceptions as a result of previous information with no direct link to our subsequent decisions.

John Bargh, Mark Chen and Lara Burrows of the University of New York performed a study[12] to highlight this

12. John A. Bargh, Mark Chen and Lara Burrows, 'Automaticity of Social Behavior: Direct Effects of Trait Construct and Stereotype Activation on Action', *Journal of Personality and Social Psychology*, vol. 71, n° 2, 1996, p. 230-244 (copyright 1996 by the American Psychological Association).

remarkable effect. Two random samples of students were each
given a list of words:

- the first group were given words associated with old age,
  which had been validated in a previous study, such as:
  'Florida', 'old', 'lonely', 'grey', etc.;
- the second group were given age-neutral words such as
  'thirsty', 'clean', 'private', etc.

Each student had to read 30 five-word combinations and
then come up with a grammatically correct phrase using four
of the words in each combination. The goal was not to check
the relevance of the answers, but to measure whether the
words implying 'old age' altered the students' walking speeds
when the test was finished! The students were timed leaving
the building, and the difference was statistically significant.
Those in the first group walked off more slowly than those in
the second!

Numerous experiments have confirmed the existence of
this priming mechanism, in which an earlier stimulus influences subsequent behavior. The process seems to work in two
stages. First, the initial stimulus activates existing mental
associations (in the Bargh experiment, this was the association
with old age). Next, these associations take effect on our
behavior.

Beyond our personal preferences and the effect of social
interaction, our behavior is also influenced by a whole range
of situational factors. These are all the elements that make up
the environment in which a decision occurs. For our brain's
convenience, however, these 'decisions' are not really decisions
per se. A high percentage of the daily choices that we make
are merely duplicates of previous decisions. That is, the repetition of habitual behavior.

Chapter 9

We are creatures of habit

Do you really decide what time you are going to get up every morning? Whether to wash first or have breakfast? What this breakfast will involve? Where will you sit at the table? What means of transport you will use to get to work? If you're anything like the rest of us, you don't really think about these decisions. There's no studying of possible alternatives, no weighing up the pros and cons of each choice option. Simply, you repeat your past behaviors. Many of our decisions are hence not really decisions as such. The weight of repetition has made them automatic actions that we may not even be aware of any more. As we shall see, however, this mechanism is a long way from being anecdotal or uncommon. In fact, it is something at the core of all human behavior. We are creatures of habit. And as such, we need to understand the mechanisms behind these routine behaviors if we want to bring about their change.

The majority of our daily decisions are grounded in habit

First of all, these routine behaviors are not peripheral. They lie at the heart of our daily lives. Various academic studies designed to measure the ratio of habitual and non-habitual decisions have concluded that our everyday choices involve roughly half of each.

By following the behavior of students from the University of Texas, Professor Wendy Wood and colleagues[1] have highlighted both the relative importance of habitual decisions and the way these vary according to the activity. When it comes to personal hygiene and appearance (showering, washing hands, brushing teeth, dressing, applying makeup) 88% of decisions are considered habitual. At 81%, this number is also high for decisions related to sleeping and washing. On the other hand, when it comes to cleaning – housework, washing up, and laundry – only 22% of decisions are the result of habits. Nevertheless, in 9 of the 12 studies carried out, habitual decisions made up more than 40% of the total.

It is essential that we, as 'choice architects', understand the nature of these habitual decisions – or non-decisions – for the following important reasons:

+ they are central to the daily behavior that makes up our lives;
+ they have a strong impact on our behavior and our lives, as, by definition, they occur daily or extremely frequently;
+ they are particularly difficult to alter as, by definition once again, they are not the result of internal deliberation.

---

1.   Wendy Wood, Jeffrey M. Quinn and Deborah A. Kashy, 'Habits in Everyday Life: Thought, Emotion, and Action', *Journal of Personality and Social Psychology*, vol. 83, n° 6, 2002, p. 1281-1297 (copyright 2002 by the American Psychological Association).

If we want to have an impact on habitual decisions – that is, help people create new good habits and get rid of bad ones – we have to understand the way they work. And so to the first big question: Why do we employ habitual behavior so frequently?

Habits: how our brains save on resources

Ann Graybiel,[2] a world expert in the study of habits and a professor in the Department of Brain and Cognitive Science at MIT, came up with a series of experiments to explain the reasons for us forming habits. And the answer was clear. We do it to arrive at quick decisions while conserving our mental resources (in comparison, that is, to times when we take new decisions in unfamiliar environments). In terms of our organism's efficiency, this is clearly a huge benefit. We have limited physical and mental powers. As for all resource managers, we must organize these efficiently to get the most out of them. And this is exactly what the brain attempts to do by forming habits. It implements a process that allows us to take rapid decisions that do not require too much attention, and which yield satisfactory results at very little cost.

Faced with having to take so many small decisions on a daily basis, the habit mechanism allows us to get on with our lives without existing in a state of permanent reflection. In terms of the survival of the species, you could even say it saves us from danger. Paying attention is difficult. Intuitively, we know that it's impossible to remain in a state of heightened awareness for a long period of time. And it's also dangerous to be continually cut off from our environment.

---

2. Ann Graybiel, 'Habits, Rituals, and the Evaluative Brain', *The Annual Review of Neurosciences*, vol. 31, July 2008, p. 359-387.

Seeing as these habitual decisions are so important – both biologically and in our everyday lives – let's take a closer look at the mechanism that controls them.

The 'habit loop'

In his fascinating book, *The Power of Habit*,[3] Charles Duhigg describes the mechanism involved in our habitual decisions. The 'habit loop', as he calls it, is made up of three sequential steps:

- a cue, which comes from the external environment and is the initial trigger for the mechanism;
- a routine, which is the core of the habit;
- a reward, which is behind the formation of the habit and the reason for it becoming so engrained.

The habit's starting point is a cue that acts as a detonator for the mechanism. This cue can come from any of the following three sources:

- internal – from our own body. For example, I get hungry every day at around 4 p.m.;
- external – from the environment in which the decision takes place. Every day, for instance, I go past an ice cream shop. Or in the morning, my alarm goes off;
- from other people's behavior – this can happen both directly and indirectly. A direct example might be a colleague who suggests a daily morning cigarette break. An indirect example would be somebody acting in a way that triggers a reaction that becomes the cue.

This cue functions as the trigger for the habit. It makes me 'decide' – although without thinking about it – to adopt a particular behavior. It is the 'routine' phase of the mecha-

---

3. Charles Duhigg, *The Power of Habit: Why We Do What We Do in Life and Business*, Random House, 2012.

nism described above. In the example of feeling hungry at 4 p.m., this cue triggers the routine that involves me getting up from my desk to buy a bar of chocolate from the vending machine in the cafeteria. The chocolate is the reward that constitutes phase three: the reward satisfied the need that was triggered by the cue. The cue and the reward are hence intrinsically linked. The routine from phase two only exists because the cue triggered a need that was later satisfied by the reward. And this is Duhigg's 'habit loop': three linked phases that activate each other and which are set in motion by an environmental trigger.

There is hence a fundamental reason for the existence of our habits. They are a means to optimize the way our brain uses its energy and attention-giving resources. There is also a specific, subtle mechanism at work – the habit loop – that is built on repetition. But these habits are not only automatic and fundamental to our survival. They are also extremely powerful, as they can impose themselves in the face of our stated intentions, and can produce behaviors that we would rather they did not.

Habits: a way of managing our time that overshadows individual will

By definition, behavior does not become a habit until such time as it is frequently repeated. And it's this repetition over a given period that allows the brain to switch from its information-processing mode to a type of automatic pilot.

Once again, an academic study[4] has attempted to establish how long it takes for a habit to be formed. Ninety-six par-

4.   P. Lally, C. H. M van Jaarsveld, H. W. W. Potts and J. Wardle, 'How Are Habits Formed: Modelling Habit Formation in the Real World', *European Journal of Social Psychology*, vol. 40, n° 6, 2010, p. 998-1009.

ticipants were invited to choose a behavior that they would like to make habitual. For example, 'run for 15 minutes after dinner' or 'eat a piece of fruit at lunch'. Their behavior was then monitored over the next 12 weeks. Results showed that it takes some time (66 days on average) for behavior to become automatic. There was also a lot of variation depending on the type of habit being formed. For instance, 'drink a glass of water after breakfast' becomes automatic after only 20 days. However, certain habits are still not formed after 12 weeks. By the researcher's extrapolations, the automation of more stubborn behaviors may take over 250 days.

It therefore takes time to form a habit. Once formed, however – and sometimes this occurs unconsciously – our habits gain in strength to the point that they can often overcome our will. This is sadly the case for me when every night after dinner I get the urge to eat some chocolate when passing by the cupboard. I'm afraid to say that I do not resist the temptation, even though I know very well that I should... However, I'm not alone when it comes to this, as demonstrated by one of the leading specialists in habitual behavior, Wendy Wood and her colleague, Mindy F. Ji.[5] Their research involved monitoring participants' fast food consumption and TV-watching habits. And their results highlighted the fact that when habits are strong, our desire to change them is largely ineffective. Not only were these habits stronger than the intention to change, but participants also underestimated the weakness of their own willpower.

The automatic nature of many of our everyday actions combines with another key feature of our behavior: inertia. The reason why we humans often do not manage to get past the status quo.

---

5. Mindy F. Ji and Wendy Wood, 'Purchase and Consumption Habits: Not Necessarily what You Intend', *Journal of Consumer Psychology*, vol. 17, n° 4, 2007, p. 261-276.

Two biases: inertia and the status quo

Faced with a dilemma, we frequently have the option not to choose anything. That is, to keep things as they are. To not choose, or decide to leave our choice till later (which is just another type of non-choice) is often the option we take. We stick with the status quo – even when the change involved is 'rationally' in our interest.

Many studies have shown this inertia to be a basic feature of our behavior. When we find ourselves in a given situation, we very often remain 'stuck' there. Early research carried out by William Samuelson and Richard Zeckhauser[6] identified this phenomenon, which they named 'status quo bias'.

Since then, many other studies have confirmed the existence of this bias. The fact is that we have a lot of trouble altering our current behavior patterns. What's more – and this suggests at least a sliver of lucidity – we all know it! Our lives are full of the results of previous decisions that are no longer relevant but whose effects we still feel. For example; phone and TV subscriptions that no longer make financial sense but which we keep paying for anyway.

The effect is so powerful because it's so deeply engrained. Scott Eidelman and Christian Crandall have made a brilliant synthesis[7] of the status quo's historical makeup. Their conclusions demonstrate that it results from a combination of rational elements and the main biases described previously. The forces that lead us to explicitly or implicitly choose 'non-change' are hence extremely strong. And our choosing the status quo may have a rational basis. That is, those times when we consider the cost of change to be greater than the expected benefit. For example, I may consider my current phone subscription satisfactory.

6.   Richard Zeckhauser and William Samuelson, 'Status Quo Bias in Decision Making', *Journal of Risk and Uncertainty*, vol. 1, n° 1, 1988, p. 7-59.
7.   Scott Eidelman and Christian S. Crandall, 'Bias in Favor of the Status Quo', *Social and Personality Psychology Compass*, vol. 6, n° 3, 2007, p. 270-281.

While another slightly better subscription may be out there, the costs – represented here by the time and thought required to hunt it down – outweigh the benefits. My choice is hence to keep things as they are, even though a better option is available. The status quo can therefore be the result of a rational decision. However, in the case of 'status quo bias' the many reasons for our basic inertia and resistance to change are essentially 'irrational'. We choose inertia – changing nothing – not because it carries any benefit but because it corresponds to the current situation. Even if the alternative option is preferable, we don't choose it. This implicit preference for the status quo comes from the following three important biases: loss aversion; fear of regret; and familiarity effects from repeated exposure.

◆ Aversion to risk and loss are expressed in the decision to not change anything. This comes about due to fear that the change will cause a loss in terms of our current situation (the reference point).

◆ Fear of regret refers to a change that might generate disappointment regarding a previous situation – and hence guilt arising from the bad decision taken.

◆ The effects of familiarity and repeated exposure are a function of the growing preference we develop for the people, contexts and objects that make up our daily lives.

Since it carries the risk of loss or regret, the change is rejected and this is even more likely when the situation in question involves the familiarity effect.

We understand the extent to which the status quo bias is rooted in all of us. And its strength is even greater since our inertia is caused by factors that are, for the most part, invisible. This leads me to another important feature of our behavior. The fact is that we are all, as Timothy Wilson confirms in the title to his important work on the same subject, *Strangers to Ourselves*.[8]

---

8. Timothy D. Wilson, *Strangers to Ourselves*, The Belknap Press of Harvard University Press, 2002.

Chapter 10

We are creatures of intuition and strangers to ourselves

Since Freud, we have known that behavior can be explained by unconscious motivations linked to events – often those occurring during early childhood – or impulses that we have repressed due to their being difficult to face on a personal or social level. This, briefly, is the basic concept of the Freudian unconscious.

Behavioral economists' understanding of the unconscious, however, is different to the Freudian model. It concerns the idea that we are unaware of many of the factors influencing our decisions. This is either because they take effect very early in the decision-making process and we don't recognize them as being influential, or because we under-estimate their importance.

Our explanations for the real factors underlying our decisions and behavior remain somewhat superficial. However, we generally believe the opposite. We aren't conscious of our own unconscious! As such, we find it easy to explain our choices, even when they don't make very much sense, as a well-known study[1] carried out by Richard Nisbett and Timothy Wilson has demonstrated.

---

1. Richard Nisbett and Timothy Wilson, 'Telling More than We Can Know: Verbal Reports on Mental Processes', *Psychological Review*, vol. 84, n° 3, 3 May 1977, p. 231-259.

The neuropsychologist Michael Gazzaniga has shown[2] that this search for causality is something deeply engrained in us. He arrived at this conclusion by studying the reactions of people suffering from split-brain. A feature of this condition is that the left and right cerebral hemispheres are unable to communicate with one another. Studies aimed at understanding the specific role of each hemisphere can therefore be carried out.

In a famous experiment, researchers set up the following protocol. First, they placed the image of a chicken leg in the visual field of a patient's left hemisphere (to their right), and a snow-covered scene in the visual field of their right hemisphere (to their left). Next, they asked the patient to choose an image from several options placed in front of them, all of which were visible to both hemispheres. The right hand picked a card showing a chicken (which was consistent with the image of the leg seen by the corresponding hemisphere), while the left hand chose a shovel (which was consistent with the snow-covered scene). The patient was then questioned about their reasons for their choosing the two cards. The speech centre, which is located in the left hemisphere, had no trouble justifying the right hand's choice. The hand had indicated the chicken leg that corresponded to the image of the chicken seen by the equivalent hemisphere. However, it was *a priori* impossible for the left hemisphere to justify choosing the shovel, as it had no way of knowing that this image corresponded to the snow-covered scene that was only seen by the right hemisphere. Most important, however, is the fact that the left hemisphere still found an explanation for its choice: 'You need a shovel to clean out the henhouse'.

For Gazzaniga, 'What was interesting was that the left hemisphere did not say, "I don't know", which was the correct

---

2.   Michael S. Gazzaniga, *Who is in Charge?: Free Will and the Science of the Brain,* Ecco, 2011.

answer. It made up a post hoc answer that fit the situation. It confabulated, taking cues from what it knew and putting them together in an answer that made sense. We called this left-hemisphere process the interpreter.'

Gazzaniga's research into split-brain patients confirmed the existence of an 'interpretation process' in the left hemisphere, where the speech centre is located. We find answers to justify our choices and behavior, even when these have nothing to do with the reality of the stimuli that influence our decisions. This is a physiological process rather than a choice.

Not only are we are unable to identify the real factors influencing our behavior. We are also convinced of our ability to explain them – and that these explanations are well grounded!

Clearly, this is an important point for marketers, academics and social science researchers the world over. At best, asking questions to try and understand people's decisions and behavior leads to the real influencing factors being skipped over. At worst, it leads to them being seriously mistaken. And even more evident when respondents are convinced of their ability to explain their basic motivations. As we will see, we have to look beyond the things that people say to get a real idea of factors underlying their decisions.

Let's end this discussion by returning to that giant of behavioral economics, Daniel Kahneman and his crucial theory of System 1 and System 2. Kahneman uses this metaphor to describe the decision-making process as simply as possible. Like a couple sharing the driving, we take decisions based on two very different systems, which he calls System 1 and System 2:

- ◆ System 1 is a sort of automatic pilot. It is consistent and unconscious. It does not require any additional effort, and is very quick to draw conclusions;
- ◆ System 2, conversely, is slow moving and conscious. It requires effort and attention. It tries to weigh up all the pros and cons of all the alternatives that confront it.

We switch between these two systems depending on the type of decision. For those we consider important – buying a car or a house, perhaps choosing where to go on a family holiday – we try and take the best possible decision, and are prepared to invest some time and effort to achieve this. These are common examples of System 2. However, the key point is that in the vast majority of our decision making, we resist this system. The reason for this is simple. System 2 requires the kind of effort we don't really like to make. Kahneman calls it 'the lazy controller'.[3] We prefer to take decisions quickly, unthinkingly, and without the mental exertions that the majority of us find very tough. System 1 is thus – to borrow the 2002 Nobel Prize winner's own expression – 'the hero of this book'. We use System 1 for the majority of the decisions in our everyday lives, for the simple reason that it's easier. It is based on routines. For example, I don't give any thought to what I have to do when I wake up. I just go straight to the bathroom and wash. System 1 uses mental shortcuts. If a product advertised as on special offer, I don't have to check that the price is less than all the others. I just go ahead and buy it. This system also uses associations that we have memorized already to enable us to make quicker judgments. For example; Apple products are innovative but expensive. Since System 1 is uninterested in calculations (this would take too long and involve some effort) it estimates, simplifies things, and doesn't second-guess itself. It is based on stereotypes and norms. If there's a picture of a child on a product, it's because the product is aimed at children. If there are lots of people in a restaurant, this is because it's better than the empty one next door.

All in all, System 1 makes our lives simpler by helping us take the bulk of the decisions we face every day, and with the minimum of effort. We therefore use System 1 most of the

---

3. Daniel Kahneman (2012), *op. cit.*, p. 21.

time and System 2 only sparingly. And the basic reason for this is that System 2 places high demands on our mental energy. Paying attention, processing information with care and consideration – concentrating, in short – uses significantly more mental energy than a simple routine decision. Our brain is the organ responsible for efficient resource management. And it optimizes these resources by using System 1 wherever possible. There is hence an important physiological reason behind the fact that we default to System 1 for the majority of our decisions.

In evolutionary terms, System 2 represents a serious flaw. Our attentions are by nature limited. By focusing on a particular subject, we are left unable to evaluate our wider environment. For our ancestors living a few million years ago, this kind of distraction could have been perilous because their environment was where the danger lurked. It's an important point, as our current brains have evolved to prioritize mechanisms that are useful for the reproduction and survival of the species. If System 1 is at the centre of our decisions, and System 2 is more peripheral, it's because this setup was the most efficient way for us to handle our environment in the past.

The important thing to remember, in the end, is that the normal mode we use for our everyday decision making is not, as we would have ourselves believe, the reflective, rational System 2. It is the spontaneous, intuitive, emotional, and automatic System 1. Since this system operates unconsciously, however, we believe that we are operating under System 2. We design actions aimed at convincing System 2 that are largely ineffective when applied to System 1. However, it's the latter that's behind the vast majority of our decisions. Let's leave the final word to Daniel Kahneman: 'Most of what we think and do originates in System 1.' In order to change people's behavior, we have to come up with actions that will influence this far more common mode of thinking.

The aim of this book, however, is not simply that of a voyage, however fascinating, into the workings of the human mind. My goal here is pragmatic: to use this knowledge as a means to produce desired changes in behavior via the design and implementation of effective strategies, or 'actions'.

The next two sections will focus on this goal. Based on our new understanding of the factors that influence an individual's decision-making process, I will address the question of how to update the model for desired-behavior outcome in the in the arena of public-policy making and private enterprise.

And so, we set off on another voyage – this time, in search of an efficient action plan.

NUDGE MARKETING APPLIED TO PUBLIC POLICY

Changing citizens' behavior

Make public policy more effective. It's an ambitious, even pretentious ambition. In light of the many difficulties currently faced by political decision-makers, however, there is an urgent need for such increased efficiency. All the more so as the levels of debt facing certain countries make their return on investment (ROI) per expenditure increasingly important. When it comes to public policy, efficiency is what's required. And this is what the Nudge approach can offer: effectiveness at very little cost.

My aim in part three is to give the reader access to the Nudge approach and its many benefits, beginning with a comprehensive understanding of all that this entails. To this end, I will use examples drawn from real life, as well as suggesting an approach for designing effective Nudges. The following three chapters will involve:

◆ a description of the general principles conceived by Richard Thaler and Cass Sunstein;

- ◆ a demonstration of Nudge's effectiveness using real-life examples and including some key questions facing public authorities;
- ◆ a suggested, practical method for designing successful Nudges.

Chapter 11

The Nudge approach: the devil's in the detail

Every time I give a presentation on the Nudge approach to an audience who's never heard of 'Nudge', I begin with an example, famous in Nudge circles for one good reason: it was used by Thaler and Sunstein, the founding fathers themselves, in the introduction to their seminal work. Gently provocative and highly visual, it does a good job of getting across the Nudge 'philosophy'. And I can't resist sharing that example here. I'm sure you'll enjoy using it yourself, should any of your loved ones ask you what this Nudge thing's all about. The example involves a fly. Or, more precisely, the image of a fly. And this image is placed in a specific location: the urinals at Schiphol airport in Amsterdam.

Now, this little fly is going to produce a powerful behavioral change. Men, who, as we know, are both hunters and big kids at heart, can't resist the temptation to take aim at this 'fly'. It's a game that results in a significant reduction in cleaning costs for the urinals at the airport. When men aim at the fly placed in the middle of the urinal, the 'splashes' are far fewer. And so is the cost of cleaning them. Aad Kieboom and his fellow janitor Jos van Bedaf, who came up with this idea

in the 1990s, did not perform any 'scientific' studies to measure the effects. Empirically, however, they put the cost reduction at around 80%.

Aside from being amusing, this example gives a simple
illustration of Nudge's basic principles:

♦ *a choice architecture* – the image of the fly positioned in a
  specific place – *aimed at altering a real-life behavior* – a
  badly-aimed stream that causes splashing around the urinal – *and encouraging a virtuous, or 'good' behavior* – a stream
  that hits the centre of the urinal, reducing unwanted
  'misses';

♦ *based on a behavioral logic for a given situation* – the men's
  playfulness – *and not on a rational logic that is assumed to be
  correct* (in this case, the presentation would generally be
  something along the lines of: 'Thank you for leaving these
  toilets in the state in which you found them');

♦ *leaving people free to behave as they wish* – the fly is merely
  an inducement to behave in a certain way. There is no
  obligation;

♦ *for which the cost of implementation is low* – the price of the
  image – *and the effects of people's behavior is high* – the greatly
  reduced cleaning costs.

Behind its trivial veneer, the fly example really does highlight the paradox at the heart of the Nudge approach. Small,
seemingly insignificant alterations can cause big changes in
behavior. The beauty of Nudge is in its combination of the
essential and the banal, the strategies and their execution, to
arrive at these astonishing results. Plus, this doesn't only apply
to airport cleaning costs. It is also highly relevant to the main
problems currently facing public policy, as we shall see.

Public action involves setting certain objectives. To reach
these goals, the action seeks to steer the behavior of citizens
or businesses in a particular direction. In democratic countries, this direction generally corresponds to the political

agenda of the elected government. To achieve this, public decision-makers have the following means at their disposal:

- The law: in this case, citizens who want their actions to remain legal do not have any alternative. They have to apply the rules laid down by the democratically elected authority. For example, the ban on smoking in public.
- Taxes and subsidies: this is a means of guiding people's economic decisions by making choice options more or less attractive. To continue the previous example, this might mean an increase in tax on cigarettes.
- Information: authorities can communicate the advantages or dangers of a particular behavior to make it more or less prevalent. This involves allowing potential consumers to take better-informed decisions. For instance, using advertising to promote the well-known message that 'smoking kills'.

Public authorities hence have a wide range of possible actions at their disposal to ensure economic agents take decisions that benefit either their organization or the wider community.

The problem with these public policies – and it would be ridiculous to suggest there weren't any – is in their effectiveness. Structural, short-term policies produce effects that we observe on a daily basis. But it is also true that during the last 40 years the world has been confronted by a stream of major crises involving some fundamental challenges. In the short term, this includes such things as high unemployment in many countries, or the extreme poverty faced by over a quarter of the world's population. In the long term, there is the environmental threat faced by our planet. The search for increased effectiveness in public policy is an incredibly important challenge where the Nudge approach is very much a part of this ongoing effort. However, this does not in any way imply a simple substitution of the three levers described above.

The Nudge method aims to complement. It works along-side the existing frameworks that are both imposed (by law), and suggested (by financial incentives and by the spread of information). It seeks neither to oblige nor to convince. Instead, it aims to steer people's decisions via the relevant choice architecture. The freedom to choose between different options remains, with the understanding that a preferred behavior exists, even though our desire to adopt it may not necessarily come from a deliberate or active choice.

Of course, ultimately, it does involve a certain logical shift. However, not even the staunchest Nudge supporters would suggest that the method be used to the exclusion of all others. On one hand, it's about making people aware of 'incentive' as a viable complement to rational and information-based approaches. On the other, it's about identifying the most appropriate response to each challenge in light of the political decision-maker's goal.

Nudge is as an example of 'last meter' marketing: a stage on which our choices can play out. Choice options in their original, unaltered state are hence of no concern. Nothing new is created by the process. Simply, the way in which these choices are presented is improved. It's about steering people towards options that bring the greatest good to either them-selves or the community, not introducing new choices or sup-pressing those already there. And herein lies both the subtlety and the difficulty of the Nudge approach. It is conducted from the sidelines, but its effects are immense – a conflict that Robert Cialdini sums up very well in the title to his latest book, *The Small Big*.[1]

Nudge's complementary nature goes beyond the simple fact of introducing a fourth way. It is also a way of enhancing the effectiveness of the three existing methods. For example, how can laws be made more acceptable and understandable

---

1. Martin Steve, Goldstein Noah and Cialdini Robert (2014), *op. cit.*

– and hence more widely followed? How can financial subsidies be made more salient to the people they are aimed at? Or how can a piece of information be made easier to process, and hence more convincing, for those receiving it? To repeat: Nudge doesn't seek to replace all other weapons in the political decision-maker's arsenal. It's more a question of complementing and strengthening these existing methods and as a consequence, improving the efficiency of public policies being implemented.

Chapter 12

Five years of Nudge: an overview

The recent TEN conference in Copenhagen, brilliantly organized and run by Pelle G. Hansen, Alberto Alemanno and Lucia Reisch in June 2014, took stock of Nudge's first five years. A few weeks earlier, the 'Behavioural Exchange'[1] conference in Sydney brought together Thaler and Sunstein, active practitioners such as David Halpern from the UK Nudge Unit, Maya Shanker from the United States, Thia Jang Ping from Singapore, representatives from Opower, and some big-name academics including David Laibson, Max Bazerman and Mike Norton.

David Halpern and Owain Service's Behavioural Insight Team, which has played a key role in expanding the Nudge approach both in the UK and worldwide, were central to this process. Not only did the team tackle some vital questions, but, as for any leading research centre, the Nudge Unit also published the results of its real-life experiments. And, what better than conclusive results coming from an official body of a major country to make other nations want to give the Nudge approach a try? Between ongoing academic studies and those carried out by the UK Nudge Unit, we now have a wealth of real-life examples by which to understand both the reality behind the Nudge approach and the results obtained.

---

1. http://bx2014.org/

The following section will set out the details of the Nudge approach applied to public policy. By taking a representative example for each of the major challenges tackled by Nudge in the following key sectors, I hope to give a clearer picture of its scope:

- Public finances
- Pension savings scheme
- Energy saving
- Public health
- Education and poverty
- Workplace performance

Nudge and public finances

Many countries are currently facing a budget deficit. Their governments are trying to manage spending as strictly as possible, as well as maximize returns on this expenditure.

My real-life example for public finances relates to this last point: maximizing fiscal returns. And this is what happened in the United Kingdom with the help of the Nudge Unit.

The United Kingdom – like most countries – has trouble getting people to pay their taxes on time. The Nudge Unit tackled this problem by reworking the contents of the reminder letter sent out to the late taxpayers.[2] In the original version, the letter was worded as follows: 'Our records show that your Self Assessment tax payment is overdue. It is easy to pay. Please call the phone number above to pay by debit card, credit card, or direct debit. You can also pay using internet and telephone banking. For more information on when and how to pay, go to www.hmrc.gov.uk/payinghmrc. If you don't believe that this payment is overdue, please

---

2. Nudge Unit – Behavioural Insights Team & HMRC, 2012.

contact us on the number above. If you have already paid, thank you. If not please act now.'

The change in the wording of the new letter was subtle. All it entailed was adding the following phrase: 'The great majority of people in your local area pay their tax on time. Most people with a debt like yours have paid it by now.' The effect of this was significant. Within 23 days of the new reminder letter going out, the percentage of people paying their tax bill increased from 33.6% to 39%. In financial terms, this amounted to 2.8 million additional pounds in the government's coffers – and that was just for the region carrying out the experiment! This is a perfect example of the Nudge approach at work. At no additional cost, it brought about a big change in taxpayers' behavior, yet these people still retained the freedom to act as they saw best. Like the example of the fly described at the beginning of chapter 11, the final action – the addition of a simple phrase – may seem completely trivial, but its effect is quite the opposite. Why is this? Because the action relies on social norms – a powerful lever identified by behavioral economics. Knowing that their neighbours behave differently creates a pressure that encourages bad payers to resolve their situation.

However, the remiss taxpayers may also be sensitive to the personal nature of the message, as demonstrated by the Behavioural Insights Team in a test[3] carried out in real-life conditions in south-west England on behalf of the Ministry of Justice (HMCTS). The experiment involved sending SMS reminders to people who were late paying fines. These messages were all different, and used the following levers:

◆ a simple text mentioning the late payment and the requirement to settle it;
◆ a text mentioning the amount due;

---

3.   The Behavioural Insights Team (ed.), *Applying Behavioural Insights to Reduce Fraud, Error and Debt*, Cabinet Office, February 2012.

+ a personalized text using the person's first name;
+ a personalized text using the person's first name and stating the amount due.

Results showed that the reminders were clearly effective, with payment rates increasing from 5.2% to 23.2%. Even more interestingly, the inclusion of the late payer's first name raised this figure to 33%. The salience arising from the personal and emotional elements attached to a first name meant that the SMS produced a significant change in behavior.

As we shall see in the following example, Nudge systematically falls back upon this principle: identify the correct lever for the behavior you want to modify, then find an appropriate way to implement it.

Funding a pension savings scheme in the USA

In France, there is a system of mandatory pension contributions designed to provide retirees with a basic level of income when they stop work. In the USA, conversely, people decide for themselves the amount that they would like to put aside for their retirement. Due to the bias that causes us to overvalue the present in regard to the future, Americans do not put enough into their pension funds. They choose to spend their disposable income rather than see it reduced by a higher rate of contributions – the negative consequence of which is a difficult retirement.

Richard Thaler and Shlomo Benartzi tackled this problem with a suggestion for a savings plan: the shrewdly named 'Save More Tomorrow' or 'SMarT Plan'. The plan has the following simple features:

+ companies offer employees the chance to agree in advance to increased rates of savings at the time of their next pay rise;

◆ employees are free to refuse to adhere to the plan, which is put to them expressly and on an individual basis;
◆ their rate of saving will increase with each pay rise until it reaches the agreed threshold for a three-year period;
◆ employees can quit the SMarT Plan whenever they want to.

The experiment led to the following results:

◆ 78% of employees who were offered the SMarT Plan accepted;
◆ 80% of subscribers are still in the plan after the stipulated three-year period;
◆ and, most importantly, as this was the ultimate goal, the rate of savings for new subscribers went from 3.5% to 11.6% in 28 months!

Once again, the underlying logic is simple but extremely powerful. It is very difficult to convince somebody to reduce their income, even when it's for their future benefit. Hence, rather than fight this bias that, as we saw previously, is so deeply engrained in human nature, Thaler and Benartzi chose to get around it. They didn't suggest reducing current income in favour of saving; rather, that people make the effort later on, at the time of their next pay rise. The plan is ingenious on two levels: it doesn't require any current effort (this potential obstacle is hence removed), and it associates the future effort with an event that is by definition positive. That is, a pay rise that will result in a net increase in disposable income, in spite of this same effort. All in all, it's not surprising that a large majority of employees took up the offer.

The status quo bias was another mechanism the researchers used to shore up the system. As we know, people don't like change. We have a strong tendency to stay glued to previous decisions, including times when preferable solutions are available. Thaler and Benartzi used this bias to embed the initial decision to subscribe to the SMarT Plan. By offering a three-year plan, the status quo effect played in their favour. The great majority of subscribers remained in the plan. One reason, no doubt, was that they were satisfied with it. But it is certainly the case that they were also victims to the inertia that affects us all.

Our personal financial decisions can hence be modified – to our benefit – via simple, inexpensive interventions, provided these are based on both a solid understanding of the factors blocking the adoption of the desired behavior and the ways to remove these obstacles.

Nudge and energy saving

Energy saving is one of the biggest issues currently facing the planet. And behavioral economics can make a major contribution, as proved by actions carried out by Opower – a company created by Alex Laskey and Dan Yates in 2007. The company's objective is both clear and highly ambitious:[4] 'Opower combines a cloud-based platform, big data, and behavioral science to help utilities around the world reduce energy consumption and improve their relationship with their customers. This helps customers lower their energy use and costs, and significantly reduces carbon emissions. Opower is transforming the way the world approaches household energy conservation.'

And the best thing is that the company achieves this using actions that are perfect examples of the Nudge approach – small changes in detail with big secondary effects – as demonstrated by the following programme established in 2009.[5]

---

4.   Opower: http://opower.com/company
5.   Hunt Allcott, 'Social Norms and Energy Conservation', *Journal of Public Economics*, vol. 95, n° 9-10, October 2011, p. 1082-1095.

The programme involved a large-scale operation comprising 600,000 households in six different countries, in partnership with 80 energy providers. Its goal (the core of Opower's corporate objective), was to reduce energy consumption in test households from the levels observed at the start of the programme. And they achieved it easily, at very little cost. All it took was a new way of showing the households how much energy they consumed. As shown in the graph below, the household consumption – 504 kWh – is not given in isolation, but in comparison with that of two specific groups: 'efficient neighbors' and 'all neighbors'. Alongside a bar chart, there was a short phrase explaining their situation – 'Last month you used 15% LESS electricity than your efficient neighbors' – and two smiley faces, followed by a GREAT (see Figure 12.1).

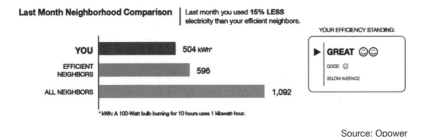

Source: Opower

Figure 12.1 Nudge by Opower

All of a sudden, the previously abstract amount of 504 kWh had a whole new meaning. When it comes to your neighbours, you are better than average. In fact, you're among the best of them. And your reward for this is two smiley faces! Next Opower applied a double lever well known to behavioral economists called 'social norms'. This is a comparison that allows us to position ourselves relative to others – by rewarding us with the smiley face it places a value on our behavior and encourages us to keep it up.

Now, you may tell me this is easy enough for a household with 'good' energy consumption. But what about when the opposite is true? When a household's energy consumption is *greater* than that of its neighbours? The answer is that the method stays the same – a piece of information that allows people to position themselves relative to others – but the content is different. In this instance, rather than thank people for their good behavior, they are presented with some simple actions to help lower their consumption levels. Once again, this involves a lesson from behavioral economics. Immediately after providing this information, Opower added a 'call for action'. This took the form of three suggestions helping people to economize over the winter. Its aim was to translate the information into new behavior.

Beyond the substance of the information in the two above examples, their style is equally striking. Their form, while incredibly simple, allows for immediate understanding. Cast your mind back for a moment to the earlier lessons outlined in these pages. Our attentional resources are limited. We can only process information that is salient and that we can interpret easily and without effort. And these are precisely the conditions on which Opower's communications are based. Images instead of words. Meaningful colours. Icons such as smileys whose meaning can be grasped immediately – a masterclass in successful execution!

And Opower aren't done yet. The company wants to make these 'good' behaviors a long-term fixture. This is why they supplement the earlier messages about consumption with personal advice on ways to reduce energy bills.

The latter is more of a classic communication than a Nudge. And this illustrates perfectly the complementary nature of the two approaches. Together, they maximize the opportunities for changing people's behavior.

Unsurprisingly, the use of relevant levers, combined with a clear and simple execution, led to significant results. Sure enough, the households in question reduced their energy consumption by 2%! This figure might seem relatively small. But when you bear in mind that it corresponds to 2 TWh (terawatt-hours) in savings – the equivalent yearly consumption of Saint-Louis and Salt Lake City combined – that smiley face seems pretty useful. Even more so when you translate the energy saved into 250 million dollars cold hard cash! When it comes to energy savings, the simple truth is that Nudge works. And this is excellent news for the planet.

Nudge and public health

Public health is one of the major challenges currently facing public policy. The long-term goal is to develop global measures to protect people's health in the widest sense of the term. This involves promoting hygienic practices, implementing effective policies for the prevention and treatment of disease, increasing health security, and developing a sense of social responsibility and concern for others.

The Nudge approach has been applied to many public health issues. Its scope here appears limitless, as indicated by a BIT[6] report describing experiments carried out in the following areas: smoking, organ donation, adolescent obesity, alcohol consumption, diet and weight, diabetes, food hygiene, physical activity, and interdependence.

The following two important examples illustrate the Nudge approach applied to public health. The first of these concerns the fight against obesity in the USA; the second, the spread of AIDS in Malawi.[7]

---

6. The Behavioural Insights Team (ed.), *Applying Behavioural Insight to Health*, Cabinet Office, December 2010.
7. Rebecca L. Thornton, 'The Demand for, and Impact of, Learning HIV Status', *American Economic Review*, vol. 98, n° 5, 2008, p. 1829-1863.

Fighting obesity in the USA

When it comes to fighting obesity, the USA is at the forefront of behavioral economics experiments. Over one-third of American adults are considered obese, as well as more than 15% of children.[8] This is a major public health issue, as proven by the personal involvement of the First Lady, Michelle Obama. Of the initiatives under development, one of the most remarkable is MyPlate.[9] Launched in June 2011 by the president's wife and the Secretary of Agriculture, Tom Vilsack, this initiative calls for a complete action plan, (see Figure 12.2), aimed at helping people cultivate a balanced diet.

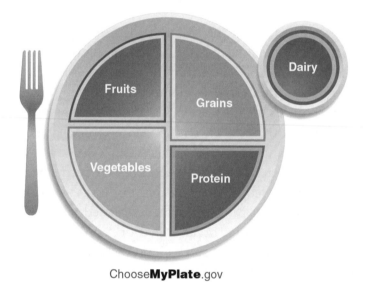

ChooseMyPlate.gov

Source: www.choosemyplate.gov/images/MyPlateImages/JPG/myplate_green.jpg

Figure 12.2 MyPlate

This graphic is intended as a constant reminder of the type and proportions of food that Americans should eat, so as to not gain weight and to maintain a balanced diet. Beyond this

8.   www.cdc.gov/obesity/data/facts.html
9.   www.choosemyplate.gov

intention, however, it's the form, chosen by the American administration, which is particularly interesting. The presentation is extremely simple, making it easy to understand – a simplicity that is especially striking when the new graphic is compared to the old one (see Figure 12.3).

Source: United States Department of Agriculture

Figure 12.3 MyPyramid

My understanding of the administration's implicit recommendation was much less immediate with the images used for MyPyramid. What do the stairs mean? What does the image say about how much you can eat in each product category? And the name itself is much more meaningful in the new programme. But beyond its name, MyPlate is a call to action. It challenges people to come up with balanced servings containing each of the different food types in the suggested proportions. The whole thing is contained in a single image. Of course, the graphic is only a banner for the more general policy that reveals itself as you delve deeper into choosemyplate.gov. But this banner is also a symbol of the new ways that the government communicates with its citizens – new methods whose basis is behavioral economics. On browsing the site, it is also interesting to see the extent to which the advice tries to be both salient and extremely simple. 'Key messages for consumers', for example, is written in bold and in red. For fruit and vegetables, the advice is: 'Put together a plate that is half fruit and vegetables'. And for dairy products: 'Choose milk that is either 0% or low in fat (1%)'. It's not surprising to learn that this simple, direct, highly visual communication was developed by officials from the American Ministry of Agriculture, in partnership with a team of nutritional specialists and communication experts, as well as Cass Sunstein![10]

The MyPlate action plan is a large-scale operation that aims to have an impact on the dietary behavior of the entire population. Of course, it doesn't rely entirely on Nudge. The emphasis on making citizens better informed demonstrates once again the complementary nature of the different approaches.

As part of its overall policy to fight obesity, the American Department of Agriculture has also enacted regulations aimed at improving the nutritional contents of school meals. School lunchrooms participating in the National School Lunch Program have to limit certain foods, such as fries, as well as encouraging children to eat fruit and vegetables. However, these bans are not especially effective, and can even produce the opposite behavior by drawing students' attention to the banned items.[11] Numerous experiments have been carried out to help change behavior – with no obligation involved – in communal eating areas at schools, universities, and compa-

---

10. Cass Sunstein, *Simpler: The Future of Government*, Simon & Schuster, 2013, p. 76-77.
11. J. O. Fisher and L. L. Birch, 'Restricting Access to Palatable Foods Affects Children's Behavioral Response, Food Selection, and Intake', *Am J Clin Nutr*, vol. 69, n° 6, June 1999, p. 1264-1272.

nies. Positive outcomes in locations such as these, which affect a large number of people on a daily basis, guarantee a significant impact on the population as a whole.

Brian Wansink performed a well-known experiment[12] in the Addison and Campbell-Savona schools districts of New York, involving students aged 7 to 12. Alterations to the organization of the lunchrooms, as well as certain employee practices, produced significant changes in behavior. As a result, 13.4% more students took a piece of fruit, and 23% more took vegetables. And, of course, the fact of taking it meant they ate more of it! To achieve this, Wansink used four main levers: salience, social norms, convenience, and attractiveness.

◆ Salience: placing fresh fruit, for example, next to the cashier, or fruit juice in the freezer next to the ice cream, puts more students in visual contact with the products you want them to choose.

◆ Social norms: lunchroom employees routinely suggesting that students take vegetables and fruits creates a social norm to be followed.

◆ Convenience: for example, a line reserved for those buying 'healthy' food (seafood sandwiches, fruit and vegetables), or salads whose packaging can act as a plate. This increases students' motivation to buy this type of product, as well as removing obstacles to their decision.

◆ Attractiveness: as we know, emotional factors play a major role in our decisions. Wansink and colleagues tried to increase the attractiveness of the products in question – a well-known tactic among marketers. Ways of doing this included introducing menus illustrated with beautiful fruit and vegetables, giving vegetables new attractive names, or placing fresh fruit in pretty baskets.

---

12. Andrew S. Hanks, David R. Just and Brian Wansink, 'Smarter Lunchrooms Can Address New School Lunchroom Guidelines and Childhood Obesity', *The Journal of Pediatrics*, vol. 162, n° 4, February 2013, p. 867-869.

This may seem like a lot of common sense. But it's still grounded in a firm grasp of the decision-making process and the understanding that students' choices are not stable and linked solely to their preferences. That is, it is possible to change their decisions given the right choice architecture for the lunchroom.

Fighting the spread of AIDS in Malawi

AIDS is just one of the many public health problems currently facing Africa. The region is responsible for 69% of all cases and 70% of deaths linked to the disease.[13] One of the proposed means of combatting the epidemic is to prioritize screening and encourage appropriate behavior among those tested. Protection, in a word. Against future infection if the results are negative, and to prevent sexual partners becoming infected when tests come back positive, which was the context of a 2008 study carried out in Malawi.[14] As part of a door-to-door operation in villages, people were offered a free AIDS test. Those tested had to get their results from a medical centre that was often some distance from their home. Due to this, only 34% received their results, hence partially diminishing the positive effect of the screening process. The question, therefore, was how to increase the percentage of people tested going to the medical centre to get their results.

The Nudge used here is one of the simplest, as it makes use of a financial incentive. Its subtlety, however, lies in the amount used: 30 US cents. Even adjusted for the standard of living in Malawi, this is a very small sum. Using money to trigger a behavior may be rightly thought of as a traditional method whose mechanism is based on added benefit. It's a very rational exchange: extra effort, in return for money. But an approach like this can be tough for the organization in

13. UNAIDS Report on the Global AIDS Epidemic, 2012.
14. Rebecca L. Thornton (2008), *op. cit.*

charge, even more so when the target population is so broad. The challenge is thus to alter behavior at the lowest possible cost. As such, we can think of the solution as a type of Nudge. It's not the amount of money that's important, but the fact that it acts as a trigger. As we shall see, increasing the amount has only a small effect on behavior:

◆ When the amount was set at 30 cents, 70% of villagers went to the medical centre to get their results. Without the incentive, this figure was only 34%. The number of people receiving results hence more than doubled.

◆ When the amount offered was increased, the percentage continued to rise – but with an asymptote. For amounts between 50 cents and 1 dollar, the figure rose to 80%. And then to 85% for amounts between 1 and 1.5 dollar.

Of course, there are other costs associated with this type of operation – something that might cause Nudge purists to object. At the same time, however, its effectiveness is clear, and these costs are very low. 'Incentives' are thus an important factor in behavioral change. Their main aim is more to act as a trigger than to truly alter the cost-benefit analysis of the various choice options. The Nudge approach hence has some very effective, low-cost solutions to offer public health. And this is equally the case for education – another central issue for the modern world, and an important part of the ongoing fight against poverty and social discrimination.

Nudge, education and poverty

To illustrate the approach's universal nature, I've chosen two very different real-life examples for the section on Nudge and education. The first of these concerns the problem of children's education in Morocco – a developing country. The second relates to social climbing by disadvantaged children in the USA – the most powerful country in the world.

Promoting education in Morocco using an unconditional incentive programme

In developing countries, education is considered an important instrument in the fight against poverty. Governments therefore want to maximize the effectiveness of actions undertaken to encourage young people to enrol at schools, first of all, and then to see their education through to its conclusion.

This was what the Moroccan Minister for Education had in mind in contacting Esther Duflo. With her team of researchers, Duflo was charged with assessing the effectiveness of a financial incentive programme[15] aimed at raising the percentage of primary school children in rural areas completing their formal education. Existing statistics showed that if 90% of these children started school, 40% of them would drop out before the end. The Moroccan authorities came up with a plan to combat this, named 'Tayssir'. A small financial incentive (5% of annual school expenses – around 60 dirhams/6 dollars per month for a 6-year-old child) would be returned to the father of the family if the child enrolled in and attended school. Esther Duflo and colleagues wanted to evaluate the impact of two possible changes to the existing programme:

♦ The first of these involved not making the financial incentive a condition of the child's enrolment at the school, while continuing its direct association with the funding of their education. Duflo calls this option 'labelled cash transfer' (LCT), as opposed to 'conditional cash transfer' (CCT).

♦ The second involved a change in the person receiving the financial aid: the mother, rather than the father.

---

15. Najy Benhassine, Florencia Devoto, Esther Duflo, Pascaline Dupas and Victor Pouliquen, 'Turning a Shove into a Nudge? A "Labeled Cash Transfer" for Education', *NBER Working Paper Series*, n° 19 927, July 2014.

The test was carried out under real-life conditions. It involved over 600 communities in 320 school sectors over a two-year period. Results were compared for the following five groups: a control group with no intervention; CCT-father; CCT-mother; LCT-father; and LCT-mother.

Whether the father or the mother received the money had no effect on attendance statistics. Interestingly, however, the programmes that performed the best were those for which the aid was unconditional (LCT). Compared with the control group, after two years of testing, these programmes brought about a 76% decrease in drop-out rates, and an 82% increase in children re-enrolling having dropped out prior to the start of the programme. While the conditional financial aid also had a positive effect, the results were statistically inferior – and with greater set up costs linked to higher administrative fees! Parents seemed to view the non-conditionality as a facilitating factor: no extra steps were needed to receive the financial aid. The clear association of the financial subsidy with the child's education was another important aspect of the programme's success. Education was assigned a value. This 'labelling' acted as a signal from the public authorities to the parents, acknowledging the important role that school plays in their children's upbringing.

A number of factors came together to make education both salient and highly valued in the parents' eyes. These included the status of the messenger – the Minister of Education; the tangible nature of the financial subsidy; and the 'labelling' that linked the aid to education (a mechanism based on the 'mental accounting' discussed previously).

All in all, a small, unconditional financial incentive for children to enrol in and attend school produced a significant change in the parents' behavior in this key area. And that's what Nudge is all about!

Helping disadvantaged US high school students go to college

The US education system faces nothing like the same kinds of issues as those in the developing world. Unlike Morocco, it's not a question of how to increase schooling for young children. The problems lie elsewhere. Specifically, how do you increase access to higher education for disadvantaged high school students, of whom only 29% go to college, as opposed to 80% from well-off families? It's a disparity that is a real impediment to social fluidity.[16] Disadvantaged students are hindered by their and their parents' poor understanding of the resources and support systems in place to help with college enrolment.

The important issue is to identify the most effective framework for supporting disadvantaged students during that critical period between high school graduation and college entrance.

Various measures have been undertaken to facilitate enrolment. In particular, the presence of councillors to assist with filling out the necessary forms. And these efforts have proved effective. College enrolment rates are between 5% and 30% higher than in cases where no assistance is provided.[17] However, this effectiveness comes at a cost – and at 100 to 200 dollars per student it is relatively high. Alternative or complementary solutions based on Nudge methods have therefore been investigated. Among these was the

---

16. M. J. Bailey and S. M. Dynarski, 'Gains and Gaps; Changing Inequality in U.S. College Entry and Completion', *NBER Working Paper Series*, n° 17 633, December 2011.
17. B. L. Castleman, K. C. Arnold and K. L. Wartman, 'Stemming the Tide of Summer Melt: An Experimental Study of the Effects of Post-High School Summer Intervention on Low-Income Students' College Enrollment', *The Journal of Research on Educational Effectiveness*, vol. 5, n° 1, January 2012, p. 1-17.

following research carried on in Dallas, Philadelphia, and Boston[18] in 2012.

The experiment involved two different types of intervention:

◆ An email campaign addressed to students and their parents going over everything involved in completing a college application. This included links to relevant websites and the suggestion that they get in touch with a school councillor.

◆ An offer of peer support from students already enrolled in college, who were trained to give assistance with the application process.

Both mechanisms essentially rely on salience: salience for the tasks the students have to carry out; and salience of the assistance offered by their peers (or school councillors).

Compared to the control group (with no intervention), the email campaign brought about a 3% average increase in college enrolment, while the offer of peer assistance saw a 4.5% rise. However, these average statistics showing a generally positive development conceal significant differences in the type of students affected. The reality is that the increase can be as much as 14% in the first instance, and 16% in the second, among certain sections of the population.

These increases may seem relatively modest. However, the email campaign has one big advantage over other traditional interventions: it is cheap. Estimated costs come out at around seven dollars per student, as opposed to the 100 to 200 dollars previously mentioned. This is hence an example of the Nudge approach complementing an existing structure. A range of

---

18. Benjamin L. Castleman and Lindsay C. Page, 'Summer Nudging: Can Personalized Text Messages and Peer Mentor Outreach Increase College Going Among Low-Income High School Graduates ?', *EdPolicyWorks*, Working Paper Series, n° 9, April 2013: http://curry.virginia.edu/uploads/resourceLibrary/9_Castleman_SummerTextMessages.pdf

actions were implemented – efficiently and at far lower cost – that produced increased social fluidity within the education system.

Improving workplace performance

Job motivation is a major factor in the performance of both public and private organizations. Without employee commitment, success is rarely sustained over the long term. Levers relating to individual motivation are thus a significant issue for public authorities, for the following three main reasons:

◆ civil servants and public officials play an important role in implementing public policy;

◆ in many countries, there are a large number of this type of employee – this represents a considerable burden for the wider community, who must therefore ensure the best ROI;

◆ the current economic climate involves major budgetary restrictions, making the proper use of public resources even more important.

Here again, the Nudge approach has an important role to play. Behavioral economists' experiments, as well as a wide range of other work in the field of human resources, have demonstrated that financial compensation is just one of the factors involved in employee satisfaction and output. It is also true, however, that given equivalent financial resources, payment conditions can have a strong effect on people's motivation and performance.

To demonstrate the effect of well-chosen Nudge levers on workplace efficiency, I'd like to share the following two very different experiments. The first is a study aimed at improving teachers' performance in US schools. The second highlights the importance of recognition for a public health campaign in Zambia.

Teachers' effectiveness in Chicago schools

This experiment[19] was performed in nine schools in the Chicago Heights district to the south of the city, and involved around 150 teachers. The aim was to measure the impact on students' performance of different types of financial incentive offered to teachers. Comparisons were made between the following schemes:

- a traditional bonus system, where teachers received money at the end of the year according their students' results;
- a system based on loss aversion that involved giving the teachers their bonus at the start of the school year, then adjusting it according to the students' final results. If these results were better than expected, the bonus amount was increased. If results were worse, then it was lowered.

Teachers participating in the second scheme received 4,000 dollars at the start of the year – a figure corresponding to the expected bonus. However, if the students' results in the end-of-year test were not up to scratch, the teachers had to return all or part of the money. Teachers in the first scheme, however, received their bonus only at the end of the year.

End-of-year results for students whose teachers participated in the second scheme were significantly better. Once again, it wasn't only the bonus that counted, but the way it was presented and the lever employed. For an identical investment, loss aversion creates a fundamentally more motivating system.

---

19. R. G. Fryer, S. D. Levitt, J. List and S. Sadoff, 'Enhancing the Efficacy of Teacher Incentives through Loss Aversion: A Field Experiment', *NBER Working Paper Series*, n° 18 237, July 2012.

Using recognition to improve a Zambian public health campaign's effectiveness

This experiment[20] was carried out as part of a 2010 campaign by the Society for Family Health (SFH) to distribute female condoms in Zambia. The researchers and SFH asked hairdressing salons to offer condoms to their clients. Lusaka, the city chosen for the experiment, has over 2,500 such salons. The recruiting process was done on a voluntary basis, batches of condoms were provided and the salons received promotional and display materials.

Four different groups were drawn up for participating salons:

♦ in the first 'control' group the hairdressers were only recruited on a voluntary basis;

♦ in the second group, the volunteer hairdressers received a small financial reward (10% of the price of the product – 50 kwacha);

♦ in the third group, participating salons receive a higher financial reward (90% of the value of the product – 450 kwacha);

♦ in the fourth group, the reward was not financial but involved the image of a thermometer showing the salon's contribution to the health of the community. The thermometer had to be placed where everyone in the salon could see it. With every sale, another star was added. After 216 packs of condoms were sold, the salon employees were invited to a ceremony held at the SFH offices.

In the first three groups, the number of sales was the same. Compared to the control group, financial rewards – even the high ones – did not result in increased performance. In the

20. Nava Ashraf, Oriana Bandiera and Kelsey Jack, 'No Margin, no Mission? A Field Experiment on Incentives for Pro-Social Tasks', *Journal of Public Economics*, vol. 120, August 2011, p. 1-17.

final group, however, the number of condoms sold was more than double that of the other groups (15 as opposed to 7). Recognition – in the case of the volunteers, as part of a humanitarian action – was a better driver than traditional financial incentives. Sales doubled, and at no extra cost, simply by identifying the right lever for the situation.

Social Nudges: an important lever for workplace satisfaction

Generally speaking, my belief is that the Nudge approach, alongside innovative HR and talent management practices, can significantly enhance workplace satisfaction and associated levels of performance.

Financial compensation is just one aspect of workplace satisfaction and motivation. It is also something that is highly over-valued by the theory of the rational man that postulates a selfish evaluation of our interests – and hence, a focus on salary. There are other major factors influencing our perceived happiness in the workplace. Among these are individual recognition, feedback, fairness, an understanding of both our own work and the wider goals of the organization, and a sense of fun and camaraderie. Of course, financial compensation is a part of this. It's not a question of pretending that organizations should no longer look at raising people's salaries. Just that they should not make this their only focus. And this is where the Nudge approach can be of help. Its role, for both public and private organizations: to reflect on how these elements are integrated into employees' day-to-day experiences. For example, how can we make employees accept company values by default? How can we create a process of systematic, regular recognition in the workplace? How can we ensure that individual and collective successes are celebrated on a regular basis? How can we organize the work environment so that everyone feels good about being there?

Some companies manage it. Others find their good intentions aren't reflected in the everyday experience of their employees. And others, caught up in short-term needs and day-to-day problems, don't even bother to think about it. However, this is not simply a moral question of worker satisfaction. It is also of great importance in terms of managerial effectiveness. Workplace happiness is correlated to both individual and collective performance, as demonstrated[21] by James Harter and colleagues from the Gallup Institute via a longitudinal analysis of 2,178 business units within 10 big companies. Results showed that the key business indicators – sales and profits – were positively affected by levels of employee satisfaction.

Professor Paul Dolan of the London School of Economics – an important behavioral economist and one of the initial members of the UK Nudge Unit – is a global specialist in happiness.[22] Dolan has done a lot of work on the link between well-being, the work environment and performance. His findings have led him to a system that he summarizes by the acronym[23] SALIENCE: Sound – Air – Light – Image – Ergonomics – Nature – Colour – Evidence. Its aim is to help companies design a work environment that simultaneously encourages well-being, creativity and productivity.

It is hence possible to design a positive work environment based on the findings of behavioral economics. That is, work culture and practices that increase employee satisfaction and the organization's overall performance. This increasing num-

21. James K. Harter, Frank L. Schmidt, James W. Asplund, Emily A. Killham and Sangeeta Agrawal, 'Causal Impact of Employee Work Perceptions on the Bottom Line of Organizations', *Perspectives on Psychological Science*, vol. 5, nº 4, July 2010, p. 378-389.
22. Paul Dolan, *Happiness by Design: Finding Pleasure and Purpose in Everyday Life*, Penguin, 2015.
23. Paul Dolan and Chloé Foy, 'Design in Mind: Stimulating Environments', *SlideShare*: http://fr.slideshare.net/obehave/design-in-mind

ber of examples, in different countries and affecting different target populations, tackles a whole range of important, unique issues, and they all demonstrate the extent to which the Nudge approach is truly universal. We can install choice architectures whose difference from one another may seem insignificant, but which produce potentially deep changes in behavior. It's just a question of identifying the right incentive and then executing it correctly. But let's turn our attention for a moment to the word 'just'. For a Nudge to be effective, it 'just' takes a good lever and the proper execution! However, this single syllable contains the difference between success and failure. Many Nudges do not work for the simple reason that the lever was not the right one, the execution was poorly conceived, or the moment was not opportune. The starting point for this book, don't forget, was: 'Behavioral change – it's possible, *but complicated.*' Nudge is a subtle art. And to succeed requires a deft and expert touch.

My aim now is to suggest a method that will maximize your chances of designing strong, successful Nudges. That is, those Nudges that effectively bring about the desired changes in people's behavior.

Chapter *13*

How to design successful Nudges

You have to be creative to come up with an effective Nudge. To design the choice architecture and execution needed to produce real changes in behavior takes a lot of imagination. Of course, there are always those rare geniuses who can conjure up innovative solutions using just the power of their mind. But not everybody can be Steve Jobs! My own belief is that creativity, in Nudge and elsewhere, should be guided and inspired by a tight, rigorous process if success is to be systematic, rather than one-off.

The process that I'm about to describe is the result of discussions with my friends and esteemed colleagues, Richard Bordenave and Étienne Bressoud, assisted by the young 'nudgers' in the BVA Nudge Unit. There were two main sources of inspiration:

◆ the processes suggested both by the UK Behavioural Insights Team and the Rotman School of Management in Toronto;

◆ our own involvement with marketers, and our research experience in the fields of creativity, design thinking, and ethnography.

MINDSPACE and EAST: two sources of inspiration from the Behavioural Insights Team

The Behavioural Insights Team, led by David Halpern, published two important documents whose aim was to give political decision makers in the United Kingdom a better understanding and ability to make use of the Nudge approach. The first of these was called MINDSPACE;[1] the second, EAST.[2]

MINDSPACE's main contribution is the checklist that makes up the letters of the title – a particularly well-chosen acronym. Each of these letters corresponds to a mechanism used by the Nudge approach (see Table 13.1).

Table 13.1 MINDSPACE

M-essenger	We are heavily influenced by who communicates the information.
I-ncentives	Our responses to incentives are shaped by predictable mental shortcuts such as strongly avoiding losses.
N-orms	We are strongly influenced by what others do.
D-efaults	We 'go with the flow' of pre-set options.
S-alience	Our attention is drawn to what is novel and what seems relevant to us.
P-riming	Our acts are often influenced by sub-conscious cues.
A-ffect	Our emotional responses can powerfully shape our actions.
C-ommitments	We seek to be consistent with our public promises, and reciprocate acts.
E-go	We act in ways that make us feel better about ourselves.

Source: Behavioural Insights Team

---

1. Paul Dolan, Michael Hallsworth, David Halpern, Dominic King and Ivo Vlaev, 'MINDSPACE: Influencing Behaviour through Public Policy', Cabinet Office/Institute for Government, 2nd March 2010.
2. Owain Service, Michael Hallsworth, David Halpern, Felicity Algate, Rory Gallagher, Sam Ngyen, Simon Ruda and Michael Sanders, 'EAST: Four Simple Ways to Apply Behavioral Insights', The Behavioural Insights Team in partnership with the Cabinet Office and Nesta.

The list contains a number of the logical and illogical processes described earlier in our examination of the reality behind the factors influencing our everyday lives. These previous examples contained clear references to a number of the above mechanisms. For instance, the social norms (N) employed by Opower; the incentives (I) on which Esther Duflo based her experiments; or the salience (S) used by the BIT for the reminder SMSs sent out to dawdling taxpayers in the United Kingdom.

For prospective Nudge practitioners with no expertise in behavioral economics, this checklist is undeniably of help. Using the acronym, you can debate the most relevant logic for designing your Nudge. Will you try to design a choice architecture that conditions the user to adopt the implicitly suggested behavior by default (D)? Or would you rather focus on emotions and affect (A)? Either way, you have in front of you a very simple, mnemonic grid that summarizes the nine logical principles on which to base your strategy. This document is hence an important step in the transition from theory to action. It allows Nudge practitioners to simply and effectively grasp the results of many years' research into the decision-making process.

Aside from the convenience of this table, MINDSPACE also details the basic principles behind a Nudge's application. Nudge is part of an overall process that involves a starting point (exploring the situation) and an end point (evaluating the planned action's effectiveness).

In Nudge, the most important evaluation tool is the experimental approach in a real-world setting. This is known as a 'randomized control trial' (RCT). The impact of each Nudge has to be measured in real life and in relation to a statistically comparable control group, in conditions where the single effect is able to be isolated.

MINDSPACE – the first document of its kind aimed at Nudge practitioners – is a significant step forward for the approach. Which is not to say it doesn't suffer from inevitable teething problems. It still lacks precision. As a result, BIT went back to the drawing board and came up with a second document, published two years later, entitled EAST. One again, the title is an elegant mnemonic acronym. This time it stands for Easy – Attractive – Social – Timely.

Armed with the knowledge gleaned from their first few years of experiments, David Halpern and his team made a twofold addition to the approach set out in MINDSPACE. First, EAST contains some simple but powerful advice regarding the main features of a successful Nudge. And, second, a suggested methodology for implementing effective actions.

The advice is hence re-formulated based on the four letters of the acronym. To encourage a particular behavior, you have to make it 'easy', 'attractive', 'social', and 'timely'. That's all it takes to come up with an EAST-type Nudge. The Nudge Unit further clarifies its thoughts by explaining the reasoning behind each of these elements. It also links them to concrete actions, using specific examples.

Rule one – 'easy' – is about facilitating the desired behavior. I'm sure you recall the status quo bias discussed previously. Well, keep it in mind throughout the implementation process – it's your number one enemy. BIT's stance here is very clear: if you want to have a shot at effectively encouraging a new behavior, you have to make it easy for the user. The Nudge Unit suggest three specific types of action that they know to be effective:

◆ utilize the power of default options;
◆ reduce the hassle linked to a behavior;
◆ simplify the messages encouraging the desired behavior.

Rule two – 'attractive' – can be split into two parts: 1) the attractiveness of the means of communication, whose goal is to grab people's attention; and 2) the attractiveness created by choice architecture, whose goal is to persuade people to adopt the desired behavior.

The first of these involves capturing the user's imagination in the moment that they make their choice. As we know, people greatly favour the choice option that seizes their attention. And we have seen how affects and emotions can be strong attention triggers, as can the power of images or the personalization of certain messages. You may recall little Rokia's impact on fundraising efforts to fight malnutrition in Africa. Or the effect of using the person's first name in the SMSs send out by BIT.

The second category involves creating positive consequences and rewards for adopting the desired behavior; or, conversely, designing penalty measures when the behavior is rejected. BIT highlights the potential benefits of four specific mechanisms:

♦ lotteries;
♦ emphasis on the rarity of a product or service;
♦ self-image and ego validation;
♦ principles taken from gaming that increase the attractiveness of the desired behavior.

These mechanisms all maximize the incentive's ROI. Given the constant cost of an incentive, the challenge is to implement it via a mechanism whose power has been previously demonstrated. After facility, attractiveness is the second key principle for encouraging people to adopt a particular behavior.

Rule three – 'social' – concerns other people: one of the main drivers for behavior. We saw previously the extent to which we are all social animals, and how social norms can influence our decisions. The 'S' in EAST hence refers to the important mechanism already seen in MINDSPACE ('M' for message, 'N' for social norms and 'C' for commitment). It is explained in detail here, however, it is particularly concerned with the potential impact of the following three mechanisms:

♦ Show those whose behavior you want to alter that the majority (or a meaningful number) or others have already adopted the desired behavior. There's a good chance their desire to conform will do the rest.

◆ Make use of networks such as Facebook, neighbours, work colleagues, old school friends, or people from the local sports club. Here again, our peers can be have a major influence on our decision to adopt the desired behavior, especially in cases where they have adopted or encouraged it themselves. Reciprocity – 'you scratch my back and I'll scratch yours' – can also be a powerful tool in the context of these networks.

◆ Encourage people to tell others about their commitment to change and their desire to adopt a new behavior. This is linked to the ego. Publicly announcing our commitment to others whose opinion we respect strengthens our urge to persevere.

The 'social' mechanism is extremely powerful, assuming it is activated in the right way and... with the proper timing.

Rule four – 'timely' – emphasizes the importance of the time factor in successfully changing people's behavior. The use of time in Nudge can be approached on the following three levels:

◆ The first level relates to the moment the Nudge is communicated and starts to take effect. The right mechanism activated at the wrong moment will have a non-existent or greatly reduced impact. The reason for this is simple. We are only open or potentially attentive to information or arguments at specific times. This 'openness' depends on where we are in our decisional cycle or our personal lifecycle. Activating a mechanism at the wrong moment is therefore like whistling in the wind. For maximal effect, we have to find the right time interval to implement the Nudge.

◆ The second level is linked to our notorious propensity to overvalue the short term – the 'here and now' – when looking to the future. We are far more influenced by the immediate consequences of an action, both positive and negative. The choice architect must hence try to design a mechanism that highlights the short-term value of adopting the desired behavior.

◆ The third level relates to planning. It involves creating Nudge mechanisms that prompt people to imagine themselves engaged in the desired behavior. Helping people anticipate a future behavior by making it more real eases the passage from simple intention into action.

EAST is thus a valuable aid for choice architects, for two reasons. First, at the general level of the acronym, these guidelines help the Nudge practitioner to stay focused on the four key elements for successfully changing behavior. And on a second, deeper level, it provides an understanding of the three main principles that it is possible to activate.

As well as these rules, EAST sets out a method for conceiving and implementing Nudges – a process which has come some distance since the basic principles outlined in MIND-SPACE.

This process involves four successive stages, as shown in Figure 13.1.

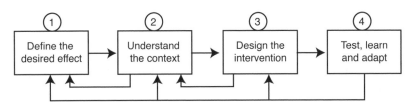

Figure 13.1 EAST methodology

In my opinion, the work carried out by David Halpern's Behavioral Insights Team is an essential starting point for any practitioner seeking an effective, intelligent application of the Nudge approach.

The Rotman School of Management's guide to nudging

The Rotman School of Management, based at the University of Toronto, have also tried to formalize the process. Their document, *A Practitioner's Guide to Nudging*,[3] is aimed at helping practitioners come up with successful Nudges. Here, Dilip Soman – the man behind an excellent online course on the same subject – and his team put forward some interesting additions to the formative work done by the UK Nudge Unit.

The first of these involves classifying four different types of Nudge according to the four main features of the underlying mechanism:

- boosting self-control vs. activating a desired behavior;
- externally-imposed vs. self-imposed;
- mindful vs. mindless;
- encourage vs. discourage.

Although conceptually interesting, this arrangement seems less useful to the Nudge practitioner than the checklists in MINDSPACE and EAST. The document is more concerned with retroactive classification than with helping choice architects design effective Nudges.

The system seeks to clarify the main principles behind various types of Nudge. As per the title of the document – a guide for practitioners – Soman and his team also outline a specific process and an overview of the main Nudge mechanisms.

This process also involves four successive steps:

- map the context: determine the main heuristics and influences;

---

3. Kim Ly, Nina Mazar, Min Zhao and Dilip Soman, *A Practitioner's Guide to Nudging*, Rotman School of Management (University of Toronto), 2013.

◆ select suitable Nudges;
◆ identify the levers for nudging;
◆ prioritize Nudges and test for effectiveness.

You will find that this process is very similar to that of the UK Nudge Unit. There is an initial phase in which we explore the context of the decision; a second phase, where the Nudge itself is designed; and a final phase, in which the process is evaluated. I will hence proceed by focusing only on the specific elements that are, in my opinion, of greatest interest to Nudge practitioners.

The Rotman team take a twofold approach to this important first phase of mapping the context. First, they highlight the importance of identifying obstacles to the adoption of the desired behavior. Second, they give four themes that need investigating to achieve this:

◆ the features of the decision;
◆ the sources of information used by decision makers;
◆ the features of the person's state of mind when engaged in the decision-making process;
◆ the environmental and social factors surrounding the decision.

These elements are useful, as they give a firm grounding to our investigation of the decision-making process.

Dilip Soman and his team also highlight specific important factors, such as the possible emotional influences involved in a decision. It's a very important and sensitive point. Important, as we have already seen the extent to which affects and emotions can influence decisions. And sensitive, as emotions are either so subtle as to be unconscious, or underestimated by people believing themselves to be rational beings, influenced only by rational factors.

An understanding of social interactions and environmental factors is essential to a comprehensive picture of all that goes into a decision. The roles of peers, messengers and networks are often central to the process. And this is equally true of environmental and contextual factors – for instance, the effects of re-organizing school lunchrooms and what students eat for lunch.

These, then, are the extra details provided by the Rotman School of Management. Later on, when it comes to designing Nudges, they may translate to insight.

In the second phase – selecting Nudges – the Rotman School sets out a solid, clear method for pinpointing the relevant factors involved. This method combines decision mapping with the identification of problems encountered at each sub-step by the decision maker in their search for the 'correct' behavior:

◆ first, stage one must identify the decision pathway;
◆ second, potential problems should be identified for each sub-decision.

This approach provides a good reflective framework for phase three – identifying the right implementation levers. Here, choice architects have to consider the mechanisms that can be used to remove obstacles or provide encouragement in key areas.

Finally, in the fourth phase of the process – 'experiment and iterate' – the Rotman team stress the importance of selecting and prioritizing Nudges. As well as the costs involved in implementing each Nudge under consideration, the authors suggest the following four criteria:

◆ choose Nudges that act upstream of the decision-making process, as they apply to a larger target. As such, they have a greater potential impact;
◆ prioritize Nudges that function automatically over those that rely on people's will. Here, again, research has shown the former's influence to be far greater;

- analyze the potential effect on different sections of the population;
- incorporate the expected long-term effects of each Nudge.

In certain instances, due to financial, time or technical constraints, it simply isn't possible to deploy the full range of prospective Nudges. Criteria that aid selection are hence an important part of the process.

To sum up, the overall process set out by The Rotman School is relatively close to that of the UK Nudge Unit. However, it does introduce certain details and extra information that may be of use to the practitioner in search of powerful, effective Nudges.

The BVA NudgeLab: guiding and inspiring the creation of effective Nudges

The BVA NudgeLab process is based on the principles outlined by both the Behavioural Insights Team and the Rothman School of Management, as well as our own expertise in human behavior, creative techniques and marketing. The key question – which was also our goal in designing the process – is simple: How can we maximize our chances of designing effective Nudges? The detailed, rigorous procedure that this entails should include the following features:

- it should be grounded in a detailed understanding of the reality behind the behavior that we would like to alter;
- it should guide and inspire creativity;
- it should incorporate barriers to the implementation of Nudges and any others linked to the customer or client.

We have tried to take the best bits from existing processes, while drawing on our knowledge gained from 30 years of research into human behavior, creative techniques applied to marketing, and implementing actions for both public and private organizations.

The BVA NudgeLab process involves six stages, as shown in Figure 13.2.

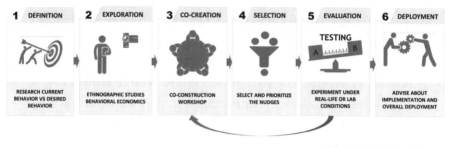

Source: BVA Nudge Unit

Figure 13.2 The BVA NudgeLab process

Stage 1: define the desired aim

As for any successful project, a clear target, understood by everyone involved, is an essential pre-condition to the Nudge approach.

This involves giving clear answers to the following four key questions:

- Is the issue raised by the client or customer suitable for the Nudge approach?
- Does the Nudge approach pose any ethical difficulties concerning the issue raised?
- What is the new behavior that we want to encourage, and how does it differ from the existing behavior?
- Which indicators could we put in place to evaluate the impact of the interventions we design?

Precise answers to these four questions will guarantee that the initiative gets off on a firm footing. It will also help ensure that the Nudges remain focused on the clients' initial demands. The Nudges will be neither ethically questionable nor inefficient due to their being poorly adapted to the issue. And their rigorous evaluation will be a relatively straightforward process.

The initial stage is even more important given that the approach is relatively unknown to potential users most susceptible to Nudge's charms. That is, the majority of public administrators. The twofold promise – effectiveness at very little cost – backed up by many successful examples, makes the approach extremely attractive to those who haven't tried it yet. This is obviously a very positive thing, and something I can only applaud as one actively involved in promoting the Nudge approach. However, remember that these positive features come with a risk. Being unfamiliar and highly attractive can lead to false expectations in terms of what the approach is able to achieve.

Nudge is an important weapon at the disposal of political decision makers. But it's not a magic wand! It is hence important to make certain, right from the start, that the approach is genuinely suitable for task in hand.

A good way to do this is to define clearly and precisely:

◆ the features of the current behavior that you want to change;
◆ the features of the future behavior that you want to encourage.

This simple question is a means to define and narrow down the issue. For example, when the BVA Nudge Unit intervened in France on behalf of the Prime Minister's Secretary General for the Modernization of Public Actions (SGMAP) and the Public Finances Directorate General, the issue was initially defined as follows: 'How can we get French people to use the digital solutions offered by the tax authorities instead of paying in person or over the phone?' The goal of the public authority – in this case, the DGFIP – was to reduce physical contact with the tax authority, and associated costs, via the use of websites such as impots.gouv.fr. Following discussions with the team initially responsible for the project,[4] it seemed that the scale of the issue was too great for the Nudge approach. We therefore tried to narrow it down by identifying a more precise wording that could be the object of effective Nudges. The following question was hence substituted for the original: 'How can we encourage French people to declare their income online via impots.gouv.fr, rather than using the standard paper form provided by the authorities?' Income tax applies to a significant number of French households (almost 20 million). And the cost of declaring using a paper form is four times greater than declaring online.[5] However, only 30% of declarants choose the latter payment method, meaning the potential savings for the French state are enormous. What we see here is:

◆ a current behavior to discourage: using the paper form to complete the tax return;
◆ a preferred behavior to prioritize: using impots.gouv.fr to perform the same action.

The indicator for evaluating the impact of the intended Nudges is equally clear. It simply involves checking the percentage of people declaring online, in comparison with a control group, as a result of the measures carried out.

We therefore have a clear objective, expressed in terms of a new behavior to be encouraged, and identification of an existing behavior that is costly to the public purse. There is also a concrete indicator for measuring effectiveness. For the

4. I'd like to take the opportunity to sincerely thank the teams from SGMAP (Françoise Waintrop, Céline Pelletier, Laure Bonneval and Leila Boutamine) and the DGFIP (Yannick Girault, Jean-Luc Jacquet and Stéphane Albisetti) for giving us the opportunity to work together on the first real-life Nudge experiment involving public authorities in France.
5. Richard Bordenave, Étienne Bressoud, Éric Singler and Françoise Waintrop, 'French Government: Nudge Me Tender,' ESOMAR, Nice Congress, September 2014.

best chance of success, this is the type of approach – and it can be very simple – that I recommend being systematically adopted at the beginning of every project.

However, we are only just getting started...

Stage 2: investigate and understand the behavior

With the goals clearly identified, the task is to gain an in-depth understanding of the behavior, and related decisions, that we would like to change. Specifically, this means understanding the decision-making process that results in the behavior that we want to discourage, and identifying the pathway leading to its modification.

This stage is vital to the process. It's here that insights first start to emerge. And the Nudges that the team designs will be based on these same insights. The goal in this instance is twofold:

◆ to identify the main decision pathways of the key segments of the population;
◆ to associate those elements that might lead one choice option to be picked – or not – over another for each of the decision stages previously identified. (Returning to the example of the income tax return, we might ask, 'What makes people favour the paper declaration?' or 'What stops people from declaring online?' and, 'What are the attractive elements that lead people to choose the internet?')

We have formalized this key process by means of the following three documents:

◆ a table of desired goals to ensure that the research gives clear answers to the established objectives;
◆ a decision pathway diagram allowing us to visualize the steps of the above table. This includes both obstacles and potential levers relating to the adoption of the desired behavior;

◆ an 'ethn'holistic' guide setting down the methodological principles to be used in arriving at a deep understanding of the factors influencing the behavior.

The Table of Desired Goals aims to ensure that project managers responsible for collecting and analyzing information have a clear idea about the purpose of their research. For each stage of the decision-making process, they have to arrive at a clear identification of both the impediments to the desired behavior being adopted, as well as the potential levers that might counteract these obstacles. As highlighted by the Nudge Unit in EAST, facilitating the change by breaking down the micro-obstacles at each stage of the decision is a key factor in its eventual success.

One of the difficulties here is that it's not simply a question of identifying people's 'explicit' aims. That is, the goals that they find easy to communicate. We also have to isolate the 'implicit' obstacles and levers. As we saw earlier, we are largely 'strangers to ourselves'. The factors influencing our choices are very often related to the environment in which the decision is made. These may be contextual factors, or related to the social interaction that we are engaged in at the moment of decision. Analysts should hence take care to research both the explicit and implicit elements influencing behavior for the entire length of the decision-making process.

In the example of online tax returns, one of the key elements identified in people choosing the paper form was simply an absence of thought linked to the possible use of the internet. This included young taxpayers who were at their computers all day long. Taxpayers were used to receiving a paper document that they completed to declare their income tax. For many years, this document was sent out to their homes. And, in the case of salaried employees – the vast majority of workers – the form was pre-filled with an amount already declared by the employer. We are hence firmly in the grip of habit and the status quo. The paper declaration is implicitly the default option offered by the French tax authority. In cases such as this, satisfied users don't think to bring up change. Why bother, when there's nothing about the existing situation that urges you to do so? This is a key element that may seem obvious, but which is nevertheless extremely important to pin down. In this case, it's the one thing that we have to thwart if we want to encourage the transition to online declarations. Of course, other more explicit elements will reveal themselves. Users are not only satisfied with the paper declarations – they are also somewhat puzzled by the idea of online tax returns. They imagine a risk of complication linked to the image of the authority – all the more so in the case of the tax office. They anticipate administrative headaches caused by mistakes that may be attributed to them and which may have significant financial consequences (and the risk of fines). They are afraid they won't be able to find all the information they need on the website and they have a general mistrust of using the internet for filing their tax returns. Also, users don't naturally perceive any benefit to declaring online, compared with the simplicity that they experience every year with the paper declaration. Finally, for those with enough curiosity who go to the site and form an opinion, logging in requires them to enter three identification numbers that they have to find by digging through the previous years' returns. There are better ways to make things easy for new users.

There are therefore numerous obstacles, all of which must be identified in detail. Only then can we proceed to thinking about Nudges that might alter this perception through the presentation of a different choice architecture. And I'll describe this to you shortly.

The purpose of the Decision Pathway Diagram is to explore the decision-making process. We want to clearly identify each of the stages leading an individual to adopt either the existing or the new behavior. This involves tracing the choice process between various possible options, as closely as possible. It spans the reflection trigger (if there is one) through to the final choice, including the decision makers' satisfaction and their related emotional state.

This audit should result in a precise, detailed decision pathway. In its most basic form, this is a question of mapping basic information about the way people assess their various choice options, from the evaluation criteria they use to the way they make their final choice. A more complex version involves closely monitoring every step of the journey leading up to the decision. As such, the pathway can be simple and automatic, or much more complicated and painstaking.

In the example of the tax returns, the pathway has become routine for the majority of taxpayers. They do exactly as they did the previous year. The trigger is the receipt of the paper forms, at home, in spring. Of course, the tax authorities hope to break this routine by providing information about the benefits of declaring online. Ah, information! That trusty method for convincing rational individuals… that none of us are. Sure enough, if you read the leaflet accompanying the paper form, you'll see all the advantages to declaring online.

The rational man, of course, reads all these leaflets. But real-life man? Sadly, he does nothing of the sort. And the desired effect on his behavior is weak as a result. What power does this written message have compared to the paper form, which is a potent default option? What chance, compared to something that encourages the receiver to use it in the same way that he always has? Or, if he is young or a first-timer, to use it in the same way as his parents, assuming they haven't directly advised him to do as they do?

Understanding the reality of decision pathways is hence an essential foundation to designing effective Nudges. And these pathways are rarely singular. More often, there are between three and five pathways involved in the same decision, linked to different segments of the target population. An accurate description of each is thus required before being able to consider which Nudges might be most suited to the situation. The goal of the exploratory study is to establish one or more detailed pathways for each stage of the decision-making process, including obstacles to the adoption of the desired behavior. However, this alone is not enough to guarantee a firm foundation for a Nudge. The aim is to understand the *reality* of the decision pathway! Not to merely skim the surface. Because there's a major pitfall associated with this type of study – a pitfall that is very much apparent in the third stage of the process, the 'ethn'holistic' guide.

This pitfall is easy enough to understand in theory, but harder to avoid in reality. It lies in the fact that simply asking or interviewing people as a way to understand their behavior does not give us the information that we want. Once again, the problem arises from our inability to express the multiple factors underlying our decisions. A researcher who confines himself to simple questioning will find that his analysis, for all its false impression of clarity, achieves no more than a superficial understanding of the decision-making process.

A methodology based on asking people questions is hence a dangerous thing. It makes no difference whether this questioning is direct (using 'closed' questions) or indirect (using 'open' questions). Even the best qualitative studies cannot coax out of us the things which we have no cognitive awareness. I'm not referring to things we have internalized. Rather, things of which we have no consciousness at all. The challenge is hence to identify both the influences we are aware of, and those that we are not. And the only way to do this is by observing how people act in the decision-making environment. That is, by carrying out an ethnographic study. This may not be a novel method, but that doesn't make it any less powerful. Understanding people through their actions is a way to get beyond the limits of what they are able to tell us. It also allows for environmental factors to be incorporated into our understanding of the decision-making process.

To really achieve its objectives, this ethnographic study should be based on data and analysis drawn from behavioral economics, with particular focus on the following three key areas:

- individual factors;
- social interaction;
- situational factors.

We have seen that a decision is the culmination of a process that combines these three types of influence. Designing well-aimed Nudges that encourage the adoption of the desired behavior hence requires that we allocate a specific role to each.

Individual factors relate to the 'internal' heuristics and biases described in part two of this book:

- the role of emotions such as arousal, regret and nostalgia in the decision-making process;
- the impact of illogical processes informing our decisions such as risk aversion; our preference for the status quo; valuing the present over the future, and things we own over things we don't; the influence of conscious and unconscious reference points, etc.;
- our own ego and the desire for validation and internal consistency.

Specifically, the ethnographic study should provide an understanding of the influence these individual factors have on observed behavior. Social interactions relate to our status as 'social beings'. The role of others in the adoption of the observed behavior should be considered in terms of the following:

- the role of the group, the community, or of peers;
- the potential influence of an authority figure on the choices taken;
- the influence of social norms;
- the impact of reciprocity, altruism, and fairness.

Once again, the ethnologist must understand the specific influence of 'social' factors in the observed behavior. As we have seen, this influence can prove stronger than that linked to our individual will or to our personal preferences.

The third focus of the 'ethn'holistic' study concerns environmental and situational factors. We have already seen the extent to which we are creatures of context, heavily influenced by conscious and unconscious stimuli that steer our behavior in one direction or another at the moment of choice. It is hence vital that we understand both the role and the relative importance of the immediate physical environment on the decision-making process. Once again, environmental factors may sway our final decision.

Analysis of the following contextual elements is therefore required:

◆ the physical organization of the space in which the decision occurs (for instance, the organization of the school lunchroom and its effect on what the students choose to eat);
◆ the type of information being provided and its salience at the time of the decision;
◆ available default options and 'hidden drivers' (for instance, the size of the popcorn bucket and its significant effect on the amount consumed);
◆ the way that choice options are communicated;
◆ potential payment methods used.

It is therefore a question of examining all the contextual factors that play a role in the observed behavior. The aim is to arrive at a precise understanding of their influence. In the majority of instances, this influence will be invisible to those experiencing it. As such, they will be unable to articulate it in response to questions posed. In light of this, my colleagues at the Brain Juicer research institute – one of those rare, truly innovative establishments – have come up with an interesting[6] 'on-the-ground' approach, using the same methodology

6. Orlando Wood, Alain Samson and Peter Harrison, 'Behaving Economically with the Truth', ESOMAR, Amsterdam Congress, September 2011.

described above. To ensure that field researchers really do incorporate all these elements, they are split into teams. Each team is focused on a specific area: the individual, social issues, the local environment, and the choice environment. This seems a good way to make sure researchers don't get swamped by the collection and analysis of all the many influences at work.

Stage 3: designing effective Nudges

Stage three is crucial. It's where theory passes into action, as the goal is to come up with Nudges that effectively encourage the behavior we want to promote.

Our Nudge creation methodology – the NudgeLab – is a significant departure from existing creative methods, particularly those related to innovation and 'design thinking'.

The NudgeLab's action blueprint can be seen in Figure 13.3.

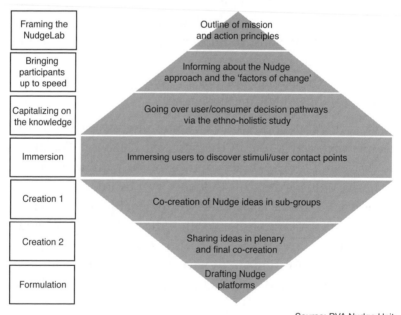

Framing the NudgeLab	Outline of mission and action principles
Bringing participants up to speed	Informing about the Nudge approach and the 'factors of change'
Capitalizing on the knowledge	Going over user/consumer decision pathways via the ethno-holistic study
Immersion	Immersing users to discover stimuli/user contact points
Creation 1	Co-creation of Nudge ideas in sub-groups
Creation 2	Sharing ideas in plenary and final co-creation
Formulation	Drafting Nudge platforms

Source: BVA Nudge Unit

Figure 13.3 NudgeLab's action blueprint

Our creative approach is designed around four main elements:

◆ a creative method: co-creation;
◆ stimulation tools: 'decision pathways'; 'the drivers of influence' involving the use of 'Nudge cards';
◆ creative support: 'the stairway to change';
◆ restitution and clarification tools: 'Nudge description forms'.

The NudgeLab creative method: co-creation

Experts behind the design of Nudges described previously – BIT, for instance – are well placed to identify the Nudge mechanics relevant to a given situation. My friends at the BVA and I believe, however, that our creative powers increase when the method is more collaborative and combines a range of perspectives and experiences.

To do this, we use a co-creation workshop involving people whose backgrounds are different, complementary, and relevant to the issue at hand.

The goal in stage two was to arrive at insights anchored in the reality of end-users' behavior. Following this, we organize one or more days of co-creation involving a group of people specially selected to increase their common creativity.

The group is made up of between 15 and 20 people from a variety of backgrounds – a diversity whose purpose is to maximize creativeness. The difference between contributors' profiles leads to conflicting viewpoints, which in turn leads them to come up with a wide range of ideas. Conversely, contributors with analogous life experiences tend to think along similar lines. The NudgeLab is hence composed of the following four profiles:

◆ experts in Nudge and behavioral economics;
◆ industry experts;
◆ those with expert knowledge of the customer or client;
◆ 'creative users'.

Others with external expertise can also be included in the group, depending on the issue being considered. At the outset, the co-creation workshop involves a group specifically structured to maximize the chances of achieving a certain level of creativity, while remaining focused on the requirements of the Nudge approach.

However, this creative capacity is strongly linked to the way the group is led and to the stimuli employed. The group is run using proven creative techniques by a highly proficient group leader (the secret to the NudgeLab's success),[7] and it is down to the leader to instill the feelings of warmth and sharing that are conducive to creativity. As well as this expert leadership, certain structural conditions also help produce the desired mindset within the workshop:

- a slightly quirky space arranged to make members comfortable with one another and aid inspiration;
- rules that encourage people to speak freely and create the best conditions for listening and exchanging opinions.

Participants are asked to say everything that comes into their heads, however hare-brained, stupid or idealistic. Even more importantly, nobody is allowed to criticize ideas expressed in the workshop. They are asked to reserve judgment, as people who fear criticism from other participants are far more likely to keep their thoughts to themselves and resist sharing them with the group. A friendly ear, and tolerance for other people's thoughts are both requested. There will be plenty of time for criticism and airing of problems in the selection phase. Quantity first, and quality later.

---

7. Special thanks to Catherine Tanitte (Catherine Tanitte Conseil), Beltrande Bakoula, Constance Dreux and Pauline Le Golvan, qualitative specialists from the BVA Nudge Unit, for their help with the design and integration of creative techniques in the NudgeLab.

A second element essential to the NudgeLab's success is a clearly and simply defined goal for participants in the workshop. This is so that there is no ambiguity regarding the aim, which we call 'the challenge'. For example: 'Identify 30 Nudges aimed at getting people to use impots.gouv.fr to file their tax return.'

Once the importance of a non-critical attitude and the goal for the day's work have been communicated, participants get stuck in with a traditional 'ice breaker' activity. Everybody makes a total fool out of themselves, allowing them the shed their inhibitions for the rest of the day.

The workshops are structured around the following four elements that function as both support and stimuli for the creation of Nudges:

- sharing the Nudge spirit and the drivers of influence via 'Nudge cards';
- decision pathways identified via the 'ethn'holistic' approach;
- the 'stairway to change';
- user contact points.

Stimulation tools

The first element, aimed at feeding the group's imagination, involves sharing the Nudge spirit. To come up with ideas for Nudges requires an understanding of what the concept entails. After stating the rules and the objective for the day, the goal is to provide participants with a whistle-stop Nudge tutorial, including the main levers influencing our behavior.

This is the goal of both the '20 elements of change' and the 'Nudge cards'. Inspired by MINDSPACE, we have created our own French acronym for the main levers influencing behavior: the '20 elements of change'. This new list complements the English version by adding some important mechanisms that do not figure in BIT's checklist (see Table 13.2).

Table 13.2 The drivers of influence checklist

Following a clear, concise explanation of all that Nudge involves, 'the drivers of influence' are presented using simple, real-life examples. This involves the use of cards that summarize in a single page (see Figure 13.4), and as visually as possible, a Nudge mechanism that has been effectively used in the past.

These cards come from a global database compiled by the BVA Nudge Unit. Examples are presented to the group, with commentary by the participating Nudge experts. The cards are then distributed among participants, allowing them to see for themselves. These cards are a simple, speedy way of getting across the 'spirit of Nudge'. That is, small details that alter the choice architecture and can change people's behavior.

With this basic knowledge in place, participants are introduced to the results of the 'ethn'holistic' phase. This is done via the 'decision pathways' described previously, and involves sharing the various stages from the reflection trigger to the final behavior. It also includes identifying obstacles to the adoption of the desired behavior. Once again, the information

 COMMITMENT without effort
1st emotional impression

 Insight | Tugging the heartstrings

The first impression naturally inspires a reaction of attraction or distancing. The emotion spontaneously evoked leads to the information being treated more or less attentively.

 Source   *Heuristic affect*

 Challenge

How to create a facilitating first impression?
Which images, colours, symbols, tones are necessary to generate a positive emotion?

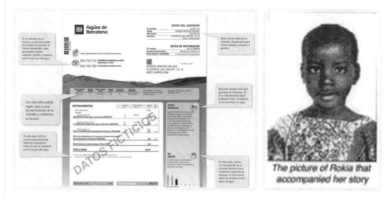

The picture of Rokia that accompanied her story

Source: BVA Nudge Unit

Figure 13.4 Example of a Nudge card

is communicated as simply and as visually as possible. These elements will act as 'insights' for the participants, and ensure that the ideas put forward are grounded in real end-user behavior. For the marketing or research experts among you the readers, this is not the usual way of presenting study results. The aim is to effectively communicate to participants, some of whom may be total novices, an understanding of what leads individuals to adopt certain behaviors. The intention is to give them a clear idea of all the mechanisms in play.

Armed with both an understanding of the decision pathways related to the issue at hand, as well as Nudge mechanics, the participants can then start coming up with ideas. And our role is to help them structure these suggestions.

Creative support: the 'stairway to change'

Another of our methods is known as the 'stairway to change' (see Figure 13.5). The aim of this is to help participants come up with potentially useful Nudges at four different stages of the decision pathway. This involves linking each stage to possible influencing mechanisms.

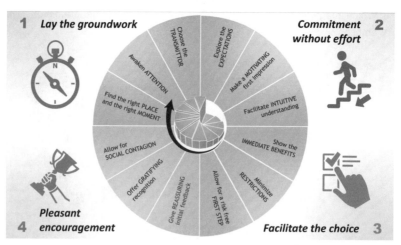

Source: BVA Nudge Unit

Figure 13.5 The stairway to change

The stairway to change is a tool that guides and structures the creative approach, making it even richer and more relevant. It should, of course, be adapted to the specific issue in question, based on the decision pathways that have been identified. For the co-creation workshops, it can be more effective to divide participants into sub-groups. Each of these is then charged with creating Nudges for a specific stage. Afterwards, the whole group comes back together to consider the ideas of each sub-group – and the collective effort benefits as a result.

The last type of stimulus that we use to help with Nudge creation involves the contact points that the decision-maker has with the decision. Specifically, the range of factors the decision-maker interacts with in the course of making a choice. And these vary greatly from one situation to the next. This can be either the physical choice environment (in the case of school lunchrooms, for instance, the physical arrangement of the lunchroom itself based on photographs) or the whole range of materials for communicating and collecting information (advertisements, websites, etc.). The decision pathways resulting from the 'ethn'holistic' study should already have identified these contact points. Furthermore, NudgeLab participants have other evidence at their disposal. That is, elements that people use, consciously or otherwise, to make their choice. These, too, offer ways for them to design Nudges based on real-life contact points. For online tax returns, for instance, the stimuli in question included: the leaflet accompanying the paper tax declaration form; the website impots.gouv.fr; emails sent to French taxpayers by the tax authority; and advertising clips made for the media campaign.

To sum up, participants in the NudgeLab are given all the necessary tools to design effective Nudges. These include a clear understanding of the obstacles to a new behavior, a knowledge of Nudge mechanisms via Nudge cards, and real-life examples (contact points). It's everything they need to set the creative wheel in motion!

Restitution tools: the 'Nudge sheets'

And so to the magic moment where participants – under the expert eye of the course leaders – start coming up with ideas. These may be small or big. Occasionally wonderful (but often not). Completely impracticable or highly pragmatic. Expressed in a few words or already fully formed. A plan or a design... At the early stages, we accept everything... and we record everything, too! This is the time when we want an abundance of input, without constraint. Where everyone can bounce around ideas, lingering on the details if they like, or quickly moving on to an alternative. It's an essential part of the process where everyone has to let themselves go, as even the stupidest, most hare-brained idea can give rise to another that is far more powerful. It's the raw material from which the group will later work towards a structured list of Nudge ideas.

After the creativity exercises comes the formulation. This involves the transition from the raw ideas – often a few words scribbled on a post-it note – to a structured concept that becomes the object of a detailed evaluation in phase four. The following two sequential stages are required to arrive at a structured list of Nudges:

♦ an initial consolidation stage;
♦ a second, drafting stage.

The consolidation stage involves going over all the ideas and collecting those that share the same logical foundations, however differently compiled. A reduced list is then drawn up containing ideas specifically related to each another.

The second stage is crucial. It involves writing out each of the Nudge ideas using a simple, standardized document – the Nudge form. Participants have to describe their idea so that it can be understood by others outside the group, who will subject it to a subsequent analysis.

The NudgeLab generally results in 30 or 40 separate ideas described using the Nudge forms.

Stage 4: a rigorously compiled shortlist

The following stage involves compiling a shortlist from the list of Nudges drawn up by the co-creation workshop. This shortlist should include those Nudges that appear most relevant to the final phase, where the impact on users or consumers is assessed.

Once again, this is a very important part of the process. Each of the ideas has to be evaluated to give the best chance of identifying Nudges that are truly effective and possible to implement.

A specific method is required to make this selection procedure as rigorous as possible. The one that I recommend is based on three main elements:

◆ an array of selection criteria;
◆ a 'Nudge matrix';
◆ a session involving both specialists and decision makers.

These standardized criteria allow for the comparative evaluation of each Nudge idea. All the elements we know to be essential in designing successful Nudges are included.

I suggest considering the following:

◆ the Nudge's potential power;
◆ the ease with which it can be implemented.

A Nudge's potential power concerns its ability to influence people and encourage them to adopt the desired behavior. This comes both from the likely force of the mechanism on which the Nudge is based, and also from the size of the population to which it is applied.

Potential force of a Nudge = force of individual incentive × size of population affected

---

A powerful Nudge that only affects a small part of the target population will see a significant reduction in its overall impact. In the same way, a Nudge applied to the whole population but with a weak incentive will have a modest final effect. Each Nudge should therefore be assessed in light of this dual criteria.

Beyond its potential force, a Nudge has different features that make its implementation more or less desirable, simple, or expensive. The second element involved in compiling the shortlist hence involves the ease with which the Nudges can be put to work. These features are as follows:

♦ external acceptability to users or consumers;
♦ internal acceptability;
♦ ease of implementation;
♦ cost of implementation.

External acceptability involves the Nudge's ethical dimension. Does the Nudge act in the interest of the individuals or communities exposed to it? Would these communities agree to be subjected to the influence if the question was put to them directly? Does the mechanism on which the Nudge is based preserve individual freedom of choice? These are crucial questions, as they go right to the heart of the 'spirit of Nudge'. A Nudge is only acceptable provided it benefits the people it is aimed at. It must also allow them the freedom to make a different choice to the one suggested. Of course, these requirements were explained in the introduction to the NudgeLab. However, as no ideas are censored in the early stages of the workshop, it bears repeating that this essential detail contains no room for compromise. A Nudge's 'internal acceptability' is determined by the agents in charge of introducing it to the target population. An action cannot be successful without the support of the people on the ground responsible for implementation, and, if needs be, giving explanations to the public. This is the standard against which each Nudge must be judged: whether the agents or officials in contact with the target population are comfortable with what they plan to do. If the answer is 'yes', we can assume that the deployment will pass without a hitch. If it's 'no', then the evaluation needs to take account of this, as the Nudge's effectiveness risks being significantly reduced or, worse, completely nullified. This would certainly have been the case for the Nudge concerning the paper tax return, where agents could have foreseen numerous complaints from disgruntled taxpayers.

Ease of implementation is the third main evaluation criterion. Nudges are, by definition, intended to be simple modifications of the choice architecture. Nevertheless, there is often a hierarchy within this simple structure. Some Nudges are truly very simple. For instance, those which involve changing a phrase in an SMS or a letter. Others – changing the physical arrangement of a school lunchroom, for instance – are a little less so. Each Nudge hence needs to be analyzed in light of this criterion that includes not only technical facility but also other hidden elements, such as legal or administrative complications.

The final criterion concerns the cost of implementation. Here again, all Nudges are inherently cheap. But there is cheap – and then there is cheap. For example, the cost of adding a simple phrase to a letter is effectively zero. Incentive triggers such as those used by Esther Duflo to encourage young children in Morocco to attend school, however, do involve a cost – even if this cost is marginal in terms of the expected economic benefits. Prospective Nudges should hence also be assessed in terms of this important criterion. Each Nudge is graded according to its potential power and its ease of implementation. Afterwards, the various Nudges are positioned in a matrix, as shown in Figure 13.6.

The X axis shows the potential power of the Nudge, starting at the left where the capacity to encourage change is perceived as weak, and moving to the right when this capacity is viewed as strong.

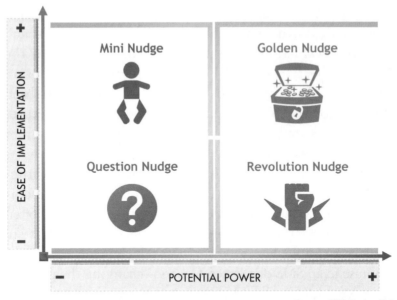

Source: BVA Nudge Unit

Figure 13.6 The Nudge matrix

The Y axis concerns the ease of implementation, as described previously (including the 'financial ease' of this). The greater this perceived facility, the higher on the Y axis the Nudge is placed.

The resulting quadrants describe the four main categories of Nudge.

◆ Bottom left, are the 'question' Nudges. This quadrant contains ideas that don't quite make the grade. These are the bad ideas that came out of the NudgeLab – those with the double disadvantage of being weak in incentive and difficult to implement. These will hence be the first to go during the shortlist phase. This box is generally rather empty, although not necessarily, as the rule of the NudgeLab workshop, with its emphasis on maximum creativity, is to let all ideas pass uncensored.

◆ Bottom right, are the 'revolution' Nudges. These are ideas that are likely to produce significant behavioral change, but which are hampered by a relatively costly or complicated implementation. This was the case for the Nudge aimed at suppressing the use of the pre-filled paper tax return. As for the majority of actions whose mechanism relies on a default option, the effect on behavior is strong, but the change can seem enforced – even when an alternative option exists. There is hence a risk of rejection by both users and agents, as well as general dissatisfaction.

◆ Top left, are the 'mini' Nudges. Their capacity to encourage the adoption of the desired behavior in seen as relatively low. However, their implementation is perceived as easy and unproblematic. Overall, these Nudges are fine to apply. But it's not worth placing too much hope in them. And they should not be at the heart of the operation, or there's a high chance of the final effect being immaterial.

◆ Upper right, are the 'golden' Nudges. These are the stellar ideas. Those which are seen as both powerful and easy to implement. For instance, Opower's restructuring of the energy bills described earlier, where the simple comparison of a person's energy consumption to that of his neighbours or other users, along with the image of a smiley face, resulted in a 250-million dollar saving!

The assessment criteria and the Nudge graph are tools used in the specialist's workshop – a central component of the evaluation phase.

This half-day workshop brings together project members responsible for the initiative. These include internal specialists charged with implementing the selected Nudges, as the process involves discussions about elements linked to technical feasibility and potential cost. By definition, the ideas are meant to be simple, as per the central idea explained to participants in the co-creation workshop. However, unexpected technical difficulties can lurk behind this apparent simplicity, which in turn can lead to hidden costs far higher than those initially expected.

Prior to this meeting, the specialists evaluate the Nudges using the grid described above. Each Nudge is then positioned on a matrix that is handed out to everybody present at the workshop.

Beyond these 'quantitative' evaluations, the specialist's workshop aims to review and debate the various qualities of each Nudge idea. It's a chance to come up with improvements, before making a final classification that usually results in the following three categories:

◆ Nudges to test;
◆ Nudges to implement;
◆ Nudges to reject.

'Nudges to test' are those with all the necessary attributes to be at the heart of the operation (often, the 'golden Nudges'). However, we need to confirm that they really do have the capacity to produce the desired changes in behavior. This is also an opportunity to rank the potential effects of competing Nudges that cannot be simultaneously applied. In the case of the reminder letter sent to people in England with unpaid fines, for instance, the Nudge Unit tested various different wordings before settling on the most powerful.

'Nudges to implement' are those whose overall process, including multiple contact points in the user or consumer's decision pathway that are completely without risk. There is no need to test these Nudges as, the expectation is, the impact on behavior is not great. These are the 'nice to have' Nudges. Generally speaking, the 'mini Nudges'.

'Rejected Nudges' are generally the 'question Nudges'. There may be a debate surrounding some of them. This might include attempts to find arrangements that strengthen their potential power or make them less difficult to implement. But when the starting point is complicated, it's uncommon for a bad idea to end up as a good one. The real discussion is mostly reserved for the 'revolution Nudges'. How can we make it possible for these Nudges, which are potentially capable of producing the desired behavioral change, to be implemented? Solutions may or may not be forthcoming, depending on how tough the problem is. For example, if the problem is with user acceptance, might there be a prior communication capable of explaining the merits of the planned action? Or could there be a re-arrangement or variation of the initial idea that reduces its negative aspect while retaining its potential power?

The specialist's workshop results in a final selection, as well as recommendations for further action. This takes the form of a 'Nudge book' containing accurate descriptions of each of the selected Nudges, including the following eight elements:

- the area covered by the Nudge – the part of the decision pathway on which the Nudge takes effect, as well as the behavior or attitude it hopes to change;
- the obstacle to change – the element hindering the desired behavior being adopted;
- the desired behavior – a description of the behavior that the user should adopt as a result of the Nudge being implemented;
- the Nudge itself – an accurate description of the Nudge being implemented;
- the alternatives – possible revisions to the initial idea should its application turn out to be problematic;
- behavioral levers – a description of the decision mechanics on which the desired behavioral change is based;
- possible visual illustrations – examples of images that act as a springboard for the Nudge's final execution;
- balancing risks – the factors which may lead to the reduction or elimination of the Nudge's influence. These need to be listed and kept in mind, in order to avoid them in the final execution;
- the conditions for success, which highlight the important factors for the Nudge mechanism. The aim is to not deviate from these conditions in the final execution.

Stage 5: Nudge evaluation

Phase four results in a shortlist of Nudges that the project group deem worthy of evaluation.

Phase five's goal is therefore simple and easy to explain, if not always to implement. It involves calculating whether the process has resulted in any Nudge ideas that meet the goals set out in phase one. That is, the adoption of the new desired behavior.

The measurement indicator should have been defined at the start of the project. In the case of online tax returns, for instance, it's straightforward: there's an increase in the number of people completing their tax returns online. Do the suggested Nudges cause a quicker transition to online tax returns, compared to the current 'Nudge-less' situation? Generally speaking, this involves staying close to the original objective. A pitfall that is often tempting and which must be resisted is the urge to create a new indicator that maximizes the chances of a positive result.

From a scientific perspective, the preferred method is a randomized control experiment. Without going into too much detail,[8] this involves testing the effect of each Nudge (or intervention, if several Nudges are at work within the same action) on behavior, compared to that of a control group who are unaffected by the Nudge. This is the main experimental method discussed earlier. In this instance, however, it is applied to real life rather than a research lab. This is because the goal is to account for the inherent complexity of the real-life environment. We need to show the real – not theoretical – effectiveness of the interventions being tested. This goal can be extremely ambitious, even impossible, in certain circumstances. However, there are many other times where it is

---

8. To learn more about the RCT method, please refer to the document published by the UK Behavioural Insights Team in June 2012, *Test, Learn, Adapt.*

very easy! The challenge is to design a real-life experiment to ensure that the effect being measured is exclusively related to the Nudge, and not the product of some other phenomenon or statistical glitch. The problem is therefore made up of the following components:

◆ technical feasibility;
◆ the construction of a rigorously designed experiment.

There is no general answer to these questions. Specific solutions have to be identified on a case-by-case basis.

Experimentation under real-life conditions is hence the preferred means of evaluation. It allows us to measure the effect of the planned intervention in a real environment. Compared to tests carried out in lab conditions, the results have a far better predictive capacity. However, this type of experiment can be difficult to implement. Reasons for this include technical complexity, legal impossibility, excessive costs, or a timescale not in keeping with the overall objectives. When this happens, there are two possible options:

◆ perform the test in a laboratory;
◆ implement the Nudge without prior testing.

Having absorbed the contents of this book, you are by now an expert in laboratory research. All the many academic studies I've described use this approach. In cases where it is absolutely impossible to perform experiments under real-life conditions, the project team has to decide whether it is in their interest – or not – to carry out the tests in a laboratory. If the answer's 'no', then the Nudges can always be applied directly. However, the fact of not having rigorously evaluated their effect is a major drawback. This is a serious problem, as the Nudge approach sets out be a scientific process. Not only as a novel incentive mechanism for government authorities but also as a revolutionary way of designing public policies. And this includes scientifically evaluating their effectiveness before deployment.

Stage 6: deployment

The deployment phase is obviously crucial. Nudgers like to say that theirs is a 'last meter', or 'last mile' approach. And deployment is the very last meter of all! The success of the entire initiative depends on the skill with which this phase is carried out. At worst, bad deployment leads to the failure of the Nudge in question; at best, a significant reduction in effectiveness. My firm belief is that the devil really does lie in the detail, and that the success of every plan rides on the quality of its execution.[9] This is especially the case for implementing Nudges, where every little feature counts. One word, for instance, is not the same as another. A particular colour can grab our attention in a way that other colours don't. Writing something by hand has a different effect to typing it. And so on… Nudge is both the science and the art of detail. And it's the mastery of these details that leads to widespread change. That is, to significant modifications in behavior. All choice architecture must therefore pay special attention to the execution of whichever Nudges are employed. In terms of overall success, a Nudge's basic concept is no more important than the skill with which it is applied. Of course, the deployment phase relies on the Nudge sheets designed previously. These act as a type of application guide. Experiment results are another source of information worth taking into account, as a way to sharpen up the Nudges being developed on the back of them.

In the case of online tax returns, the first changes that we implemented concerned the wording of the text sent to French taxpayers. The aim of the Nudge, you will recall, was to encourage people to use the website impots.gouv.fr. (see Figure 13.7).

---

9. If this subject interests you, see *Execution: The Discipline of Getting Things Done* by Ram Charan, Larry Bossidy and Charles Burck, Random Business Books, 2011.

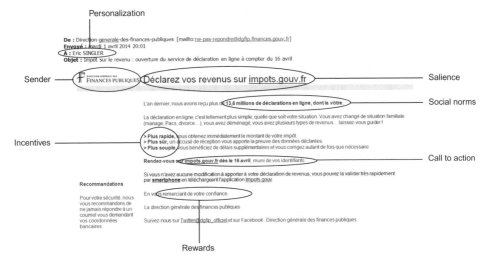

Figure 13.7 A promotional email campaign

First and foremost, we wanted to draw taxpayers' attention to the online option as a means to break the habit attached to the paper form. We needed to create salience, which we did via an email addressed directly to the taxpayers. The senders' name – the Public Finances Directorate General – was intended to grab their attention. It was a way to get them to first open and then read the email. The subject heading 'File your tax return at impots.gouv.fr' was another simple, direct message aimed at generating clarity.

Beyond the salience of the message, we mainly used the two action levers described previously: social norms and 'incentives', including obstacles and potential benefits (speed, security and flexibility) identified in the upstream phase known as the 'ethn'holistic' study. Finally, we used the following 'call to action' to make taxpayers begin to plan the behavior: 'From 16th April, go to impots.gouv.fr with you login details'.

The email campaign was carried out about 10 days before the declaration period. It had to be close enough that the message was of interest to taxpayers, and far enough away to play a warning role.

The primary support for the 2014 campaign was the leaf-let accompanying the paper declaration form that taxpayers received at home. The letter was addressed to everyone in France who had not filed their tax returns online before. Also, it was directly linked (it was sent at the same time and in the same envelope) to the main document – the paper declaration form. In such a way, we managed to reach the whole of the target population, maximizing the chances of the leaflet being read. The goal was to arrive at a complete reformulation of the previous year's leaflet. We wanted to make online declara-tion the default option explicitly recommended by the tax authority.

Below is a comparison of the 2013 and 2014 leaflets (see Figure 13.8).

Figure 13.8 Leaflets sent with the tax return

The 2012 leaflet contains a lot of information about online declaration. It talks about passwords, 100% online tax returns, and the possibility of filing via smartphone. The advantages of online declaration are even mentioned at the end of the document.

The problem with this, however, is the inability of the leaflet to instantly grab the reader's attention – something shown by the 'ethn'holistic' study to be low in this instance. Specifically, the problem related to two areas: the existence of online tax returns, and the benefits most likely to trigger the desire to use the online method.

The new leaflet tried to generate this instant understanding. It used a heading that was visually powerful: 'I declare online'. The information was all focused on online declaration and its various benefits. The facts were not diluted, merely re-centred on a singular message concerning all the upsides to an online tax return. The former heading, 'Leaflet to assist you in completing your 2012 tax return' became 'Complete your tax return at impots.gouv.fr, it's so much easier...' The former categories – 'new developments', 'calendar', and 'smartphone declaration' – were replaced by 'Developments for 2014 making online declaration easier' and 'Online declarations deadlines'.

In light of the results, the 2015 initiative will involve an email campaign at the start of the declaration period. The text of these emails will correspond to the most effective Nudges, and there will be a permanent link to import.gouv.fr encouraging people to click through and complete their tax return. The website is also being redesigned to make it more simple, flowing, and intuitive. The goal is to keep moving towards the principles set out in EAST, in pursuit of maximum effectiveness.

To sum up, the deployment phase is not simply the last step of the design stage. It also consists of the intelligent application of ideas. To maximize the impact on desired changes in behavior, choice architects have to stay involved and alert throughout the entire implementation process. The huge potential power of the Nudge approach lies in the real possibilities it offers public authorities to gain low-cost, additional effectiveness in an economic climate that demands it, furthermore a rigorous approach to every stage of the conception and evaluation of these Nudges means the opportunity is not wasted.

However, the applications of Nudge marketing aren't limited to the public sphere. Private companies and marketers the world over can utilize the revolution to increase effectiveness and ROI. The final part of this book will take a closer look at how this happens.

PART FOUR

FROM NUDGE TO NUDGE MARKETING

Increasing marketing effectiveness using behavioral economics

Whatever the sector, the final goal of marketers the world over is the same: to encourage consumers, clients, or users to adopt specific behaviors. That is, to first purchase the product or service offered by the company, then to use it regularly as a result of having had a positive experience.

Every marketing action includes both a current behavior and a desired behavior. The goal is to get current non-consumers to buy the product; to increase the frequency with which small buyers make their purchases; to increase the quantity bought or consumed each time; or to generate positive word-of-mouth recommendations by fans of the brand, etc.

The Nudge approach, with its focus on behavioral change, is particularly well suited to helping marketers in their daily work. Just as for Nudge applied to public policy, it's about adding to the marketer's armoury, with a view to making actions more effective.

The Nudge approach hence involves a movement away from 'conviction marketing' and towards 'incentive marketing'. The Nudge marketer is a new type of expert in behavioral change, whose skills involve both a fresh mental framework and novel activation levers.

Chapter 14

The Nudge marketer's mental framework

System 1, choice architecture, and new levers

Today's marketer uses yesterday's (false) knowledge

Marketers are still largely influenced by the theory of the rational man. We are secretly guided by the obsolete impression of an individual who listens, thinks, reflects, deliberates, assesses, and weighs all the pros and cons in choosing the action that maximizes his interest or his satisfaction. That is, an individual who we must first inform, then use the right positioning to convince about the benefits he will receive and of his 'reason to believe'.

Current marketing is about seeking the conviction, affirmation, and evidence presented to a consumer or client that leads them to choose a particular service or product. As you know, this individual – the imaginary Superman – does not exist. Or rather, he does not exist outside the heads of theoretical economists, whose thought has largely been usurped by behavioral economics. But, it still endures in the minds of we marketers, and is unconsciously imprinted on the levers we employ. Modern marketing is awash with this vision of the *homo economicus*. As seen in the way we still seek to understand behavior by asking direct questions, in the belief that people have the first idea about their motivations. Or in the way we try to convince those using AIDA (Attention-Interest-Desire-Action) models that hammer out the same tired tune about competitive advantage. And of course, if you get the basic diagnosis wrong – the way consumers take decisions – there's a real risk that the actions you come up with will be ineffective when it comes to steering their behavior. And this, sadly, is exactly what the market is telling us. Just look at the soaring failure rates for newly launched products. This statement may be difficult to make and to hear – but that doesn't make it any less true. In his insightful book *How Brands Grow*,[1] Bryron Sharp, Director of the Ehrenberg-Bass Institute for Marketing Science, writes, 'Marketing managers operate a bit like medieval doctors working on impression and myth-based explanations.' To drive the point home, Sharp stresses that his observation doesn't only apply to bad marketers, but also to those star performers with the top jobs in the biggest companies: 'Even the most intelligent marketers, in the best organizations, routinely make mistakes. Because many marketers operate using incorrect assumptions about how buyers buy and how marketing works, they emphasize the wrong things and ignore important points, consequently making mistakes.'

Nudge marketing is a way to use this updated knowledge about the factors influencing consumers, and our understanding of their behavior, to create more effective actions. In terms of Nudge's underlying philosophy, this is, of course, for the ultimate benefit of the consumer.

Specifically, Nudge marketing is both a new mental framework *and* a guide to action.

---

1.   Byron Sharp, *How Brands Grow*, Oxford University Press, 2010, p. 8.

The Nudge marketer's mental framework

The Nudge marketer's mental framework is based on three main pillars (see Figure 14.1).

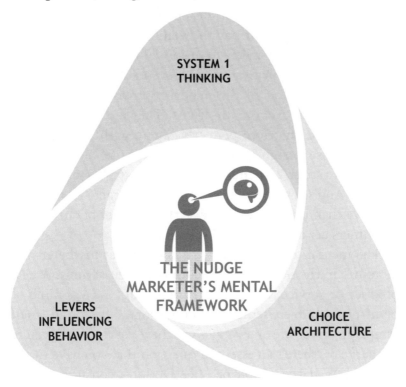

Figure 14.1 The Nudge marketer's mental framework

Design 'System 1' actions

Daniel Kahneman's System 1 is the cornerstone of the Nudge marketer's new mental framework.

As you know, consumers take the majority of their decisions based on System 1. That is, quickly, intuitively, often unconsciously, and using mental shortcuts. In a word, without really 'deciding' at all. Furthermore, they do this ultra-quickly, as a result of environmental triggers that they process automatically. The benefits to System 1 are considerable, as it requires no concentration or effort from the lazy creatures that we all appear to be at heart.

The main problem lies with the fact that marketers frequently design actions that are best addressed to System 2. That is, to people who pay attention prior to taking a decision. Those who process information, weigh up the pros and cons, and then decide with a view to maximizing their interest. The inclination to favour System 2 is even stronger given that these marketers are, in the majority of cases, intellectuals steeped in high-level qualifications. They are accustomed to reflection, and therefore perfectly happy with sophisticated actions whose design is to convince. Because they think in terms of System 2 themselves, they create System 2-type actions. And these frequently miss their target – or are less effective than imagined – because the majority of clients and consumers act and decide using System 1.

The mental revolution hence demands that marketers use System 1 in the design and execution of their actions. A new product or service; a change in packaging; a TV, online or point-of-sale advertisement; a promotional offer or an email campaign; a website or an app – whichever of these that you're in charge of, there's an essential question that you have to ask yourself. Will the action be effective for a consumer/client using System 1 thought processes?

This crucial question can be broken down into four subquestions:

◆ How can you attract the attention of somebody who is not paying attention and does not intend to?

◆ How can you communicate your message and make it instantly understandable to a consumer who does not process – or who processes very superficially – the information you present?

◆ How can you convince the consumer to change their behavior, given that they are a creature of habit, routine, and the status quo?

◆ How can you encourage the consumer to build habits that benefit your product or service?

My aim here is not to come up with yet more suggestions in response to all these questions. It's to encourage you to ask the questions systematically for every action you design. The operative word being 'systematically'.

To develop successful marketing strategies and actions, you have to be able to consider them in terms of System 1 thinking, right down to the smallest detail. By this I mean, think more in terms of visual images than words. Take simplicity and ease over comprehensiveness. Prefer immediate understanding to a glut of complex arguments. Choose emotion over reason.

Think globally: choice architecture and perceived value

The second pillar of this new mental framework concerns choice architecture: the environment in which the consumer takes their decision.

You have already seen the extent to which our decisions are sensitive to this. A default option in one direction or another and tens of thousands of people are ready to sign up to an organ donation programme. Shift the focus away from hundreds of thousands of people in need of saving and onto little Rokia, and donations go through the roof. A letter containing the person's first name rather than an impersonal greeting, and confidence rates change dramatically. *The Economist* presents a range of subscriptions containing one choice option of no interest to anybody, and everybody takes the offer that's most profitable for the magazine. All these actions are within your grasp. It's you who gets to choose.

A marketer is hence essentially a choice architect. And, as such, you are able to design a choice environment that alters the salience and the perceived value of your product or service for potential clients, relative to other competing options. A good choice architecture will encourage your client to make the right decision, while strengthening perceived value compared to the alternatives.

The role of the choice architect involves more than contemplating a specific action. It also refers to the environment in which the action occurs, and the interplay between these two. It requires a more holistic thought process. A movement away from singular or closed-off ways of looking at the problem.

Of course, there's nothing new about all this. Many marketers do it on a daily basis. Just like Molière's *bourgeois gentilhomme* who speaks in prose without realizing it, marketers have been designing 'choice architecture' for a long time without giving it a name. It has long been known, for instance, that the choice of distribution network has a strong effect on a product's image, or that the makeup display on which a line of lipstick is placed is not merely a means of distribution but also a way of assigning value. The basic idea behind choice architecture is hence already known to marketers. But what's needed now is the extra step. That is, to integrate it into every level of the process. Because from top to bottom, from the largest to the smallest element, it's all choice architecture! And once again, the fundamental question is easily expressed: How can we design a choice architecture – and this applies at every level, from top to bottom – that encourages the client to adopt the target behavior via a change in the perceived value of different offers?

Use new incentive levers

The third element involved in the Nudge marketer's new mental framework concerns incentive levers.

System 1 thinking leads to effective communication with the target population. Choice architecture leads to the design of an environment that steers the client or consumer towards the right decision. And these new incentive levers are the final mechanism by which theory becomes action and the desired behavior is adopted.

Specifically, the Nudge marketer has to go beyond the regular conviction-based techniques that he uses to design his actions. As previously discussed, public policy Nudges work because they complement traditional methods such as the law, financial incentives, and information. The same applies to private enterprise, where the Nudge approach seeks to increase effectiveness by working alongside existing marketing levers.

Classical marketing logic is based on the capacity to convince a potential buyer about the specific benefits of a particular offer, compared to other competing offers. 'My product leaves whites whiter, is fresher, more natural, easier to use, cheaper, state-of-the-art...' There is hence a triple challenge for the marketer: the benefit has to be motivating for a significant portion of the target population; it has to be believable; and the customer's experience must conform to the initial promise. Over the decades, with markets becoming hyper-segmented, this process has grown more and more complex. Accordingly, the promises have become the subject of intense scrutinization. Modern consumers are experts in the products that they use, as well as sceptical of promises they hear.

It's not a question of disputing the validity of the conviction model. Rather, it's about making it more effective. We do this by addressing the levers involved in designing these actions. Not only the levers traditionally used as a means of convincing people, but also, once again, those levers that apply to the irrational, emotional, social, and situational beings that we all are.

This new mental framework hence provides the basis for Nudge marketing. These are the foundations from which it will be possible to design and implement increasingly effective actions. The next step is to put these general principles – the three pillars of our new mental framework – into practice. And the transition from theory to action is centred around the following question: 'What is the best approach for designing and implementing efficient marketing actions – that is, actions that are both effective and which make the best use of available resources?'

The process that I am about to suggest is built around the following three main questions:

- What type of base should effective actions be built upon?
- How can we steer consumers towards the desired decision?
- How can we predictively evaluate the effects of actions prior to their deployment?

Chapter 15

A base for the construction of effective actions

Understanding the System 1 consumer

It's not the goal that is new here, but the means of achieving it. The ultimate goal is both clear and well known in marketing circles: an effective action cannot be designed without understanding the consumer. But the 'how' part of the question is where behavioral economics really comes into its own. *How* can we arrive at a real understanding of consumer behavior?

Behavioral economics shows that this real understanding – a prerequisite to any successful marketing action – requires significant changes to current practices. We need to know both the core elements of the decision-making process, and the specific features of its context.

Understanding the core elements of a decision and the specific features of a situation

The first of these concerns our knowledge of decision-making fundamentals and human behavior. As a marketer, your subject matter – the one thing that comes before all thoughts of brands, packaging and price – is people. Your job is to come up with actions that will modify people's behavior. It all comes down to this: you have to know what motivates these people and what influences them in their decisions. Not what you might *think* motivates them, but what you *know* moves them to act – for a fact! And at this point in the book, you can think of yourself as one blessed with this basic knowledge.

However, this knowledge is a prerequisite, not an end in itself. Understanding consumers requires not only a general knowledge but also a specific understanding of the situation in which the behavior takes place. You know by now the extent to which it all comes down to details and context. You know that people, and hence consumers, are sensitive to a particular situation or environment. That they are influenced by a whole range of features – from their own emotional state to what other people are doing – as well as by the way the choice options are presented.

And this happens via an approach that goes beyond the words and statements that lead, at best, to a superficial comprehension of consumers' behavior and at worst, to a complete misunderstanding! As we shall see, this search for the reality behind the factors influencing behavior calls into question many of the research techniques currently in use in some of the world's largest companies. These are techniques that they employ to take crucial decisions… which can lead to some very unpleasant surprises.

More than words: ethnography, neuromarketing, and big data

In marketing, understanding customers or clients involves three fundamental 'moments of truth'. These are: the moment prior to purchase; the decision itself; and the experience of the product or service. If your product or service performs well at each of these key moments, then it has every chance of succeeding in the marketplace. This refers to two types of traditional marketing research: shopper studies on one hand, and usage and attitude studies on the other.

The goal is identical: to gain a deep understanding of people's behavior at each of these key moments. What is the decision-making process that leads people to choose one mobile phone service provider over another? To buy an iPhone instead of a Samsung? To choose Tide over Omo? And what is the behavior and satisfaction level that results from driving a Ford or a Chevrolet? Eating a fruit yoghurt made by Yoplait or Danone?

When it comes to behavioral economics, however, these studies contain two potential pitfalls. The first of these concerns the words themselves; and the second, their meaning.

First of all, the problem of words. That is, the use of direct questions, where shoppers or consumers are asked to explain their own behavior. This technique only allows us to collect information from consumers that are a) consciously aware, and b) able to articulate. Worse yet, this is a reinterpretation. It's what the individual *believes* to be at the root their behavior – a belief that is filtered by the dual biases of internal coherence and social conformity. At best, direct questions can only provide one possible source of information. And this is never the only – or even the main – source that there is.

Of course, my qualitative-marketing friends will tell me that they're long past using simple discourse as a means to dig up hidden or repressed motivations. They'll say they have specific techniques for this – both forward-looking and analytic methods – that have proved to be successful. And they are right. But only partially! As we know by now, there are two limiting factors at work here. First, a cognitive limitation – we don't have access to the early stages of our perception and the way we process information. And, second, a limitation in conscious awareness linked to situation or social factors influence our behavior and which we then have difficulty articulating.

New generation ethnographic research: the key starting point

Happily, new technologies have led to a resurgence in ethnography! The aim of this technique is to grasp objective reality by observing people's behavior. To go beyond what is *said*, by paying attention exclusively to what is *done*. Ethnographic studies, by their very nature, transcend the spoken word. They involve observing and recording, as faithfully as possible, the behavior of people in their natural environment – for example, at a point of sale or in their home.

Evolving new technologies have led to new and highly sophisticated observation techniques. These include:

◆ far more powerful video devices;
◆ blog for tracking behavior;
◆ the advent of the smartphone – a new 'self-reporting' tool.

Video devices have got dramatically more powerful in the last ten years. Cameras have become so small that they can be installed practically anywhere. At point of sale and reception areas, of course, but also in people's homes (in their kitchen or in their bathroom) or in their cars. The capacity for storing images has also seen a phenomenal increase due to the portable nature of memory cards and disks. One of these can be given to a shopper as they make their way around a store, and the process can be tracked without any data storage problems. These technological improvements make ethnographic studies increasingly relevant, particularly in regard to limiting the bias caused by the presence of the observer, which is always a sensitive issue in this context. By taking the ethnologist away from the middle of the lounge or the passenger seat of the car, and replacing them with a miniature camera, the observation process is made less disturbing, even more objective, and the observer less intrusive. The data collected is hence potentially more reliable.

Aside from its questionnaires and online focus groups, the internet has given rise to new types of studies based on blog platforms. Institutes set up blogs on an *ad hoc* basis, allowing samples of participants to share their feelings, for instance, about a product that they use in their home. Every evening, participants post photos and videos of their product experience, while saying how they feel about it all. Forums can be set up for participants to exchange viewpoints and swap opinions. The research institute can also intervene by asking participants specific questions about observed behavior and related comments. Or course, this approach is not as 'pure' as direct observation by an ethnologist in the home. But it does allow for longitudinal tracking over a sufficiently long timeframe to justify the cost of the study.

It's the smartphone, however, which is the real revolution in gathering information to improve our understanding of behavior. People who own smartphones can be asked to act as their own private investigators; to film anything they see that relates to the issue being studied; or to engage with a particular behavior in order to identify the factors involved as part of a later analysis. The availability of geo-tracking and the fact that it all happens in real time is of great advantage here. Smartphones are especially useful for understanding the contact points in the preparation phase of the buying decision. For instance, a smartphone-owning representative sample of the target population can be recruited. These can then be tracked over a fixed timeframe, during which they are asked to identify the contact points they have with a particular product category. This contact might include watching an advert on TV, discussing the product with friends and family, visiting the website of a specific brand or a related forum, going to the point of sale to get information, etc. In such a way, the whole range of contact points with an upstream influence on the decision can be identified. Their power can be measured by examining the proportion of the target population affected. Once the purchase has been made, the influence of these contact points can be calculated in relation to the final decision. With all this information at his fingertips, the marketer, can then invest in those for which the ROI is highest.

As well as sending photos, videos, and SMSs, a smartphone app can be downloaded allowing participants to be asked specific questions about the observed behavior.

All these assets make ethnographic studies an integral part of any approach seeking to understand behavior. However, the technique contains a notorious pitfall. That is, the problem of meaning. However rigorous and relevant, observation and behavioral data can be extremely deceptive for a marketer in search of 'insights' that will help him have a positive impact on the business for which he is responsible. What use is it to know, for example, that shoppers approach the shelf containing washing products from the right? That they are usually alone in the week, but with their children on Saturdays? That they stop twice and spend 16 seconds in front of the shelf before buying one product, on average, without hesitating or reading the back of the packaging? Not much use at all, if we can't give this information any meaning! Clearly, it's for the analyst to give significance to the observations. That is, to transform facts into 'insights'. For example, a very fast decision-making process requires a packaging design that communicates information clearly and convincingly at a glance. Of course, this presents quite a challenge. An ethnographic study without meaning is hence no more than a giant stack of data that is basically useless to the marketer in search of insights.

What this shows is that no one single approach is able to capture the full complexity of issues involved in the decision-making process. The methods and the tools – ethnographic, qualitative, and quantitative – hence need to be combined. Clearly defined objectives need to be assigned to each, without losing sight of the basic direction that comes from behavioral economics. That is, to understand the respective role of the three main influencing factors: social interactions, the situation, and personal considerations. In the end, as always, it is rich and rigorously gathered data, in conjunction with concise, detailed analysis, which leads to the big insights.

Beyond the right combination of approaches, however, studies aimed at understanding behavior have been gradually revolutionized by two radically different methods. One of these is centred on the individual; the other relates to our behavior *en masse*:

◆ neuromarketing;
◆ big data.

The aim here is not to give a comprehensive overview, or even a summary, of these two giants who have stormed onto the scene. Rather, my intention is to show how their contributions may be so important for understanding behavior.

Neuromarketing: getting past what people say

I know that this word can scare people, including a good number of marketers and specialist researchers. When I founded a think tank on the subject within Adetem (the National Association of French Marketing Professionals), I was careful to avoid the term 'neuromarketing' and use 'neuroscience and marketing' instead. That word has negative connotations – especially in France. Marketing is already considered by many to be the science of consumer manipulation. And so neuromarketing must be some kind of demonic unconscious tampering. A way of infiltrating people's brains and causing them to make decisions of which they have no knowledge.

So let's try and inject a little calmness into the debate by examining both the real-life contributions – of which there are some important examples – as well as certain limitations, as these are also present. Neuromarketing uses methods derived from neuroscience to better understand the issues involved in consumer decisions. The goal is to get beyond the limited nature of what people can articulate, and to address their physical responses to certain stimuli. The idea is hence to better understand the reality of the decision-making process by analyzing brain activity (the 'central' system) and that of the rest of the body (the 'peripheral' system). What happens in my brain when I take this or that decision, or when I adopt a certain type of behavior? How does my body react to a certain thing happening? Is it my body, in fact, that leads me to decisions?

Once again, my intention here is not to give a panoramic overview of the techniques involved, but to dive straight into the ones which seem most interesting to practitioners in search of deeper understanding. I refer those readers who want to explore further to Olivier Droulers and Bernard Roulet's book,[1] or to the excellent review paper[2] by Olivier Oullier, Dwight Merunka and Olivia Petit.

The first technique that I consider indispensable to a heightened understanding of consumer behavior is 'eye tracking'. This allows us to pinpoint what a person is looking at. Be it a commercial, a television programme, a website – eye tracking shows us the focus of a customers' gaze as they move around a retail outlet or buy something in a store. As well as this, it lets us know the time spent in each area, and the order in which these things are watched. While we may believe that our gaze is relatively stable, eye tracking reveals that we absorb environmental information at high speed. Our gaze is constantly shifting, and, even more importantly, this movement is not random. Analysis of eye-tracking results reveals

1. Olivier Droulers and Bernard Roulet, *Neuromarketing. Le marketing revisité par les neurosciences du consommateur* [Neuromarketing: Marketing Revisited by Consumer Neuroscience], Dunod, 2010.
2. Olivier Oullier, Dwight Merunka and Olivia Petit, 'Neurosciences et comportement du consommateur 1 et 2' [Neuroscience and Consumer Behaviour 1 and 2], *Revue française du marketing*, n° 247 and 248, June and September 2014.

a system of information gathering that is governed by our brains.

Using eye tracking makes it possible to understand what is and is not seen. We can identify which information is potentially being processed, and which is not. And we can examine these results in light of the final decision taken.

Eye tracking hence contributes a diagnostic process to a crucial aspect of all marketing: the link between attention and decision. In a world so heaped with information, is the element that the marketer wants to communicate actually seen by the consumer? A specific reference on some packaging, a new product on a shelf, an advertising banner on a webpage... And in a more general sense, what does a person's system of information gathering reveal about what counts for them in making a decision? In choosing a cherry yoghurt – one of my guilty pleasures – do I compare brands? Do I look at the price? Or is my gaze focused on the cherry as depicted on the yoghurt pot? The thing I look at shows both what matters to me in the context, and the order in which I find these things important! Of course, clients don't buy everything they see. When it comes to an action's capacity to persuade somebody, or to get them to make a purchase, we know, thanks to the work of Joseph LeDoux and colleagues, that emotions have a major role to play. But emotions also come with a problem, in that they are often felt unconsciously, and hence not something that we can articulate.

Here again, neuroscience can make a real contribution. There are several techniques that allow us to measure the emotion caused by a particular stimulus. As we know, when we are gripped by a strong emotion, our body has a number of ways of showing it. Our heart beats faster. Our breathing quickens. We begin to sweat. When something makes us happy, we tend to smile. And when the opposite is true, we frown. All these physiological manifestations can be gaged using specific techniques that reveal the emotional involvement. Even when these emotions are weak – and therefore unconscious – it is nevertheless possible be measure them.

The main techniques suitable for use in marketing are given in Figure 15.1.

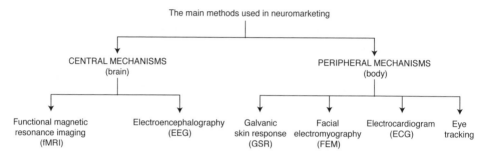

Figure 15.1 The main methods used in neuromarketing

All of these techniques have the same aim: to get beyond the things we say, and measure bodily responses to stimuli such as advertising, shop design, websites, new products, packaging, or even the smell or the experience of using a product.

The techniques differ according to the type of response being measured and its possible interpretation. That they remain so little known and sparsely used is due to a range of reasons including cost, complexity, their ability to add value, and legislation that exists in certain countries.

Apart from eye tracking, the two most commonly used methods are EEG (electroencephalogram) and GSR (galvanic skin response).

- EEG is a means to evaluate the intensity with which we process information, and hence the attention level aroused by each stimulus. For example, which stimulus grabs my attention and makes me process information at length when I am doing my shopping?
- GSR measures the intensity of the emotion via micro-secretions of the skin. Does seeing a certain stimulus – an advert or some packaging, for instance – result in an emotional reaction?

The preferred technique for decision neuroscience researchers who want to understand the biological foundations of our behavior is fMRI. However, my feeling is that it poses too many ethical and technical problems to be used in marketing. Two other methods at the fringes of neuroscience are also being developed to better understand the nature of emotions and unconscious reactions:

◆ Facial decoding. Based on the work of the psychologist Paul Ekman, this involves deciphering a person's facial reactions to a stimulus, to identify the type of emotion being felt.
◆ Implicit association tests (IAT) that indirectly measure the unconscious association generated by a stimulus.

These techniques taken from neuroscience should be viewed with interest, as they already contribute – and will do even more so in the future – some complementary information that is useful for understanding consumer behavior. However, they also require a certain caution and a critical perspective when considering how best to use them.

Big data: a wealth of free, real-time behavioral statistics?

Big data is the other major revolution leading to a better understanding of behavior. Companies currently enjoy a source of information that is both free and which gets bigger by the day. Vast amounts of behavior-related data are collected on a daily basis from clients in a wide range of sectors including banks, major telecommunications companies, distributors, e-commerce sites, or even the huge GPS-based car network that will soon be a reality. How many times per day does an Orange client use their cell phone? What is their average call time? When do they make their calls? In which area? All this data can be used to put together user types, giving meaning to the figures and allowing for 'behavioral models' to be drawn up and researched.

Of course, big data is a beast that we must tame in order to draw any useful conclusions. The amount of information is overwhelming. It is often without structure, and in a state of constant change. These are all significant difficulties facing a new breed of worker: the 'data scientist'. However, researchers the world over are investing time and money to gain a better grasp of this continuous, free data source that we provide every day via Facebook, LinkedIn, Twitter and all kinds of blogs.

No doubt, there is a long road ahead before the true value of this data is realized. However, I don't doubt for one instant that, given the challenges presented by big data and the power of the parties involved, increasingly better solutions will appear. With each day that passes, practitioners' jobs will get easier. Certainly, we will have to find out *how* to extract meaning from this great weight of information. But for any behavioral economist, this cornucopia of data is an extremely positive starting point.

Our understanding of consumers hence comes from a diverse range of sources. These include a better understanding of individual decisions and the way that markets work. On an individual level, this comes via 'ethn'holistic' studies, combined with clever qualitative methods and new tools taken from neuroscience. And more broadly, it is achieved through the proper analysis of behavioral information thrown up by big data. This true understanding therefore makes it possible to design efficient action plans.

Chapter 16

The five phases of Nudge marketing

Nudge marketing aims to bring about desired behavioral change in a target population.

This new type of incentive marketing is built around the following five phases:

1. Prepare people's mindsets by building familiarity, reciprocity and trust;
2. Attract their attention with salience and good timing;
3. Steer their behavior in the desired direction using choice architecture;
4. Use the right levers to coax them into action;
5. Solidify the change and make the behavior more widespread by forming habits and encouraging social contagion.

The following diagram (see Figure 16.1) shows the rationale that links these different stages. It identifies both the main Nudge mechanisms and relevant action levers, as well as the marketing materials required for each action.

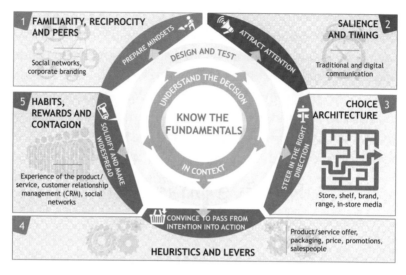

Figure 16.1 The Nudge marketing dashboard

Each stage lays the groundwork for the next: it's a holistic vision where the last phase leads back to the first.

Phase 1: preparing people's mindsets

Incentive marketing gradually steers the consumer towards the behavior that the choice architect (the marketer) would like them to adopt. With the exception of phase four, the goal of which is the transition to action – that is, the decision itself – this doesn't mean that each of these steps in indispensable. Rather, that the work carried out in each step paves the way for the 'right' final decision.

And this is where phase one comes in: 'Preparing people's mindsets'. This phase involves designing actions that create a favourable mental attitude in the client towards the brand or business in question. It is not about selling products or services. Rather, it's about creating a mindset that leaves the client with a positive perspective on the decision to come.

The first step in phase one is familiarity – and it's a simple one. First of all, we impart knowledge. Then, we generate complicity with the company or its products. Familiarity is a means of creating preferences: we prefer things that we know. And in contexts where the inherent features of competing offers are either unknown or equivalent, familiarity can be the deciding factor in the consumer's final choice. There are two main tools used to generate familiarity. Advertising, in all its forms, builds popularity while seeking to create an image in line with brand positioning. But this does not necessarily mean 'heavy' advertising – that is, involving large investments in high profile media, such as prime time television. Familiarity can also come about via brand reminders that pop up in the course of our daily lives. Examples of this – and there are many – might include the presence of a brand on a pedestrian crossing, an image on the side of a delivery truck, etc.

Familiarity, and subsequently preference, can be created on an unconscious level. As Professor Julien Intartaglia[1] has shown, the presence of advertising banners that visitors to websites can't remember seeing, still improve the perception of the brands in question through implicit association.

Other than the different forms of brand communication, the use of the product itself is of course a way of generating familiarity. This is the strongest means of creating proximity with both the brand and its image, which need not necessarily have been communicated beforehand.

The marketer hence has many potential materials at their disposal to create familiarity. Nevertheless, to truly lay the groundwork takes a little more than this.

---

1. *L'Influence et la réception de la publicité sur les jeunes consommateurs. Du processus de socialisation aux effets sur la cognition implicite* [The influence of advertising and its reception by young consumers: From socialization to the effects on implicit cognition], thesis defended by Julien Intartaglia on 20th November 2013.

The main challenge of this first stage is how to use social logic to create reciprocity. If you want people to buy your product or service, you have to act upstream of the sale itself. That is, at a time when you'd be least expected to do it for commercial reasons. So do your consumers a favour. Help them out. With the understanding, of course, that nobody is fooled any more in this, the age of the expert consumer – an expertise that covers sales and marketing techniques! Your clients know you have a vested interest in it all. But this is no way an attempt to deceive them. To do so, in fact, would be a huge strategic error. It's about creating the conditions for reciprocity while acting in a way that truly benefits your clients. By being of service to them. By valuing them, even when there's no direct link between you doing this and the eventual sale of your products. If you want to create conditions for your brand's sustainable success – or, even more importantly, your company's – it's vital that you create a sense of real, all-consuming trust. This should come about as a result of both your words and your actions. It should entail the common vision of a win-win partnership. You win via the sale of your products. And your client wins too, not only in the positive experience that your product brings but also via his belief – generated by you – that you have his long-term interest at heart. That you're concerned with more than just his wallet. And make no mistake about what all this involves. Of course, it's a wonderful thing when ethics and results collide. But it's behavioral change – that is, these same results – that is behind my suggestion that you take the time to act this way.

Specifically, what does it mean to pave the way for a positive attitude using mechanisms linked to reciprocity and fairness?

First of all, it's a type of mindset. It's about thinking of the client's current and potential interest in a way that extends beyond the product offer. Next, it's the real and visible execution of this mindset. To create a favourable mindset in the consumer takes more than mere lip service (the worst of traps, leading to all sorts of deceit). Rather, it needs real and genuine action. Many marketers, of course, merely reaffirm this with their slogans, adverts, sales patter, and all manner of sycophancy. The main difference with traditional corporate campaigns that also try to create a positive image for the company lies in one factor. It's not a question of directly promoting a business and its brands or products and going about things in a top-down manner. Rather, it's about providing your target population with a service that goes right to the heart of their best interests. If you really want to feel their reciprocity, you have to make a genuine investment that benefits your clients.

Some companies know how to do it very well. Let's look at few examples to illustrate the process.

First, the Facebook page of Pampers.

Source: https://fr-fr.facebook.com/PampersFrance

Figure 16.2 Pampers Facebook page

This big Procter and Gamble (P&G) brand's Facebook page shows how much they want to generate complicity with their clients beyond the simple use of nappies. 'Welcome to our Facebook Community, where you can connect with parents, ask questions, and make the most of your baby's journey.' Further on, the site adds, 'Pampers has been celebrating, supporting, and protecting babies for more than 50 years. The Pampers Facebook page is meant to be a fun environment for our fans to share ideas and to discuss Pampers products and promotions.' Of course, there is a constant reference to Pampers products. At the same time, however, there is a real desire to provide young mothers with useful, complementary services. These include offering ways for them to exchange views and opinions, or providing little moments of happiness such as the Baby Book (see Figure 16.3).

Source: www.facebook.com/Pampers/app_267595473377411

Figure 16.3 Extract from the Pampers Facebook page

As well as the personal service offered to its visitors, Pampers also makes use of an important social lever: altruism and fairness. It does this via a project carried out in conjunction with Unicef (see Figure 16.4).

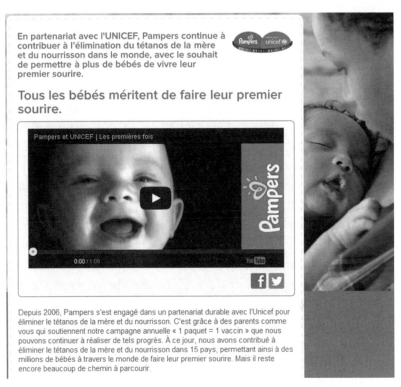

En partenariat avec l'UNICEF, Pampers continue à contribuer à l'élimination du tétanos de la mère et du nourrisson dans le monde, avec le souhait de permettre à plus de bébés de vivre leur premier sourire.

Tous les bébés méritent de faire leur premier sourire.

Pampers et UNICEF | Les premières fois

0:00 / 1:08

Depuis 2006, Pampers s'est engagé dans un partenariat durable avec l'Unicef pour éliminer le tétanos de la mère et du nourrisson. C'est grâce à des parents comme vous qui soutiennent notre campagne annuelle « 1 paquet = 1 vaccin » que nous pouvons continuer à réaliser de tels progrès. À ce jour, nous avons contribué à éliminer le tétanos de la mère et du nourrisson dans 15 pays, permettant ainsi à des millions de bébés à travers le monde de faire leur premier sourire. Mais il reste encore beaucoup de chemin à parcourir.

Source: www.pampers.fr/unicef

Figure 16.4 Extract from the Pampers website

On the main Pampers website, people are asked to watch or share a video clip to receive a free vaccine. On the Facebook page, the campaign is broken down as follows: 'So more babies get to smile for the first time: share a photo of your baby's first smile and we will give you a vaccine against infant tetanus.' And there is also a more traditional promotion, where buying the product triggers the same offer. Of course, there is clearly some attempt at manipulation in the Cincinnati company's campaign. And it's undeniable that there's an underlying aim to the whole process. However, there's no denying the reality of the ensuing commitment, as well as Pampers' altruistic approach to this important subject for young mothers.

In terms of behavioral economics, the aim is clear and the mechanism appropriate. Reciprocity and familiarity for the Pampers brand is created by providing mothers with real complementary services that go to the heart of their individual or general best interests. And these services are independent of the products themselves – it's not a question of selling them directly. This is what separates the approach from traditional corporate communications. And it's *this* that makes the former both more powerful and more effective.

Another worldwide giant, Coca-Cola, is equally proficient at creating a favourable mindset in its clients. The mechanisms that it uses are different, however, as seen in the company's French-language Facebook page (see Figure 16.5).

As for P&G, the aim of Coca-Cola's Facebook page is clear. It's not about selling or promoting its products, but showing that it values its clients. 'The Coca-Cola Facebook page is a collection of your stories showing how people the world over have helped make Coke what it is today.'

The mechanism used by Coca-Cola makes use of another social dimension. This time, the target population is teenagers and young adults, whose central preoccupation is their own self-image and their friends. We all know the extent to which adolescents are concerned with both their ego and their peers. The global proliferation of the 'selfie' is proof enough of this. First names on Coke bottle labels, and the accompanying possibility of taking a picture and posting in on the Facebook page, are hence a platform for staging and self-actualization, with the brand acting as a symbol of this happy moment.

The power of this ego-related mechanism once again creates both familiarity and reciprocity with the brand. And the

Source: https://www.facebook.com/cocacolafrance/photos_stream?ref=page_internal

Figure 16.5 Extract from the Coca-Cola Facebook page

hope is that the target population, in return, will end up buying the product. But Coca-Cola also wants to activate other powerful motivators in young people. In direct contrast to the ego, these involve the timeless values of freedom and fairness. On the site, there are quotes from Nelson Mandela (used on the Facebook cover photo – see Figure 16.6) which act as a call to virtuous behavior by associating personal happiness with that of others.

Finally, Coca-Cola develops actions to demonstrate its commitment to wider causes through its partnerships, such as the 'Vote for a better world' initiative with the UN (see Figure 16.7).

Source: www.facebook.com/cocacolafrance?brand_redir=1

Figure 16.6 Extract of photos from Coca-Cola's Facebook cover page

As for P&G, this approach combines actions of specific interest to the target population (helping young mothers in the case of Pampers; giving young consumers an increased sense of self-worth in the case of Coca-Cola) with others of a wider humanitarian nature. Together, these build the desired corporate image, as well as laying the foundations for a reciprocity lever. How could you not consume these products that are so concerned with both yourself and with the world?

Social networks, with their interactive nature and their powerful ability to disseminate information, are thus central to the execution of stage one strategies for 'the preparation of a favourable mindset'. However, there are other far less sophisticated measures that can also be of great assistance here.

This is the case for all the men and women who interact with clients or prospective buyers. Those 'front office' employees who are the human face of a brand or company. Beyond

Source: vote.myworld2015.org/cocacola/

Figure 16.7 Coca-Cola's 'Vote for a better world' initiative

their main function, which in many cases is to sell or give out information, they have a great capacity to generate reciprocity, which in turn will benefit the business (or not, as the case may be). Everything that the client perceives as 'above and beyond' goes some way towards the gradual creation of a mindset that is favourable to the company and its products. Of course, this is obvious enough, and far from original. But it's even more important to remember just how difficult this is to implement and to apply in an on-going, stable manner. It's not enough that the front office simply does a good job. What's needed is that they go the extra mile to convince the client that the company takes a special interest in their satisfaction. Beyond the products themselves, it's this extra effort that creates both short-term reciprocity and long-term trust in the business.

Phase 2: attract attention

Creating a favourable mindset is an important, but not indispensable first step. Your brand or product can still do well without this upstream reciprocity. It's an extra feature that is neither obligatory nor a guarantee in itself of success. An upstream differentiating factor that builds or consolidates client relations. However, there is still a long way to go to persuade clients to buy your product or service.

Phase two aims to draw the attention of the target population to the message or product in question. Somewhat tautologically, it follows that something which is not observed – even unconsciously – cannot have any influence. Simply, if your message isn't seen, it won't build anything at all. This salience is one of the central concepts of the Nudge approach. And it can be very difficult to grab the attention of your target – even for a few short moments.

So what should we do to make our little voice ring out above the constant din that is the modern world?

Attracting attention: timing it right

Before thinking about how to attract attention, it's important to consider the timing of the action being implemented. There are both good and bad moments to communicate a piece of information. Moments when the potential receiver is open to processing the message, and those when they are not – as is more often the case. In short, we are far more receptive to messages, or to processing information, when we are interested in the broader area that they relate to. This is also true for moments when we're close to taking a decision.

However, for the vast majority of products and services – particularly when it comes to day-to-day purchases – this simply isn't the case. We are not in this specific, receptive mindset, and marketers have to fight to win our attention before it quickly shifts towards another message, product, or piece of information. As it's here that the question of timing is most crucial. Our capacity to attract attention depends as much on this as on the features of the action itself. When it comes to timing, the basic rule is simple enough. People pay attention to things that are of short-term use to them. This is particularly the case for decisions that need to be taken in a short timeframe. Conversely, the further away the action is from the decision, the less the chances of it grabbing our attention. This is why point-of-sale communications (assuming they can stand out from the chaos) often capture people's attention better than those attempted earlier. This is also the reason why new promotional systems which send an SMS to your smartphone with a specific offer when the GPS shows you entering a catchment area show a very high rate of return. They catch you at the perfect moment. You are interested in receiving the information because you are right on the point of making a purchasing decision.

But of course, there is no absolute rule as to what determines good timing. It will depend on the decision course particular to each product category, as well the desired goal – beyond simply getting people's attention – of the action in question. Are you more concerned with building popularity and image? In this case, the timing can be less linked to the decision to buy. Is the action aimed at persuasion? In which case, proximity to the decision will be a determining factor, and timing will be crucial.

Whatever the circumstances, the important thing is to think about timing before considering the design of the action itself. Although this is, of course, still a fundamental part of the overall process.

Salience: the revolution and its cues

Actions which emerge from the constant bombardment of information and grab our attention adhere to the following two mechanisms.

- ◆ The first relates to their capacity to 'break out' of the environment in which they operate. We call this the 'awakening power' of a stimulus. When the red fire truck hits its siren, for instance, it automatically grabs the attention of surrounding drivers. This involves doing something different, or in stark contrast to the environment.

◆ The second concerns the meaning of the thing communicated by the stimulus. And it's the relevance of this meaning, in terms of what we want or other factors spontaneously communicated by the environment, which leads to our attention being held.

Attention hence has two dimensions to it. There's a 'bottom-up' action, where a stimulus stands out from the environment due to its unique status. And there's a 'top-down' action, where our attention is spontaneously attracted by messages or objects that resonate with our mindset at a given moment. That is, they relate to something we are actively in search of at that time. This salience is the result of a double mechanism that makes us interested in a particular object or message from within a sea of other stimuli. And one doesn't work without the other.

The ideal theoretical mechanism is so-called 'relevant rupture'. On one hand, we want to create the rupture – that is, the environmental schism – that automatically attracts attention. On the other, we need to maintain relevance in terms of the person's mindset and expectations at the moment of their being exposed to the information or object. The rupture awakens the attention, and the relevance allows a longer processing of the stimulus. This may come about via advertising, packaging, or any other form of communication.

When Danone's Activia – now called Bio – was launched in France, its green colouring was a first for fresh dairy products. No other brand of yoghurt used such an overpowering colour. But this visual rupture brought about the desired salience. At the same time, its greenness was consistent with ideas of health and naturalness that Danone's marketers wanted to convey. The colour has an automatic association with these qualities, with no further explanation necessary.

The colour difference therefore both engaged and communicated. In terms of Activia's brand positioning, the decision made very good sense.

The difficulty here is to make the basic signifiers both different and relevant. If we want to attract attention using novelty, but the novel element comes from an entirely different sphere, the visual rupture can generate the opposite effect – a low level of visibility. This is even more the case for System 1 buyers who don't take the time to carefully decode the information. Hence the need for 'relevant rupture' – to attract people's attention, the two elements need to be working in harmony.

This leads me to two other fundamental concepts related to the complex phenomena of attention and perception: the 'implicit anchor' and 'brand cues'.

Interpreting without processing: implicit anchors and brand cues

In a general sense, we perceive the world in light of our past experiences. These experiences are committed to memory, and later re-mobilized – a method that allows us to rapidly process all kinds of information. This is both the strength and the weakness of System 1 thinking. Its strength is that it allows for high-speed processing that is mostly accurate, as it is based on the sum total of our life experiences. It allows us to take effective, effortless decisions. However, this system of association can also lead us into error. It is hence important to bear in mind that all the signifiers being used – for instance, a colour, a shape, a material, or the position of a product on a shelf – are implicit anchors that consumers will interpret, at high speed, as part of their decision-making process. To generate salience, the marketer thus has to be able to identify these implicit anchors, to ensure that there is resonance between the signifiers used and the decision maker's mindset.

An example of implicit anchors – very important in marketing circles – is what are known as 'brand cues'. Brand cues are signs whose associations are so deeply engrained that consumers spontaneously recall a brand without it being specifically referred to.

Brand cues are not only logos and icons. They can be a piece of music or a song. It could also be a smell or even a distinctive style, like that of the Apple adverts. Often, these are colours or combinations associating a colour with a specific element. All these indicators, or brand triggers, are essential assets for brands seeking to implant themselves in the minds of their consumers. The whole story of the brand is captured in a simple sign. The mere seeing (or hearing) of this sign triggers a series of associations related to the consumer's past experiences. The capacity to create these brand cues, and to manage them across a range of communication materials, is a great advantage for any brand. It's an excellent way to capitalize on previous actions and strengthen ROI.

However, brand cues are not limited to the heavy hitting signifiers of big-name brands. They can also be the many little signs associated with a brand or a product that are used by shoppers, consciously or otherwise, to quickly and easily locate the product they are looking for. To distinguish them from brand cues – their big brother, if you will – I call these 'recognition indicators'. They work according to the same logic, with one big difference: while brand cues take effect across the board, recognition indicators only work in a given situation.

The modification or suppression of one or more recognition indicators following a change in packaging can hence be a dangerous pitfall. The effect on sales can be dramatic. And the reasons for an unsuspecting marketer falling foul of it can be very harmful. We call this trap – one of the most common that we see – the 'destabilizing revolution'. Recognition indicators are often unconscious, and not something that consumers can articulate. Their loss, however, causes a systematic, significant reduction in sales. The decrease can be as much as 30%. So don't use purchasing intentions as a sole means to justify a change in packaging. And take care to identify these recognition indicators so they can be carried forward in the event of any change.

For all your marketing actions, pay at least as much attention to salience as you do to the message being communicated. Capturing attention is an obligatory step on the road to success. And yet the challenges involved are often underestimated.

Phase 3: steering consumers in the right direction

The central idea of this phase is the construction of a choice architecture that steers the decision maker towards the option that we want them to take. That is, towards the purchase of our product or service. As we know, a choice option can be selected much more frequently depending on the way it is presented. The key point here is that our preferences are not stable. They are influenced by both the context and the situation. Specifically, this means that the competitiveness of an offer can be significantly altered by its context, all other things being equal. You can make your offer more attractive by presenting it in an environment that creates a favourable mindset in the consumer – and that's the only change you ever need to make.

Phase three is hence not about working on the product offer itself. Rather, its focus is on the features of the environment that will make it more attractive.

In marketing, across the board, for actions big and small, the subject of choice architecture comes back to the following main questions:

◆ merchandising implementation;
◆ sales location – physical and virtual (ecommerce) stores;
◆ branding;
◆ product mix.

An offer's performance is incredibly sensitive to its environment. This is because the latter plays a major role in the following three essential areas:

◆ the salience of the offer;
◆ the offer's perceived value in respect of comparison points created by the environment;
◆ the mindset that it generates in the decision maker.

If choice architecture provides a product with a higher level of salience – that is, it seizes potential buyers' attention during the decision-making process – its likelihood of being selected automatically increases. In situations where a product's ability to convince is identical, performance will be boosted by a larger base of potential buyers (i.e., those who have seen it).

In the same way, if the perception of a product's value is strengthened by a choice architecture containing reference points that make favourable comparisons to competing offers, then the final performance will be similarly improved. Again, given identical levels of salience, the higher confidence rating will strengthen eventual sales. The choice environment also has an influence on the decision maker's mindset. It creates expectations, reactivates associations, and encourages a suitable decision logic. Situational factors hence generate a client mindset that is more or less favourable to the desired behavior.

Merchandising implementation

I will illustrate the three mechanisms affecting the performance of a brand or group of products via two case studies where merchandising implementation is drawn from the very different worlds of laundry and toilet paper.

The first of these concerns a new product launched by a big-name brand in the world of laundry products. The challenge is to find a way of getting it onto the shelves that maximizes its potential. The new offer is endorsed by a market leader with top-end positioning. However, its unique selling point is its low price. Two options are hence possible: 1) introduce it to the market segment containing low-price offers; or 2) introduce it to the segment containing products in its umbrella brand. In short, should it be placed next to its direct competitors or with other members of its brand? The results are unequivocal. The number of buyers more than doubles when the new product is placed next to its direct competitors. And the reason for this is simple. Shoppers for whom price variation is an important choice criterion generally head for the portion of the shelf containing bargains. The new product is therefore seen far more widely by the portion of the target who are interested in good quality at affordable prices. Greater salience for the most relevant target hence generates higher sales than the same offer placed alongside other products in the same umbrella brand – a section that is mainly visited by shoppers less motivated by price variation. As well as this, the cannibalization of umbrella brand products is reduced.

All in all, the same new product, with a perfectly identical mix, will see a significantly improved performance given the right implementation (choice architecture). The mechanism at work here is more sophisticated than in the previous example, which only relied on the salience of the product group. In this instance, the base effect is an enhanced salience. But the perception of value in regard to other competing products is also altered. In terms of the immediate competitive environment, buyers perceive the new offer as a 'better' proposition: a high-end brand at an affordable price. However, this is not the case for 'premium' buyers, for whom the same new range seems like a lesser offer. The product may be cheaper, but to their mind this must mean lower quality. The benchmarks for this type of buyer are not the same. They generate a different comparative logic that results in different choices. The competitive environment has thus altered the way in which the value of the offer is perceived.

The second example concerns the launch of a new toilet paper for young children. The product is designed to help them learn to use the bathroom by themselves. In terms of its use, the logic could be to place it on a shelf for other toilet paper, for which the visitation rate is very high. In terms of its features, however (it is similar to a type of baby wipe), and above all in terms of the target (mothers of young children), the new product could be introduced to the shelf containing baby wipes and other baby related products (lotions, shampoos, etc.). So once again, there are two possible options that show very different results. In tests, the number of buyers was six times higher when the toilet paper was placed on the shelf containing other baby products.

The main explanation for this gap in sales is the difference in perceived value caused by each of the environments. When placed on the shelf with other toilet papers, the price of the new product seemed prohibitively high to the majority of potential buyers. The wipes cost almost 3 dollars for a pack of 50, in a product environment where the amounts offered are generally far greater (often 6 to 12 rolls) for more or less the same price, and sometimes even less (the store brand frequently offers 12 rolls for a little over 2 dollars). Beyond this fact-based comparison, the new offer seems like a premium product at first glance. A sophisticated little plastic box when all around are big and basic-looking packs of toilet paper. Entering this section, the shopper's mindset is generally geared towards getting good value for money. The purchase is made quickly – it takes a dozen seconds or so – and with little emotional investment. As a result, this part of the market is very important for store brands or products whose prices compare favourably with well-known labels.

However, the consumers' mindset in the baby products section is the complete opposite! When it comes to their young children, mothers are inherently motivated by the quality of what they are about to choose. The purchase hence takes much longer and involves far more attention. In this environment, assigning a value to the quality of a product is central to the decision-making process. As well as this, the products surrounding the new offer are generally expensive. Baby wipes, baby shampoo, and other cotton-based materials all have a unit value of more than three euros. It is therefore unsurprising to note that the price disincentive was far less in the baby section than in the toilet paper section, and that the final purchases were much greater. The choice architecture hence significantly alters perceptions about the value of the product, as the shopper's mindset and immediate reference points are different in each instance.

Sales location: the case of Abercrombie & Fitch

The decision maker's mindset is also influenced, often implicitly, by situational factors such as music, smell, or lighting. Each of these variables has a specific effect on clients' behavior at the point of sale. Abercrombie & Fitch is an example of a company who make full use of these sensory variables to encourage people to buy their products. Professors Jean-François Lemoine and Olivier Badot have performed a study of this luxury US chain store[2] highlighting their use of the following three levels:

◆ the ritualization of the client's journey through the store;
◆ the exacerbation of sensory stimuli;
◆ the redefinition of store employee roles.

These three levers use emotional over-stimulation to create a point-of-sale atmosphere that produces a customer mindset favourable to impulse buying. The ritualization of the in-store

---

2. Jean-François Lemoine and Olivier Badot, 'Gestion tribale de la marque et distribution spécialisée : le cas Abercrombie & Fitch' [Tribal brand management and specialized distribution: the case of Abercrombie & Finch], *Cahiers de recherche PRISM-Sorbonne.*

journey involves a succession of steps, including the now-famous handsome guy and beautiful girl who welcome clients and offer to take their photo.

This is just the beginning of the journey whose aim is to rouse the clients' senses via the heady presence of A&F perfume, techno music more suited to a nightclub than a clothes store, and low lighting that, helped by exterior shutters that block out the natural light, make for very limited visibility. The exception to this is the micro-lights that cast their aura over certain key products and the images of beautiful young men and women that adorn the walls, enhancing the general feeling of eroticism. Employees have a key role here. Recruited for their physical attractiveness, they 'play the game' their employer requires of them. They are an integral part of the ambiance and its exaggerated sensuality, which they create by dancing, playing music, and smiling eagerly at clients. These elements all contribute to Abercrombie & Fitch's unique atmosphere, as well as helping clients shed their inhibitions. In the end, it all comes back to products and sales. But they get there via a wonderful detour and a unique choice architecture in which customers can let go – before buying things.

The brand as a basic structure that creates associations and expectations

Choosing which brand will be included in a product offer is clearly a vital decision, as it will immediately give the offer a specific image. The brand's presence reactivates both conscious and unconscious associations created by our knowledge of its potential use. And these associations are transferred from the brand to the product, generating a specific set of expectations. The issue doesn't apply to single-brand companies. But for those with a portfolio of various brands, it's a very important decision. It will have an effect both in terms of people being persuaded to buy it, and also on perceptions about the way the product is used. This has been demonstrated by both blind tests and those in which the brand has been identified. In a taste test, for example, the same product shows different results when the brand is visible, compared to a blind evaluation. Brands are hence an important 'primer' that colors the entire product experience. The choice of brand should therefore be considered both in terms of the offer's capacity to convince, and also its ability to fulfil expectations. And if this isn't the case, then the problems can be twofold: dissatisfaction with the product experience, and a change in the overall brand image, which can lose its coherence.

When it comes to choosing a brand, Nudge marketing and traditional marketing are on the same page. This is a fundamental decision that goes right to the heart of an offer's success, and whose influence extends beyond the product's individual features.

Structuring an offer and the decoy effect

Choice architecture involves more than just the sales location or choosing one brand over another. On a deeper level, there is also the question of the way the offer is structured. The profitability of each reference can never be identical. It can be in your interest to push one offer in a certain way, and another in quite a different direction. But this is still a question of choice architecture – internal, this time, to the offer you're presenting.

A decoy offer is created using the following method. There is an offer that you want to prioritize – let's call it option A. You then have to create option A+ or A- whose features are similar to option A, and which give the latter a marginal benefit or the former a much higher cost for a slight difference in value. The proximity of options A and A+/- achieves two things. First, it encourages potential buyers to compare the two offers more closely than other propositions. Second, it results in option A being clearly identified as the better option.

Of course, this is easier to implement this method in markets where the decoy offer doesn't have to be produced and is not required to demonstrate its profitability. By definition, it's not designed to be successful; rather, to enhance the success of another strategically positioned offer. For the consumer goods market, the decoy reference is hence to some extent constrained. Demand must exceed a certain level to be acceptable to both the producer and the distributor, who may discontinue the produce in the event of insufficient sales. But in many other areas where the offers are more 'virtual', the decoy strategy can be extremely profitable.

Your aim is to come up with a choice architecture that steers your client towards the 'right' decision. The decoy establishes a salience for your offer, generating both comparison points and a customer mindset that strengthens its perceived value in comparison to other competing offers. All that remains is to ensure that the client makes the transition from intention into action. That is, they go ahead and make the choice. And this is the purpose of phase four.

Phase 4: from intention to action – the levers of change

The question here concerns which lever to activate at the exact moment of a client's choice, to make sure their decision is final.

The good lever: a balancing act between the lever, the aim, the target and the situation

The method I suggest involves using the '21 drivers of influence' checklist. You should match each of the potential levers to the aim, and give thought to the materials required for the action to be implemented. As we know, each of these levers can have a significant impact on the final decision. However, their effectiveness depends on the specific features of the situation to which these are applied. A lever is not effective in a vacuum, but in respect of a particular target and in a given situation.

To identify the relevant lever, we have to understand both the factors impeding the desired behavior being adopted, as well as the materials needed for deployment. As part of the initial selection process, each potential lever must be matched against materials the marketing team would like use. Then, if the stakes are high, the various options should be tested to measure their actual impact on the target's behavior.

To illustrate this, I will examine the successful use of several major action levers by large global brands.

Creating product benefits via consumer engagement and appealing to the ego: Converse and Build-A-Bear

Engaging the consumer in the product they're about to buy as a way to make the offer more attractive can be a very effective mechanism. This approach is based on two different levers:

◆ the ego;
◆ personal engagement and the endowment effect.

The ego is a powerful lever, and the personalization of a product by consumers themselves is one way to bring it into play. An example of this is Converse's 'Design your sneakers' campaign.

Clients were invited to choose a generic model whose base colour and main details could be personalized. As such, the product was not perceived as identical for everyone, but designed by the client for themselves. It became an expression of their personality. Of course, this lever has some issues relating to industrial feasibility. However, Coca-Cola's mass personalization involving first names on their bottles shows that it is possible – even for mass markets – to use this lever to improve a brand's performance.

Engaging a client in a product can have an even stronger effect when it includes a personal experience of the product being made. Build-A-Bear is a good example of this lever.

This US cuddly toy company offers their clients – who are children – the unique experience of designing their own toy, step by step, in the shop. It's this experience that creates the value. The child chooses the type of animal (bear, dog, cat, cow, monkey, etc.), that is, the empty body of the animal which they'd like to assemble, and then a sound, one from a range of animal noises or a sound that they record themselves. The child then uses a pedal to fill the body with cotton stuffing – another personal engagement with the product. There follows the 'heart ceremony', where the child chooses a heart, rubs it against their body, and makes a vow before inserting it into the cuddly toy. After being sewn up, the toy is 'washed' using an air shower. The child then picks out some clothes for its new friend, before giving it a name that is printed on a birth certificate. Finally, the child is asked to make a 'pet's promise' that seals the bond with their new toy.

After a journey such as this, the value of the cuddly toy – both emotional and financial – is some distance from that of an identical toy in the same final condition. It's the experience, more than the product itself, which creates the value. The use of commitment and creation levers – and the corresponding emotions – are therefore central to both the positioning and to the product offer.

Creating a default use that boosts sales: fruit compote in a pouch

When it comes to changing people's behavior, the 'default' mechanism often wields the most potential power. It allows you to make a long-standing suggestion about a behavior, without having to convince your target of specific repeatable actions. You don't have to hope for voluntary change, and there is no additional will involved on the part of the client.

Before the 1998 launch of Maternes de Pom'Potes, the French fruit compote market was practically dead. However, the new snack pouch packaging generated a fresh wave of enthusiasm for the product.

The former industrial-looking tin was replaced with playful, modern packaging that gave the product a completely new image and implicitly suggested a much more frequent usage. The pouch design is both modern, easy to hold in your hand, and lets you eat it on the move – anytime, anywhere.

What's more, the pouch is generally stored in the fridge. This increases visual contact – salience – and means the product is more likely to be eaten, given that the fridge is opened very frequently. The tin, however, suggested the opposite. It recalled images of an industrial product, difficult to open, that had to be eaten on a plate and was generally kept at the back of a cupboard. The pouch packaging hence acts as a permanent encouragement – by default – to consume.

At the end of 2013, five million French households bought Pom'Potes[3] – a 50% market share, with 27,000 tons of pouches being sold. So try to think of possible default options for your offer. It may well be that there's an alternative – your own take on the fruit compote pouch – that will revolutionize the market.

Creating a favourable price anchor: Steve Jobs and the launch of the iPad

At the iPad launch meeting, Steve Jobs made wonderful use of the anchor mechanism to make people believe that the high price of his new product was perfectly acceptable. How did he do it? Let's take another look at his brilliant presentation.

---

3. Panel Kantar, 2013, and the Nielsen panel, December 2013.

As was his way, the Apple founder turned up in his famous jeans and black jumper. At the end of the presentation, he asked his audience, 'What should we price it at? If you listen to the pundits, we're going to price it at under 1,000 dollars. Which is code for 999 dollars.' Next, Jobs put a giant 999 dollars up on the screen. He left it there long enough to sink into the minds of everybody present, while the tension in the room crept up. Then he said, 'I am thrilled to announce to you that the iPad pricing starts not a 999 dollars but at just 499 dollars.' Then, the screen showed the 999 dollars being crushed by a falling 499! And finally, the various different iPad prices were displayed.

The brilliant Jobs had just made use of anchoring. He created a virtual anchor – 999 dollars – which acted as a reference point and made the iPad's price range appear cheap in comparison... to a price that had never existed.

The important thing to take away from this is that the same price can be perceived differently according to the way it is presented.

Play on their emotions: the Evian babies

The year 1998 saw the first instalment of what would become the 'Evian babies' advertising saga. In this short movie, the babies dive gleefully into a swimming pool and give an astonishing demonstration of synchronized swimming. Ten years later, the success continued with the 'Roller babies' commercial, seen over 60 million times on YouTube, and then again with the current 'Spiderman' campaign.

The advertising idea is based on the emotion generated by using babies, as well as the quirkiness of the scenes and the power of their humorous content. The writers' great achievement is to use emotion in a way that benefits both the brand and the product itself. The emotion is not artificially tacked onto the brand, which would risk it having no association and no potential spillover. It is also a means of communicating the 'live young' concept. The clear, strong message is that water is the stuff of life, and growth, and that drinking Evian will help you to 'live young'. There may be a link with the product, but Evian is not being sold directly. Rather, it's the concept – an idea that transcends the drink itself. And it's this concept that gives Evian an edge in a market where product differentiation is difficult to communicate, even though the gap in price between this and the cheapest brands is more than 50%!

Keeping it simple to encourage action: one-click buying on Amazon

When dealing with System 1 consumers, any idea that makes things simpler is welcome. As you no doubt recall, we humans hate making an effort. Which means that by making life easier for your client or consumer, you make them more inclined to act as you would like.

Amazon understood this very well in creating one-click buying.

No longer any need to enter your personal information and address to receive the product. No bank details required. While neither of these processes requires much time, they are still cumbersome enough to discourage certain buyers from acting. One-click buying maximizes the transition from desire into action. One tap on the mouse, and the product is yours. What better way to encourage people to make impulse purchases?

Let people try things to create a feeling of possession: Warby Parker's five-day trials

Warby Parker is an online company that sells glasses. Beyond the models that it offers, it has a unique business proposition: '5 pairs. 5 days. 100% free'. It's a trial offer that allows you to pick five pairs of glasses from the site and try them out at home. For free, of course.

Warby Parker thus combine two levers that we know to be extremely powerful: loss aversion and possession valorization. The trial period creates a feeling of possession towards the glasses, while the idea of not being able to keep them generates a feeling of loss.

Once again, the products' competitiveness is strengthened by creating a choice architecture that encourages potential clients to take the leap from intention into action.

Strengthening belief using social norms: Tripadvisor peer reviews and the P&G authority figure

As described in stage one, brands can activate the social norms lever far upstream of the relationship with the consumer. And this mechanism can be equally effective in the final phase of the transition from intention into action. When there's hesitation, social norms are a good way of convincing people of the soundness of their choice.

This is the lever that booking.com uses in placing such strong emphasis on user ratings for the hotels that they offer.

Potential travellers consider peer ratings to be extremely useful. These are people they identify with, whose appraisals they believe are honest and not linked to the company (whose business they are in fact promoting). The challenge for all those sites that rely on client feedback is hence to assure people of their honesty. To do this, booking.com makes special reference to its 'honest feedback'.

Once again, it's interesting to think of ways this lever could be used to convince people to stop thinking and start acting.

Proctor & Gamble also play on social norms. For the launch of their new toothbrush, the 'Oral-B Trizone Power Brush', they use the authority figure lever. Their advertising pack concludes with the following line, 'Number 1 toothbrush brand recommended by dentists worldwide'.

Clearly, dentists are a highly relevant authority figure when it comes to toothbrushes. As well as several different product benefits stressed by the advert, the reference to the dentists' support for the brand can only strengthen the offer's credibility. And hence push clients into action.

Phase 5: solidify the change and make the behavior more widespread by forming habits and encouraging social contagion

Eureka! Your product or service has made its first sale! It was difficult, but you got there in the end. You succeeded in generating the desired change in behavior. But without sustainable foundations, this initial success will float away like petals on a breeze. This is why phase five is so important. It's both the end and the beginning of the process. Like a relay baton passed between two athletes: if it touches the ground, you're out of the race.

All markets contain the same non-negotiable imperative: customers' experience of your product or service must be *at least* as great as the expectations that you have created. So after this first sale, you have to solidify the burgeoning relationship. If possible, you should also encourage social contagion to build on your success.

Solidify relationships by giving the client a magical experience and creating habits

Of course, at the heart of the client experience is a product or service whose inherent qualities are a priority. There is no client satisfaction if a company can't meet the basic expectations that it generates with actions carried out in the preceding phases.

This said, behavioral economics brings three additional elements in the pursuit of this elusive of 'magic touch':

- ◆ the importance of everything other than the product, from small, peripheral details to the sense of overall appreciation;

- the importance of two key moments: the 'peaks' and the 'end' in the client's perception of the overall experience;
- habit creation, which is crucial.

A key factor in being highly successful is the ability to create habits.

First of all, a product's inherent qualities aren't everything. In terms of overall perception, the product experience is coloured more or less strongly by everything around it. Once a product has been defined, it is hence worth paying special attention to the way it we give it value. This value comes from classical elements including branding, presentation or packaging, 'food shape' in the case of edible goods, or website design if you're selling things online. When it comes to the client experience, it all counts. Would the iPhone have been so successful based only on its technical features, without the aesthetic aspect – that is, the smartphone itself, the box that it comes in, its accessories and its user guide? If you want give clients a little bit of magic, you have to think about the big picture.

This leads me to the second point: the perception of an experience's quality follows specific rules that are often very different to those you might image. The 'peaks' and the 'end' of an experience play a major role in our overall perception of it. This rule was first discovered by Daniel Kahneman and a team of researchers as a part of their studies into the perception of pain[4] in a medical setting.[5] The findings were later confirmed as having a broader application, and they could be adapted to aid our understanding of other areas, such as our

4. Barbara L. Fredrickson and Daniel Kahneman, 'Duration Neglect in Retrospective Evaluations of Affective Episodes', *Journal of Personality and Social Psychology*, vol. 65, n° 1, July 1993, p. 45-55.
5. Barbara L. Fredrickson, Daniel Kahneman, Donald A. Redelmeier and Charles A. Schreiber, 'When More Pain Is Preferred to Less: Adding a Better End', *Psychological Science*, vol. 4, n° 6, November 1993, p. 401-405.

perceptions of package holidays.[6] The overall perception of an experience is not the result of a mathematical equation involving all constituent parts. If a client experiences 'peaks' – specific positive or negative moments – and if the end is memorable, these moments play a key role in their overall perception. Otherwise put, it can be very profitable for 'experience architects' to ensure key elements in the client experience – such as the end – generate the emotional peaks that have an important bearing on the overall positive perception.

The third point is without doubt the most important. How can we create habits that generate the purchasing frequency or sense of indispensability that lead to sustainable success?

To create habitual behavior, we have to consider the final reward that makes someone take up and continue a habit, as well as the trigger mechanism involved. Of course, the basis of the reward should be the benefit offered by your product or service. The benefit itself should be viewed as something that can be incorporated into habitual behavior. However, not all products can do this. Far from it, in fact. We therefore have to consider the specific actions that can lead to these habits being developed. And this is where the trigger comes in: How can you create a habit trigger that will increase the success of your product?

In his excellent book, *Hooked*,[7] Nir Eyal sets out the following main types of trigger:

◆ 'external' triggers that come from the environment, such as seeing an ice cold Coke on the side of a vending machine;
◆ 'internal' triggers, which come into our heads through association with a particular moment, behavior or emotion.

---

6. Christopher D. B. Burt, Laura Furneaux and Simon Kemp, 'A Test of the Peak-End Rule with Extended Autobiographical Events', *Memory & Cognition*, vol. 36, n° 1, January 2008, p. 132-138.
7. Nir Eyal with Ryan Hoover, *Hooked: How to Build Habit-Forming Products*, Portfolio, 2014.

For example, at 8 p.m. you get the urge for a cocktail. Or if you're watching football on TV with friends, a cold beer seems like just the thing.

External triggers contribute to making us think about a product. However, they also contain one major drawback: they generally cost a lot of money. The ultimate goal is hence to create internal triggers, which are free. And this is a real challenge. Many companies try, and few succeed, as people's life experiences are not the same.

The Nudge marketer has to find ways of building these habits by focusing on the following four elements:

- the capacity to mentally associate the product or service, as strongly as possible, with a powerful need in the target;
- the creation of an internal or external trigger that provides a regular reminder of both the need and the associated product;
- a solution that the user finds easy to implement;
- a reward contained in the client experience that meets expectations.

This satisfaction can lead to social contagion, giving added momentum to a product's initial success.

Generating social contagion

Contrary to what you might believe, social contagion – the capacity to benefit from powerful physical or digital word of mouth – has nothing to do with chance or luck. Neither is it the result of a product or service's high quality, exceptional price, or brilliant advertising. As the Wharton professor Jonah Berger demonstrates in his inspirational book *Contagious*,[8]

---

8. Jonah Berger, *Contagious: Why Things Catch On*, Simon & Schuster, 2013.

there is a set of rules to follow if you want to profit from this potent lever.

Word of mouth is a hugely important lever – not only since the arrival of the internet. In a study[9]examining the conversations of a representative sample of Americans, the authors calculated that brands were mentioned more than three billion times every day in the course of a few hundred million conversations.

These conversations contribute to consumers' choices and decisions. According to the *McKinsey Quarterly,*[10] 'word of mouth is the primary factor behind 20 to 50 percent of all purchasing decisions'. And herein lies the power of the social lever. There are two features of these exchanges that make them so important and convincing. First, the information is believable. When a friend recommends a restaurant, a movie, a brand of shampoo or a website, you believe them. And the reason is that generally, you trust their opinion. Of course, this isn't the case for every type of brand-related communication. Consumers' critical faculties are not always so fully engaged. But word of mouth's great strength comes from the fact that it is ultra-focused on the target. You only talk about a subject with a friend, colleague, or family member if you think that it will interest them. The intimate knowledge that we have of those close to us means that these conversations are perfectly targeted. And of course, their effectiveness is far greater than any advertising communication, which could never achieve the same level of precision.

---

9.   Ed Kerrer and Barak Libai, 'A Holistic Approach of the Measurement of WOM: Its Impact on Consumer's Decisions', ESOMAR *World Wide Media Measurement,* 5th May 2009.

10. Jacques Bughin, Jonathan Doogan and Ole Jørgen Vetvik, 'A New Way to Measure Word-of-Mouth Marketing', *McKinsey Quarterly,* April 2010 : www.mckinsey.com/insights/marketing_sales/a_new_way_to_measure_word-of mouth_marketing#

Word of mouth is hence an extremely powerful and efficient tool. Jonah Berger's efforts to understand it have led him to a methodology, the use of which will increase your chances of profiting from this crucial lever. The method comes from the systematic analysis of products, brands, YouTube clips, and other places that have seen the benefits of 'good buzz'. It is based on the following basic question, 'What rules do these social contagion success stories all obey?' Berger goes on to identify six general principles, which are summarized – once again – by an acronym, STEPPS:

- Social Currency
- Triggers
- Emotion
- Public
- Practical value
- Story

The first principle, social currency, returns to an area already covered at some length in these pages: the importance of social factors in our decisions and behavior. In all of our social actions, we seek the reflection of a positive self-image. This impulse is related to the ego and to the desire for recognition. And this is also what we're in pursuit of when it comes to word of mouth – an important form of social interaction. We're sharing information that we believe will make other people – especially our loved ones – think more highly of us. This is what Berger calls 'social currency'. A subject conforms to the image that we want to project of ourselves – consciously or otherwise. And this is what makes us want to share. It is the basis of all social contagion.

The second principle is identical to the one described previously regarding habits. That is, a trigger. To benefit from word of mouth, we must be able to translate it into action. Berger cites the wonderful case of a restaurant in Philadelphia called Barclay Prime, whose 100-dollar cheesesteak created such a buzz. While lots of restaurants serve this traditional dish for no more than a few dollars, Barclay Prime offers something different. Theirs is a high-end gastronomic experience involving a homemade brioche roll squirted with homemade mustard, thinly sliced Kobe beef, caramelized onions, peeled tomatoes and a triple cream of Taleggio cheese, topped off with black truffles and Maine lobster-tail butter. The dish has become a symbol of the restaurant's quality. It has also benefitted from a magnificent trigger: the presence of so many adverts for Philadelphia cheesesteak. Every time someone comes across this type of restaurant, it triggers the association with Barclay Prime and its famous 100-dollar meal!

The third principle, emotion, is another of the big levers that we looked at previously. We share things that touch us or which we find moving. Look at the amount of videos and photos of ill-treated animals on Facebook. The number of humorous photos on Instagram. The YouTube clips of songs that tug at our heartstrings. When a subject touches us, we have the urge to share that emotion. As we saw with little Rokia, emotion is a fundamental lever governing human behavior. And it is also a powerful driver when it comes to word of mouth.

The fourth principle, the public, is somewhat technical. To create word of mouth, a person must find it easy to make their thoughts public and have the urge to communicate their experiences. An image, a video clip, a story in a few words… these are the types of things that make us want to share. Complex issues are far less suited to this kind of interaction.

The fifth principle, practical value, relies on altruism – another powerful driver. We like helping others. And we like showing others that we like it even more. We share information that we believe they will find useful. This is particularly true in the case of our loved ones. The practical value of a piece of information is hence a potentially important driver for word of mouth. The greater the perceived social utility of the information, the stronger our desire to share it with others who may find it important.

Johan Berger's sixth and final principle, story, is a classic element of all types of communication. We don't share facts. However, we like sharing stories that other people find interesting and which capture their imagination. If possible, we prefer these stories to be short and colourful, as these are the easiest to impart.

Berger also states that you don't need all six of these principles to generate buzz. Emotion and practical value, for instance, can work in competition with one another. However, each of the levers, used individually, still have the same capacity to trigger word of mouth.

To conclude, the main lesson to take away is that it is possible to design a product or a marketing action with this set of rules is mind. Doing so gives us the best chance to profit from the well-known, ultra-powerful lever that is social contagion.

17

Predictive testing

Context, behavior and timing

So there it is: you've designed an action that seems genuinely relevant, one that is anchored in a real understanding of the client or user's experience and based on a powerful lever. Now, the time has come to test it. However, two major pitfalls may hamper the method selected by either you or your chosen specialist and they are context, and timing.

Choose your context badly and you'll end up with a weak evaluation

The first of these pitfalls comes from a simple but important idea, which Dan Ariely expresses perfectly: 'Most people don't know what they want unless they see it in context.' Any environmental difference between the test conditions and the real-life context of a choice will by definition modify the eventual decision.

I would like to illustrate the seriousness of this pitfall using a real-life example. The case involved updating a merchandising implementation. It required travelling to the United Kingdom on behalf of a multinational drinks company. And the challenge was simple. The client's marketing and merchandizing teams thought that the supermarket layout of non-alcoholic drinks seemed out of date. The products were segmented mainly according to 'producer' categories, as follows:

◆ water;
◆ juice and adults;
◆ fizzy;
◆ sports and energy.

The basic idea was hence to rework the merchandizing organization so that it resembled a more modern segmentation based on shoppers' perceptions. Drawing on information gained from consumer focus groups, we swapped this 'producer' segmentation for something more conceptual. The new arrangement involved the following sections:

◆ a 'leisure time' section for sports and energy drinks;
◆ an 'busy lives' section for flavoured water, squash, and drinks to accompany lunch boxes;
◆ an 'everyday' section for waters, colas and fruit juices.

Since shoppers mentally arrange the drinks market in this way, we tried to present them with a merchandizing layout that matched their natural perception.

The two configurations were set up as shown below (see Figure 17.1).

The study we performed to test shoppers' reactions was simple enough. The following two groups of shoppers were presented with each of the configurations that we wanted to evaluate:

◆ the first 'control' group were given the current 'producer' configuration;
◆ the second 'test' group were given the new 'concept' configuration.

Flavoured water	Functional water / Table water	Still water	Sparkling water
	Water		
	Juice & Adult		
Squash	Sports and Energy Posh squash	Sports and Energy	Adult/ Mixer drinks
Lunch box	Lunch box	Other fizzy (cans)	Colas (cans)
	Cans & Lunchbox		
	Fizzy		
Fruit juice	Other fizzy (bottles 1.5L)	Colas (bottles 1.5L)	Colas (bottles 1.5L + packs)

Sports and Energy	Functional water / Sports and Energy	Posh squash / Table water	Adult/ Mixer drinks
	Leisure time		
	Busy-lives		
Flavoured water	Squash	Lunch box	Lunch box
Other fizzy (cans)	Other fizzy (bottles 1.5L)	Sparkling water	Still water
	Everyday		
Colas (bottles 1.5L)	Colas (bottles 1.5L + packs)	Colas (cans)	Fruit juice

Figure 17.1 The two merchandizing layouts for non-alcoholic drinks

The test protocol involved two distinct parts:

- first, participants from each group made an *in vivo* shopping trip in a test store containing a drinks aisle whose layout corresponded to their group;
- next, participants were questioned individually using a photo of the layout in which they had just done their shopping. Data was gathered about their perception and appreciation of the configuration in question.

The results for each group were as follows. When questioned about each of the layouts, participants had a clear preference for the 'concept' organization, which received better marks for the majority of items. The shelves were seen as clear and better organized. They could find the product they were looking for without difficulty. The level of appreciation for shopping in the drinks section was higher. Participants felt encouraged to buy a greater number of products. In short, the new organization scored better on all the important points. The shopping experience was more pleasant, potential purchases were higher, and there were no complications when it came to participants being able to find their regular products.

But what happened when the 'concept' configuration went live? Well, this was something of a surprise! Non-alcoholic drinks revenues dropped by more than 12% as a result of the new layout. The same layout, that is, which had received such rave reviews in the test phase.

How, then, to interpret these results that the shoppers themselves could not anticipate? The answer is fairly simple, and comes back to two fundamental principles of behavioral economics: simplicity and salience.

Simplicity, first of all. By creating a new 'everyday' section in which shoppers could find the drinks they consumed on a daily basis – colas, waters and fruit juice – their lives were made much easier. They no longer had to trawl through the various aisles to find the products they were looking for. Doing this, however, caused a salience problem for other, more marginal, products. The feature of marginal products is that shoppers do not automatically set out to buy them. The desire to purchase is triggered by the fact that they can be seen. Under the new configuration, sales of these products hence plummeted.

What this case illustrates, other than people's inability to anticipate their own behavior, is the role of situational factors in decisions and behavior. It is very difficult to come up with predictive indicators for future behavior by putting people in a study context that contrasts sharply with the real-life decision environment.

As highlighted and demonstrated by behavioral economists on so many occasions, situational factors have a strong influence on our behavior. It's a huge challenge for research institutions to pre-test marketing actions in a realistic environment, and to predict the actual behaviors that people will adopt. But it's a challenge that is also indispensable. Misconceived immersions can also be a siren song's, as we shall we in the following experiment[1] carried out by Professor Pierre Desmet of Paris-Dauphine University and a BVA IN VIVO team.

---

1. Pierre Desmet, Richard Bordenave et John Traynor, 'Differences in Purchasing Behaviour Between Physical and Virtual Laboratory Stores', *Recherche et applications en marketing*, vol. 2, n° 28, July 2013, p. 71-86.

The aim of this research was simply to compare the behavior of shoppers in a real physical environment – an *in vivo* experimental store – with their behavior in an identical virtual reality 3D space. The question they sought to answer was, 'Can a store that is virtually reconstructed using 3D technology produce natural behavior in shoppers?'

The product that we chose was coffee. The same coffee section was constructed both in a real-life experimental store, and in virtual reality. There was no noticeable difference between the way the reconstructions looked.

Two comparable groups of coffee buyers then did their shopping in one or other of the stores. One of the groups had a supermarket cart, the other tapped on a computer keyboard that allowed them to enter the store and virtually manipulate the products before making their choice.

And what were the results? Generally speaking, the shoppers behaved differently both in their decision-making process and when making their final decision. These differences were as follows:

- the average length of the purchase was around 15 seconds in the physical environment and over 35 seconds in the virtual environment;
- 39% of shoppers stated that they examined the price in the physical environment, as opposed to 10% in the virtual environment;
- in terms of brand visibility, two differences were observed:
  - shoppers in the virtual store saw more of their regular brands than other brands;
  - the visibility of different brands on the shelf was greater is in real environment.

- finally, the number of shoppers buying Carte Noire (the control brand for the study) was significantly greater in the virtual store than in the real store among buyers who regularly bought this brand. Conversely, in the real store, shoppers bought a higher number of competing brands.

The overall conclusion, confirming many similar behavioral economics findings, is clear: the environment in which a decision occurs is a highly influential factor. By changing the environment, we also change the decision-making process. It is therefore extremely presumptuous to imagine that we can predict consumers' real future behavior via a test where a new variable is evaluated in a 3D environment. In the present case, the differences in behavior can be explained by two main factors.

- ♦ Using the 3D interface to move around and pick up objects, as simple as it may appear, is different to the actions involved when shopping in a real store. Virtual reality requires that we mobilize some of our attentional resources, which translates to a choice process that is more focused on the products we habitually buy. Shoppers focus on what is simplest, as part of their attention is taken up by the virtual tool. This is why it takes them longer to make a purchase, why they see their favourite brands more often, and why they purchase these familiar brands more frequently.
- ♦ Also, shoppers are unable to use their five senses in a virtual reality environment. Feel, touch, smell and so on. As we know, emotions, which stem from all of our senses, are central to the decision-making process. In a virtual world, the choice is by definition different, as it only involves sight.

This isn't to say that virtual reality has no place in marketing. But it can be dangerous when the aim is to predict behavior in response to an action whose effects we want to test. Which leads me to another major pitfall awaiting pre-test methodologies. Its name, as stated previously, is time.

Given enough time, everybody understands

Time considerations are a fundamental aspect of decisions. Consciously or not, people adapt their decision-making logic according to the amount of time they give themselves (or which is given to them) for a decision. Different amounts of time lead to different logics, and, depending on the type of logic used, potentially different choices. Time is hence something that marketing actions have to take into account if their aim is to predict the consumer's final decision.

Below is a real-life study carried out a few years ago concerning the impact of this 'time' variable following a change in tea packaging.

The brand in question was a market leader, and its aim was to further strengthen its position by highlighting a new health benefit: the presence of antioxidants in its tea. The new packaging involved a green band with the words 'new selection', as well as a round 'AOX' insignia printed on the box.

Two equivalent samples of consumers were questioned to measure their purchasing intentions in regard to the two types of packaging. The first group was asked about the current packaging, and the second about the new 'AOX' packaging. Participants answered a 25-minute-long questionnaire about the box design. They were then asked to state their purchasing intentions. And the results were unequivocal: 34% had 'strong' purchasing intentions in the first case, and 54% in the second. The AOX insignia thus made the product significantly more attractive.

The interesting thing, however, was to observe what these same participants, faced with the same offers, actually bought. That is, the purchases they made *before* answering the questions. Here, the whole thing played out rather differently. In fact, 26% picked the current version from the shelf, while only 24% chose the tea with the new packaging. The AOX insignia hence led to a decrease in sales. As is often the case, participants think one thing and do another. Intention and behavior are different. So what happened in this case to make consumers act so differently to how they said they would? The reason isn't complicated. Purchases in the teabag market are made very quickly – often in less than 10 seconds. They are often made out of habit, especially in the case of a brand leader that is easily recognizable thanks to its powerful yellow colour. Simply, the presence of the green band and the AOX insignia changed the way the packaging was deciphered. This was confirmed by eye-tracking results.

For the original packaging, consumers mainly looked towards the centre of the box. That is, at the brand insignia and the name 'Yellow label tea'. For the new packaging, however, a significant number focused on the left-hand side. The green band, and its contrast with the dominant yellow, attracted their attention. And what should have been an advantage – the eye-catching benefits of AOX – became a huge problem as it brought the notorious 'time' variable into play. Since shoppers make decisions about teabags very quickly, they didn't take the time to read the information closely. The majority didn't get beyond perceiving the colour green. And what does this colour communicate when it comes to tea? Mint tea, or lime tea! The green band was meant to draw shoppers' attention to the new benefit. Viewed quickly, however, it misled them by evoking a different flavour, rather than their regular tea with an added benefit. So the number of buyers decreased, even though their purchasing intentions showed that the initial idea was sound. The fact that consumers don't take the time to process information – be it packaging or any other type of communication – is a crucial point that should be factored into any research protocol. If not, there is a real risk of incorrectly predicting the reality of consumers' behavior. The vast majority of traditional research techniques give participants time to think – too much of it, in fact – before coming up with a response. This applies to both qualitative groups and quantitative studies based on questionnaires relating to new product concepts where everything is described on the packaging, as in the case outlined above.

The challenge is therefore to come up with research protocols that allow us to understand people's initial, spontaneous reactions to the planned marketing action.

Taking the lead from behavioral economics, we can say that studies aiming to reliably anticipate consumer behavior should employ a methodology that seeks to:

- observe people's decision-making behavior in a natural context, or in an environment that represents it with a high degree of realism;
- include a timeframe for processing information that corresponds to that used in real life. If a participant takes only a few seconds to examine a product's packaging before deciding, then don't give them half a minute.

You now have everything you need to design effective strategies for producing behavioral change. Use them wisely. That is, to achieve sustainable growth for your company by building trusting relationships with your clients via product offers that match their expectations and contribute to their well-being, both now and in the future.

Conclusion

By way of conclusion, I'd like to do the following:

◆ recap the three main ideas behind the effective design and implementation of actions leading to behavioral change;

◆ consider some ethical questions raised by the Nudge approach;

◆ make two suggestions for increasing Nudge's use in French public policy.

The three things to remember if you want to change people's behavior

The first of these is the most important. We are not superhuman beings who, faced with any given choice, perform a rational analysis of all available information to identify the option that maximizes our selfish interest, before acting in a way that achieves a clearly defined objective. On the contrary, we make logical errors – including those times when we are actively pursuing our best interests. We use mental shortcuts to spare our attentional resources. We are influenced by the image that we want other people to have of us. By what these others do and think. By the emotions that we feel. By the way that different choice options are presented to us. And by the situation or the environment in which we find ourselves at the time of taking a decision. We act quickly, automatically, intuitively, out of habit, and without thinking about things very deeply.

All in all, we act more with our heart than with our head, with more regard for others than ourselves, and in close interaction with our environment. Human decisions and behavior are hence the result of a complex interplay between a range of internal and external influences. Behind this complexity, however, there are still a set of operating rules. Our 'irrationality' is not chaotic. Conversely, research carried out by behavioral economists, as well as actions implemented by Nudge practitioners, have shown that it can be understood, anticipated, and integrated into effective plans to achieve the desired changes in behavior.

The drivers of influence checklist (see Table 13.2) is aimed at helping practitioners by giving them a means to systematically review the main factors influencing behavior.

My first suggestion is that you use this checklist to identify one or several levers that might increase the effectiveness of the action that you plan to implement. By taking this rigorous, systematic approach, you can ensure that you don't overlook a potentially powerful lever.

My second suggestion concerns your understanding of the behavior that you would like to change. Good levers don't exist in a vacuum. Rather, levers are more or less relevant depending on the given situation. And a detailed understanding of this situation is a prerequisite for any effective action. A concise analysis of the decision pathway, particularly the whole range of explicit and implicit obstacles to the adoption of the new behavior, is required to identify the most appropriate levers, to remove associated obstacles, and to activate the desired change. Effectiveness is rooted in our understanding of the user, consumer, client, or citizen's behavior. And this understanding should not be limited to people's explanations of their own behavior. Rather, it should be based on a combination of approaches, an essential one of which is ethnographic observation. Identifying the role of a whole host of unconscious factors means being able to get beyond the words that people use. The important thing to remember here, then, is to begin each Nudge initiative with a deep understanding of the behavior in question.

My third suggestion concerns the way that Nudges are evaluated prior to deployment. Nudge is a fiercely scientific discipline. First of all, we have to arrive at a scientific understanding of the factors influencing behavior. But we also have to scientifically evaluate the impact of the planned actions on the way that people act. This is a very important point for public policy, as it involves testing the Nudges before applying them to ensure both the soundness of their design and their effectiveness. It's a basic reversal of logic – particularly in France – which places pragmatism over ideology. We design, we test, and then we deploy. It's a three-step process, rather than the simple, direct application of an ideological plan. To achieve our goal means battling the three Is – 'ideology', 'ignorance' and 'inertia' – denounced by Esther Duflo[1] as the major obstacles to effectiveness in public policy. A crucial aspect of this is the scientific, rigorous evaluation of our Nudges. That is, measuring people's actual behavior – and their intentions – in a real-life situation, with a control group acting as a reference point, and test groups to isolate the effects of each Nudge being assessed. This is the third key point for the implementation of a successful behavioral change strategy. However, effectiveness isn't everything – not even for Nudges. Ethical considerations are also at the heart of any new initiatives.

Nudge and Ethics

The Nudge approach has a precise goal: to encourage people to change their behavior. And this raises a legitimate question regarding ethics and manipulation. This is especially the case

---

1. Esther Duflo, in 'Le Grand Jury RTL, *Le Monde*, iTélé' [The Grand Jury: RTL, *Le Monde* and iTelevision], 4th January 2015.

when the mechanisms take effect at an unconscious level. For instance, the use of default options in choice architecture.

Following the publication of their book, Richard Thaler and Cass Sunstein were subjected to some heavy questioning about the ethics of their approach. And when the Obama administration made it known that it planned to install Sunstein at the head of OIRA, some leading figures in the Republican party went all out against what they termed the 'regulatory Tsar'. In a chapter entitled 'The most dangerous man in America', Sunstein describes[2] the extent to which he had to fight in order to be able to do his job: a monster of manipulation was about to destroy American democracy. Of course, reactions such as these were the minority. But they refer to a valid debate that should not be avoided, and which Sunstein and Thaler were in fact the first to raise.[3]

Yes, the Nudge approach tries to influence people's behavior. And yes, it uses unconscious drivers, not only as a means of gaining active acceptance. For me, however, the approach is both legitimate and more importantly useful. *If*, that is, the two fundamental rules that I will outline in a moment are adhered to. And as long as ethical evaluation is conducted in a specific, pragmatic – rather than a generalized, theoretical – fashion.

First of all, the Nudge approach is only acceptable if the following two key elements are respected:

- ◆ ongoing freedom of choice;
- ◆ the individual or collective benefits linked to the desired behavior.

---

2. Cass Sunstein, *Simpler: The Future of Government*, Simon & Schuster, 2013.

3. Richard Thaler and Cass Sunstein (2010), *op. cit.*, chapter 'Objections', p. 225; Cass Sunstein, 'The Ethics of Nudging', *Social Science Research Network*, 20th November 2014; *Why Nudge? The Politics of Libertarian Paternalism*, Yale University Press, 2014.

The first of these is an important point, as it differentiates the Nudge approach from the law. Nudge leaves people the freedom to choose. There is no reduction or modification of the available choice options. The only changes are those relating to the work done on choice architecture. You don't have to sign up to the NHS organ donation programme, even it says that 'thousands of people' have done so. You don't have to buy a single can of Campbell's soup, even if the buying limit is set at 12. You can print that document in colour, even if the default on your printer is set to black and white. In short, Nudge undertakes to steer people towards the right choice, while insisting on the fact that complete freedom of action is preserved. The only real Nudges are those which respect this freedom – a principle that lies right at the heart of the approach's ethos.

The second point is equally important. As highlighted by the sub-title to Thaler and Sunstein's book in its French edition, Nudge seeks to 'inspire the right decision'. This is the ultimate justification for the approach. That is, to make it so that the decisions we take are indisputably better for ourselves, for our communities, or for the planet. For many of our individual challenges, it's just a question of a helping hand with the transition from intention into action. I'd like to lose weight, but I can't seem to manage it. I'd like to do more exercise to be healthier and live longer. I'd like to save more money to give myself a more comfortable retirement. I'd like to be more ecologically responsible to increase the chances of the planet being left in a better state for future generations. When the Nudge approach helps people take good decisions from their own perspective – that is, decisions aimed at things which they themselves desire – then ethics is not an issue.

When there is a collective benefit to the behavior being encouraged, then the ethical question refers to the legitimacy of the public authority. Who is responsible for defining the 'right' target behavior? Here, my own opinion is that a democratically elected government can legitimately make this definition. As long as the actions' objectives are clearly and publicly announced, I don't see why the Nudge approach should be any less ethical than the government's right to draw up laws whose aim is equally to modify behavior. If the goal is to reduce tobacco consumption, why should a law banning smoking in public places be ethical, but not an advertising message that uses a Nudge lever to increase the desired effectiveness? If the end-point really is the common good, if the power being exercised is democratic, and if the objective has been clearly announced, then it follows that the Nudge approach is ethical.

The question of interest is trickier in the case of private enterprise. Here, the 'social purpose' is not the well-being of the community, but the pursuit of profitable growth. While this has undeniably positive consequences for the community, such as providing jobs and contributing to the country's economic performance, it is nevertheless true that the desire for profit lies at the heart of corporate strategies and decisions.

So can the Nudge approach help businesses influence behavior, with their clients or prospects as the beneficiaries? My answer is based on the following two points:

My heartfelt belief is that a business whose goal is sustainable, can only achieve year-on-year growth by building strong, trusting relations with their clients, based on products or offers that live up to expectations. If, as a consumer, you have bought a product that's not right for you, will you not buy it again and your image of the company will be damaged. As well as this, there's a risk that you will give the product and the company negative publicity (we have seen the power of word of mouth). Of course, as for all marketing in a general sense, the Nudge approach can cause the consumer to be 'tricked' from time to time; but not in a sustainable manner. I know of no long-term success story based on products that don't deliver the expected benefits to the consumer. Short-term planning that involves actions that run contrary to clients' interest is a sure-fire way to medium-term collapse. Especially in these times when consumers can make their dissatisfaction known so easily via everybody's favourite bullhorn: the internet.

In my opinion, this belief is shared by the vast majority of international business executives. They know that the only way to build solid, sustainable growth is to take account of consumers' long-term interests. I believe, therefore, in the ethical use of the Nudge approach, including its application to the world of private enterprise. The self-regulation of the market is guaranteed both by the consumers themselves and by companies who understand the fatal consequences linked to tricking the consumer.

It's true that this reasoning is limited by people's capacity to identify their own interests. If they're not capable of this, then self-regulation by the market will be either bad or non-existent. Cigarettes are an example of this problem: the pleasure of smoking outstrips the risk, however well known the reduction in life expectancy caused by the behavior. Since the benefit is immediate and the risks are more or less distant, a good number of people continue to smoke. In such instances, it's for the public authorities to intervene via the law and other means at their disposal. Their job is to make citizens informed and encourage them to adopt the right behavior.

It's my opinion that the ethics of the Nudge approach for private enterprise are guaranteed by both the companies' own interests and the consumers' behavior. However, public authorities must remain in a state of constant alert to possible abuses, and legislate against them when necessary.

Rather than discuss the ethics of Nudge in a general sense, I think it's more fruitful to examine the question on a pragmatic level. That is, in terms of how these Nudges are produced. To consider Nudge's acceptability not in a vacuum, but relative to planned ideas for a given challenge. Specifically, this means that I suggest including – just as we do in the NudgeLab – an ethical checklist that considers the following:

- ◆ At the start of the process, do the project team responsible for the issue raised by the client consider the Nudge approach to be an ethical way of encouraging citizens or clients to adopt the desired behavior? In the case of organ donation or using the phone while driving the answer seems clear. But there are other times it may be less so.
- ◆ Following the Nudge creation phase, there should be an evaluation phase in which ethics of each idea is put under the microscope. Certain default mechanisms – for instance, making the non-default option too long or complicated – might twist the target's arm in such a way that freedom of choice is no longer guaranteed.

Rather than keeping ethics at a theoretical arm's length, it seems far better to me that it stays central to the creation and evaluation of Nudges. This will guarantee that a vital dimension of the process will be genuinely taken into account. To reject Nudge out of hand for ethical reasons seems both impossible to do, as well as making no sense in respect to the approach's fundamental utility.

How do you implement the Nudge approach in France?

It's this social utility that motivates my commitment to bringing Nudge's effectiveness[4] to the big issues currently facing public policy.

---

4.   It is with this mindset that I have funded the change tank Nudge-France – that you're very welcome to join – with my friends and experts on the subject, Françoise Waintrop, Alberto Alemanno, Richard Bordenave, Étienne Bressoud and Olivier Oullier.

I would like to see the Nudge approach being systematically used in my own country. Of course, this would be complementary to all the other resources that the public authorities have at their disposal. It's about adding to, rather than replacing the range of current interventions such as the law, financial incentives, and the spread of information. As we have seen via the many examples in this book, this complementary approach can have a significant impact on effectiveness, at no extra cost. Using the levers of change identified by behavioral economists, along with the rigorous evaluation of their likely impact prior to deployment, would be a major asset to the effectiveness of French public policy.

So how to make it happen? This comes down to a question of political will, as the technical solutions are simple, and could include the following:

- the creation of a 'Nudge Unit' in France, called something like the 'Behavioral Science Unit';
- a training programme for high-level officials and public decision makers.

The first thing would be to set up a 'Nudge Unit' similar to the one in the United Kingdom. Working in close contact with the bodies responsible for public policy (regions, city halls, etc.), the unit's task would be to help the reinforcement of public policies' efficacy, using the Nudge approach as well as knowledge gleaned from behavioral science. The unit would comprise a multidisciplinary team, including specialists in behavioral economics, experimental economics, behavioral psychology, ethnography, decision neuroscience, statistics, modelling, design, communication, marketing, and big data. It would be made up of people with different yet complementary profiles. These would include high-level officials with an intricate knowledge of the French administration system, professors specializing in the disciplines mentioned above, and Nudge practitioners.

The unit could be operated under the direction of the Prime Minister's office. This would both legitimize it in the eyes of other ministries, as well as allowing it to work on their behalf. The Secretary General for the Modernization of Public Actions (SGMAP), which carried out the first Nudge experiments in France, could incorporate a team like this. Equally, a stand-alone team affiliated to the Prime Minister and working on behalf of SGMAP may result in greater visibility and autonomy. The creation of smaller Nudge Units within each ministry, or a state-owned agency run independently of the government, might also be possible. But it's not so much about the legal form or the positioning. Rather, it's a question of setting up the unit so that Nudge can progress from the ad hoc status that it currently enjoys in France towards a systematic usage, allowing public policy to reap the full benefits of the potential increase in effectiveness. That is, to make the shift from craftsmanship to the type of industrial status that would be of great service to our country.

Aside from its operating budget, the Nudge team should receive sufficient financial support to be able to include a working network of communication agencies, marketing and opinion studies, data processing, and specialists in the necessary fields (nutrition, the environment, energy, etc.). Financing would also extend to the evaluation tests that lie at the heart of the approach. It may cost a few dozen million euros to set up this remarkable effectiveness lever, steering people towards the desired behavior, but in the end, it could save a few hundred million.

The group's effectiveness should of course be monitored. The reason for its existence, and the yardstick that lies at the heart of the whole operation, is simply this: How much does it cost? And how much does it bring in?

As well as this first mission, the Behavioral Sciences Unit should have a second, equally important function concerning the training of high-level officials and public policy decision makers. It's a question of making the approach known to those liable to use it, both now and in the future. In the case of current decision makers, this training would be carried out via conferences involving specific examples of Nudge's real-life application to public policy. There would also be simple, easy-to-use presentation guides, or a website, for practitioners to share their experiences. As for any training plan, this would involve defining a target audience – public decision makers – and creating conditions to inform them about the Nudge approach, even on a very small scale. We might think of this as 'nudging the Nudge', if you will. That is, examining the needs and constraints of the target and designing training programmes that are as attractive and stimulating as possible.

It would also be a good idea to train the high-level officials of the future. This could involve making Nudge a part of ENA or Sciences Po students' knowledge base. They could then incorporate the approach into the various issues that they face as they go about their daily work.

It seems to me that a Behavioral Sciences Unit and its two functions would be easy to implement. Since the basic mechanism is the lever effect, there is huge potential for improving the ROI of French public policy.

Of course, its success would be dependent on certain key factors. In my eyes, the following three are the most important:

♦ Political will in high-level government to get the process off the ground. That is, the will to set up a French Nudge Unit. And also, even more importantly, to give it the necessary support during its first two years. This support would call for both the validation of the group and its role, as well as its systematic use for important issues, working in partnership with government ministers. For any change process, support for the new entity, be it a government or a private company, should be total, in order to break established habits. After two years, this support should be less necessary, as the Nudge Unit will have proven itself through its results. And if not, then it would end up being disbanded.

♦ The quality and enthusiasm of the members of the Nudge Unit are also key. The team should be able to both design genuinely powerful Nudge actions, as well as communicate their belief in the new approach to those without whom it would not exist. The team therefore must be experts in behavioral change, and able to design and implement effective strategies. They should also be brilliant communicators with a strong belief in what they're doing, to generate contagion and make others want to use their services.

♦ The French administration should also demonstrate their open-mindedness in saying 'yes' to change. Nudge is a revolutionary approach that challenges many of our basic beliefs. Its success in France would only be possible if high-level officials were fully on board. That is, they should leave preconceived ideas and habits at the door, and become open to innovation. I must say that the last two years I have spent amongst these people have convinced me this is possible.

Times of crisis can equally be a time for change and the birth of new ideas. That's all that I want for my country, and I'd like to lend whatever skills I have by way of contribution. I hope to have convinced you, over the course of this book, that Nudge can offer a solution.

Please don't hesitate to fan the fires of the debate by joining the change tank NudgeFrance via my twitter account (@ thobava, on LinkedIn or via email eric.singler@bva.fr).

Bibliography

I have chosen only to list the main books I have used, the research articles are quoted throughout the book.

Acemoglu, D. and Robinson J. (2012), *Why Nations Fail*, Crown Business

Akerlof , G. and Shiller R. (2009), *Animal Spirits*, Princeton University Press

Andler, D. (2004), *Introduction aux sciences cognitives*, Gallimard

Augier, M. and March J. (2004), *Models of a Man*, MIT Press

Ariely, D. (2012), *The (Honest) Truth about Dishonesty*, HarperCollins Publishers

Ariely, D. (2010), *The Upside of Irrationality*, HarperCollins Publishers

Ariely, D. (2008), *Predictably Irrational*, Harper Perennial

Ariely, D., Hreha, J. and Berman, K. (2014), *Hacking Human Nature for Good*, Irrational Labs

Behavioural Insights Team (2013), *Organ Donor Registrations: Trialling Different Approaches*

Behavioural Insights Team (2013), *Applying Behavioural Insights to Charitable Giving*

Behavioural Insights Team (2012), *EAST: Four Simple Ways to Apply Behavioural Insights*, Cabinet Office

Behavioural Insights Team (2012), *Test, Learn, Adapt: Developing Public Policy with Randomised Controlled Trials*, Cabinet Office

Behavioural Insights Team (2012), *Fraud, Error and Debt: Behavioural Insights Team Paper*, Cabinet Office

Behavioural Insights Team (2011), *Behaviour Change and Energy Use: Behavioural Insights Team Paper*, Cabinet Office

Behavioural Insights Team (2011), *Helping Consumers Make Better Choices and Better Deals*, Cabinet Office

Behavioural Insights Team (2010), *Applying Behavioural Insight to Health: Behavioural Insights Team Paper*, Cabinet Office

Banerjee, A. and Duflo, E. (2011), *Poor economics: A Radical Rethinking of the Way to Fight Global Poverty*, PublicAffairs

Barden, P. (2013), *Decoded: The Science Behind Why We Buy*, John Wiley & Sons

Bardleys, N., Cubitt, R., Lommes, G., Moffatt, P., Starmer, C. and Sugden, R. (2010), *Experimental Economics*, Princeton University Press

Benartzi, S. (2012), *Save More Tomorrow*, Portfolio Penguin

Berger, J. (2013), *Contagious: Why Things Catch On*, Simon & Schuster

Brooks, D. (2011), *The Social Animal*, Random House

Brown, T. (2009), *Change by Design*, Harper Business

Camerer, C., Loewenstein, G., and Rabin, M. (2004), *Advances in Behavioral Economics*, Russell Sage Foundation

Cialdini, R. (1984), *Influence, the Psychology of Persuasion*, Harper Business

Congdon, W., Kling, J. and Mullainathan, S. (2011), *Policy and Choice: Public Finance through the Lens of Behavioral Economics*, Brookings Institution Press

Damasio, A. (1996), *Descartes' Error*, Penguin

Dean, J. (2013), *Making Habits, Breaking Habits*, Da Cap Press

Dolan, P. (2014), *Happiness by Design*, Hudson Street Press

Dolan, P., Hallsworth, M., Halpern, D., King, D. and Vlaev, I., (2010), *MINDSPACE: Influencing Behaviour through Public Policy*, Cabinet Office/Institute for Government

Droulers, O. and Roulet, B. (2010), *Neuromarketing: Le marketing revisité par la neuroscience*, Dunod

Duhigg, C. (2012), *The Power of Habit*, Random House

Dunn, E. and Norton, M. (2013), *Happy Money: The Science of Smarter Spending*, Simon & Schuster

Edelman, G. (1990), *The Remembered Present: A Biological Theory of Consciousness*, Basic Books

Edelman, G. (2007), *Second Nature: Brain Science and Human Knowledge*, Yale Universty Press

Eyal, N. (2014), *Hooked: How to Build Habit-Forming Products*, Nir Eyal

Fogg, B. J. (2003), *Persuasive Technology*, Morgan Kaufmann Publishers

Frijda, N. (2007), *The Laws of Emotion*, Lawrence Erlbaum Asociates

Frith, C. (2010), *Comment le cerveau crée notre univers mental*, Odile Jacob

Gazzaniga, M. (2011), *Who's in Charge?: Free Will and the Science of the Brain*, Ecco

Gazzaniga, M. (1987), *Social Brain: Discovering the Networks of the Brain*, Basic Books

Gazzaniga, M. (1970), *The Bisected Brain*, Appleton-Century-Crofts

Gigerenzer, G. (2014), *Risk Savy: How to Make Good Decisions*, Viking

Gigerenzer, G. (2008), *Gut Feelings: The Intelligence of the Unconscious*, Penguin

Gigerenzer, G. and Selten, R. (2001), *Bounded Rationality: The Adaptative Toolbox*, The MIT Press

Glimcher, P., Camerer C., Fehr, E., and Poldrack, R. (2009): *Neuroeconomics: Decision Making and the Brain*, Academic Press

Glimcher, P. and Fehr, E. (2014), *Neuroeconomics*, Academic Press

Gneezy, U., and List, J. (2013), *The Why Axis*, PublicAffairs

Goldstein, N., Martin, S., and Cialdini R. (2009), *Yes! 50 Scientifically Proven Ways to Be Persuasive*, Free Press

Hartford, T. (2008), *The Logic of Life*, Random House

Hartford, T. (2006), *The Undercover Economist*, Abacus

Heath, C. and Heath, D. (2010), *Switch: How Change Things When Change Is Hard*, Broadway Books

Heath, C. and Heath, D. (2007), *Made to Stick*, Random House

Henrich, J., Boyd, R., Bowles, S., Camerer, C., Fehr, E. and Gintis, H. (2004), *Foundations of Human Sociality*, Oxford University Press

Heukelom, F. (2014), *Behavioral Economics: A History*, Cambridge University Press

House, J., Lyons, E. and Soman, D. (2013), *Towards a Taxinomy of Nudging Strategies*, Rotman School of Business, University of Toronto

Hsieh, T. (2010), *Delivering Happiness*, Business Plus

Issenberg, S. (2012), *The Victory Lab*, Crown Publishers

Iyengar, S. (2010), *The Art of Choosing*, Twelve

Johnson, J. (2014), *Designing with the Mind in Mind*, Elesevier

Kahneman, D. (2011), *Thinking Fast and Slow*, Farrar, Straus and Giroux

Kahneman, D., Diener, E., and Schwartz, N. (1999), *Well Being: The Foundations of Hedonic Psychology*, Russell Sage Foundation

Kahneman, D. and Tversky A. (2000), *Choices, Values and Frames*, Cambridge University Press

Karli, P. (2011), *Le Besoin de l'autre*, Odile Jacob

Kenrick, D. and Griskevicius, V. (2013), *The Rational Animal*, Basic Books

Laflay, A. and Charan R. (2008), *The Game Changer*, Crown Business

Laflay, A. and Martin, R. (2013), *Playing to Win*, Harvard Business Review

Le Bihan, D. (2012), *Le Cerveau de cristal*, Odile Jacob

LeDoux, J. (1998), *The Emotional Brain*, Simon & Schuster

Lehrer, J. (2009), *How We Decide*, Houghton Mifflin Harcourt

Levine, D. (2012), *Is Behavioral Economics Doomed?*, OpenBook Publishers

Lieberman, M. (2013), *Social: Why Our Brains Are Wired to Connect*, Crown Publishers

Lindstrom, M. (2008), *Buy.ology: Truth and Lies About Why We Buy*, Doubleday

Loewenstein, G. (2007), *Exotic Preferences: Behavioral Economics and Human Motivation*, Oxford University Press

Loewenstein, G., Read, D. and Baufmeister, R. (2003), *Time and Decision*, Russell Sage Foundation

Low, D. (2012), *Behavioural Economics and Policy Design*, World Scientific Publishing

Lunn, P. (2014), *Regulatory Policy and Behavioural Economics*, OECD Publishing

Ly, (Kim), Mazar, N., Zhao (Min) and Soman, D. (2013), *A Practitioner's Guide to Nudging*, Rotman School of Management, University of Toronto

Ly, (Kim) and Soman, D. (2013), *Nudging Around the World*, Rotman School of Management, University of Toronto

Martin, S., Goldstein, N. and Cialdini, R. (2014), *The Small Big*, Business Plus

Medina, J. (2008), *Brain Rules: 12 Principles for Surviving and Thriving at Work, Home and School*, Pear Press

Mullainathan, S. and Eldar, S. (2013), *Scarcity: Why Having Too Little Means So Much*, Time Books

Montague, R. (2006), *Why Choose This Book?*, Dutton

Montague, R. (2006), *Your Brain Is (Almost) Perfect: How We Make Decisions*, Plume Books

Michel-Kerjan, E. and Slovic, P. (2010), *The Irrational Economist: Making Decisions in a Dangerous World*, PublicAffairs

Oliver, A. (2013), *Behavioural Public Policy*, Cambridge University Press

Oullier, O. and Sauneron, S. (2010), *Nouvelles Approches de la prévention en santé publique*, La Documentation française, n° 25

Pinker, S. (1997), *How the Mind Works*, W. W. Norton & Company

Pradeep, A. K. (2010), *The Buying Brain*, John Wiley & Sons

Ross, L. and Nisbett, R. (1991), *The Person and the Situation*, McGraw-Hill

Samson, A. (2014), *The Behavioral Economics Guide 2014*

Schwartz, B. (2004), *The Paradox of Choice: Why More Is Less*, Harper Perennial

Sharp, B. (2010), *How Brands Grow*, Oxford University Press

Shiller, R. (2005), *Irrational Exhuberance*, Broadway Books

Slovic, P. (2010), *The Feeling of Risk*, Earthscan

Sommers, S. (2011), *Situations Matter: Understanding How Context Transforms Your World*, Riverhead Books

Sunstein, C. (2014), *Why Nudge? The Politics of Libertarian Paternalism*, Yale University Press

Sunstein, C. (2013), *Simpler: The Future of Government*, Simon & Schuster

Surowiecki, J. (2004), *The Wisdom of Crowds*, Doubleday Anchor

Thaler, R. (1994), *The Winner's Curse*, Princeton University Press

Thaler, R. and Sunstein, C. (2008), *Nudge: Improving Decisions about Health, Wealth and Happiness*, Yale University Press

Vincent, J.-D. and Lledo, P.-M. (2012), *Le Cerveau sur mesure*, Odile Jacob

Wansink, B. (2006), *Mindless Eating: Why We Eat More than We Think*, Bantam Books

Weinshenck, S. (2011), *100 Things Every Designer Needs to Know About People*, New Riders

Wilson, T. (2002), *Strangers to Ourselves*, Belknap Harvard

World Bank Group (2015), *Mind, Society, and Behavior*, World Development Report

Zajonc, R. (2004), *The Selected Works of R. B. Zajonc*, John Wiley & Sons

Zaltman, G. (2003), *How Customers Think*, Harvard Business School Press

About the author

As CEO of the BVA group – one of the world's leading marketing research institutes – Éric Singler is responsible for mass-market studies carried out by IN VIVO BVA, as well as the BVA Nudge Unit.

Over the past twenty-five years, he has developed his expertise in behavior and the decision-making process by advising some of the world's largest companies, including L'Oréal, Danone, Unilever, Nestlé, Colgate, Palmolive and Procter & Gamble.

The founder of the NudgeFrance change tank, he is at the forefront of the Nudge approach in France. His clientele includes both public authorities (the Ministry of the Interior, the Health Ministry, the Treasury) and privately owned global corporations in the fields of health, energy, and consumer goods.

He is a member of the scientific board of the French national marketing association (Adetem), and co-founder of two LinkedIn groups: Neuroscience and Marketing, and Behavioral Economics for Marketers. He also works in partnership with a number of prestigious schools and universities (HEC Paris, INSEAD, Paris-Dauphine University, and ENA), and he gives regular conferences in France and abroad (ESO-MAR, Innovate Asia, The Market Research Event).